Mission-shaped Questions

Reviews for *Mission-shaped Questions*

'At last! A book on mission which doesn't duck questions or offer simplistic answers.'

Vivienne Faull, Dean of Leicester

'Exciting, challenging, difficult, hopeful – this book marks a decisive shift. Mission is the new culture and the old questions about church now have a vital currency.'

Simon Downham, Vicar/Senior Pastor,
St Paul's Church, Hammersmith

'Wise, big picture stuff, rooted in real life.'

Lucy Moore, Associate Missioner for Fresh Expressions
and part of the leadership team of Messy Church

Praise for *The Future of the Parish System* – also edited by Steven Croft

'Reading this is a bit like encountering the *Ocean's Eleven* of church literature . . . visionary, theological and extremely practical.'

Sally Hitchiner, writing in *Christianity* magazine

'A radical and challenging title which deserves to be read carefully and applied as appropriate, offering hope for the future while at the same time not rejecting the values of the past.'

Mark Clifford, Manager of Sarum College Bookshop,
writing in *The Sarum Link*

Mission-shaped Questions

Defining issues for today's Church

Edited by Steven Croft

CHURCH HOUSE
PUBLISHING

Church House Publishing
Church House
Great Smith Street
London SW1P 3AZ

Tel: 020 7898 1451
Fax: 020 7898 1449

ISBN 978–0–7151–4153–3

Published 2008 by Church House Publishing

*The opinions expressed in this book are those of the authors and
do not necessarily reflect the official policy of the General Synod or
The Archbishops' Council of the Church of England.*

Cover design by S2 design and advertising

Typeset in Rotis Sans Serif by RefineCatch Limited, Bungay, Suffolk

Printed in England by MPG Books Ltd, Bodmin, Cornwall

Contents

Contents

The Contributors

The Revd Canon Professor Loveday Alexander is Professor of Biblical Studies in the University of Sheffield and Canon Theologian at Chester Cathedral.

The Revd Dr Martyn Atkins is Principal of Cliff College and the current President of the Methodist Conference.

The Revd Dr Linda Barley is Head of Research for the Archbishops' Council.

The Revd Dr Steven Croft has been Archbishops' Missioner and Team Leader of Fresh Expressions since 2004. He was previously Warden of Cranmer Hall, St John's College, Durham.

The Revd Canon Tim Dakin is General Secretary of the Church Mission Society.

The Revd Professor John Drane is part of the School of Theology in Fuller Seminary, California and formerly professor of Practical Theology in the University of Aberdeen.

Professor James D. G. Dunn is Emeritus Lightfoot Professor of Divinity in the University of Durham. He is a Methodist Local Preacher and a lay Canon of Durham Cathedral.

Professor John M. Hull teaches in The Queen's Foundation, Birmingham and was Professor of Education within the University of Birmingham.

The Revd Dr Alison Morgan is a writer and theologian. She is part of Resource and of the ministry team at Holy Trinity, Leicester.

The Revd Angela Tilby is Vicar of St Benet's, Cambridge and was previously Vice-Principal of Wescott House, Cambridge.

The Revd Dr Graham Tomlin is Principal of the St Paul's Theological Centre, Holy Trinity, Brompton and was previously Vice-Principal of Wycliffe Hall, Oxford.

The Rt Revd Lindsay Urwin OGS is a professed member of the Oratory of the Good Shepherd and has been Area Bishop of Horsham in the Diocese of Chichester since 1993. He is a founder member of the Archbishops' College of Evangelists.

The Revd Canon Martin Warner is Canon Pastor of St Paul's Cathedral, London and was previously Guardian of the Shrine of Our Lady of Walsingham.

The Revd Dr David Wilkinson is Principal of St John's College Durham and Wesley Lecturer in Divinity in the University of Durham.

Introduction

The Church of England is no longer messing about when it comes to God's mission. Since the beginning of the Decade of Evangelism, we have made a determined attempt to set God's mission to a changing world at the heart of our life. The same can be said of the Methodist Church and many of the other mainstream denominations.

As we have moved forward, we have discovered different and practical ways to renew traditional congregations in mission and evangelism. We are learning now many new and creative ways to plant and sustain new communities: fresh expressions of church.[1]

However, this engagement with God's mission has provoked deep theological questions particularly about the nature of that mission and its relationship with God's Church. What is the relationship between the Church and the kingdom of God? What was the biblical warrant for the kind of thinking contained in mission-shaped Church? How should we describe or recognize a fresh expression of church? What should we call 'church' in any case? Are there dangers and risks in embracing a mixed economy of church life? Is mission-shaped Church simply a pragmatic response to our changing culture or something deeper still? How will fresh expressions of church develop into the future?

These are not questions that can be answered in five minutes. Fresh and deep thinking is needed to address new questions in both an Anglican and a Methodist context.

As a contribution to this thinking, in 2007 Fresh Expressions sponsored the 'Hard Questions' series of day conferences in seven different venues between Easter and Pentecost. We invited two theologians each to address a different hard question at each conference. Each 40-minute address was followed by questions to the speaker and a panel discussion with practitioners and church leaders.

This book is one of the fruits of the reflection, thinking and dialogue that took place around those day conferences. Each author has revised their material in the light of feedback, questions and responses and in the light of other people's contributions.

What has emerged from this process is, in my view, an extremely helpful resource for deeper thinking about mission and fresh expressions of church within a mixed economy. It is our hope that these essays will be helpful to anyone who wants to engage in an accessible way with reflection on the nature of the Church in a changing world. We hope it will be provoke thought and discussion among practitioners – ordained and lay ministers in every kind of church, among the pioneers, those engaging in fresh expressions, but equally among the permission givers – district chairs, bishops and those working at national level.

Each chapter in the book addresses a different question and each author approaches the issue from their own perspective and areas of expertise. In selecting the contributors we aimed for a balanced field of scholars of academic distinction and credibility combined with a commitment to the life and health and mission of the churches. All of the essays provide genuinely new and original resources to the questions they are addressing. Many direct some new hard questions back to the churches and particularly to those developing or reflecting on fresh expressions of church. As expected, what emerges is not a single neat or uniform answer to any of the issues but a varied – and in some places sparkling – set of new perspectives on the questions we face.

The essays are arranged in the order in which they were delivered in the series of day conferences. This is I think a good order in which to read them as a series but each can of course be read independently. In many ways the essays here build on the material in *The Future of the Parish System*.[2] The opening perspective is a more developed version of material I delivered at the start of each day conference. My final chapter attempts to draw together some threads and perspectives on ecclesiology and fresh expressions of church.

I would like to express my sincere thanks to the contributors for being willing to engage in the conferences and in the writing of these chapters within a tight timetable and also to say thank you to Canon George Kovoor, Principal of Trinity College, Bristol, who gave a memorable lecture but was unable, due to other commitments, to contribute a chapter to the book.

Thanks also to all those who came to the day conferences, who both asked questions and gave us their insights. There was a sense throughout of quality debate. Particular thanks go to those who served on the panels for the day conferences and made a very helpful contribution to what emerged (in order of appearance): Michael Moynagh, Paul Roberts, Ward Jones, Maggi Dawn, Ian Mobsby, Elaine Lindridge, Pete Pillinger, Ben Edson, Steve Hollinghurst, Geoff Langham, Pam Macnaughton, Yvonne Richmond, James Bell, Nick Haigh, Norman Ivison, Jean Kerr, Kerry Thorpe and Andrew Roberts. The tour would not have happened at all without the outstanding contributions of Rob Marshall, our media adviser, who had the original idea and helped carry it through, David Neaum, our ordinand on placement from Wescott House who handled all the practicalities with aplomb and asked some memorable hard questions, Rachel Kirkby of 33RPM, who did the original scoping and setting up of venues and the unflappable Ben Clymo, who handled bookings and administration. The Hard Questions tour represented a considerable financial investment by Fresh Expressions and thanks, as ever, go to the Lambeth Partners and the Lambeth Fund for their generosity, vision and prayer support for this and other ventures. Finally, our thanks and appreciation go to Church House Publishing for their commitment to the project and particularly to Kathryn Pritchard, who has been involved at every stage and, as with *The Future of the Parish System*, has again shared in editing the material with her customary blend of rigour, encouragement, wisdom and good humour.

Steven Croft
August 2007

1

Fresh expressions in a mixed economy Church: a perspective

Steven Croft

Before engaging in depth and detail with the questions we are facing, there is a need to set a context. It is valuable therefore to begin with an overview of the story so far and a perspective on our present situation.

The story so far

There is now a broad acceptance across the Church in England of the logic of the mixed economy: that we need fresh expressions of church alongside existing and traditional churches. The relationship between church and society has been changing for some time. The Church finds itself no longer at the centre of uniform and clearly recognized culture – the situation which has pertained for many years and which we know as Christendom. Instead, we recognize a growing gap between where much of the Church is and where much of our society now is. At the same time, British society is becoming itself much more diverse. This means it is no longer enough to imagine that the Christian Church can change in one particular direction (such as introducing guitars or informality into its worship) and so move with the times. That may appeal to some, but it will alienate others. Different parts of our culture are actually moving in different directions. How is the Church to respond?

For some years now, the Church has been responding by listening again to the commission of Jesus to go and make disciples. While we have continued to learn how best to invite people to come and join existing churches there has also been an identifiable, if still fragile, new movement of Christians going to different parts of our culture and communities. For the most part, these new missionaries within British culture have gone in humility and in love and, while they have been clear about their calling, they have had no fixed methodology. They have sought to listen before they have spoken. They have gone looking to serve and bless others in the first instance. Out of that service new communities have emerged. In the midst of these new communities, men and women, children and young people have found Christ. Instead of attempting to draw such people back into membership of existing and traditional churches, the new missionaries have felt their way towards establishing new Christian communities connected to the wider Body of Christ but seeking to grow in ways appropriate to a particular culture yet faithful to the wider Christian tradition.

In the middle of the 1990s this new movement had begun to be noticed and to be studied. The earliest stories and studies were the series of booklets, *Encounters on the Edge*, produced by the Church Army's Sheffield Centre and mainly written by its Director, George Lings. In 2002 the Church of England set up a working party chaired by the Bishop of Maidstone, Graham Cray, to reflect on the changes which had taken place since the 1994 report on church planting, *Breaking New Ground*. This working party, which had Methodist representation, produced the report, *Mission-shaped Church* in early 2004.[1]

Mission-shaped Church has proved to be a landmark report for the Church of England. Its total sales so far (more than 22,000 copies) have far exceeded any other Church of England official report ever published. The working party adopted a primary methodology not of creating a strategy but of listening to what God is doing – to what is emerging – across Church and society and reflecting that back to the Church of England as a whole.[2] The ideas they captured and commended in the report have resonated across much of the Church in the United Kingdom and, indeed across many parts of the world over the last four years.[3]

Two factors emerged as distinctive and particularly helpful in all that was good in *Mission-shaped Church*. The first was to create some helpful new language for describing a range of disparate phenomena with some common threads and themes. The term 'fresh expressions of church' was first used in print in the report and chosen as a neutral term to describe a range of 12 different types of activity, all of which reflected a desire and movement to go to where people are and let the culture, the context and the mission of God shape the resulting new community.

It is worth quoting in full the paragraph where the term is first introduced and explained in the report:

> The phrase **fresh expressions of church** is used in this report. The

Preface to the Declaration of Assent, which Church of England ministers make at their licensing, states 'The Church of England . . . professes the faith uniquely revealed in the Holy Scriptures and set forth in the catholic creeds, which faith the Church is called upon to proclaim afresh in each generation'. The term 'fresh expressions' echoes these words. It suggests something new or enlivened is happening, but also suggests connection to history and the developing story of God's work in the Church. The phrase also embraces two realities: existing churches that are seeking to renew or redirect what they already have, and others who are intentionally sending out planting groups to discover what will emerge when the gospel is immersed in the mission context.[4]

The 12 loose groups of examples included as fresh expressions of church were (in alphabetical order): alternative worship congregations, base ecclesial communities, café church, cell church, churches arising out of community initiatives, multiple and midweek congregations, network focused churches, school based and school linked congregations and churches, seeker church, traditional church plants, traditional forms of church inspiring new interest, and youth congregations.[5]

The new language has in itself been immensely releasing and encouraging to many local initiatives, enabling them to give a name to tentative new steps forward in a particular direction and helping them to connect to a wider movement of mission. As we shall see, the rapid adoption of the new language has not been without its problems but overall this has been a positive and helpful move.

The second piece of new language, coined originally by Archbishop Rowan Williams while he was Archbishop of Wales, was the equally helpful phrase 'the mixed economy Church'. This catches the view that for the Church of England (and for the Methodist Church) the establishing of fresh expressions of church is not being done at the expense of or in competition with existing or traditional congregations. Because of the changing nature of our society, we need a range of different kinds of church, each attempting to reach out and to share in God's mission and connected to one another in the wider Body of Christ. The 'typical' parish, benefice or circuit is now and will increasingly be a collection of several different communities. Some will meet on Sunday mornings and look and feel like traditional church services. Others may meet on a Saturday in the early evening or midweek after school or monthly in the village hall. These communities are likely to overlap and be interconnected but also to have their own distinct common life.

The second major and lasting contribution of *Mission-shaped Church* is that it provided the vehicle for the Church of England to say that the development of fresh expressions of church should no longer be marginal but central and normative in our common life and our understanding of God's mission. In effect, the report says, the development of fresh expressions of church within a mixed economy is more than a very good thing: it is an essential part of our life and witness within British society at the present time. This overall endorsement of a way forward is followed through with a number of far-reaching recommendations, the majority of which have now been taken forward and translated into policies.

It is one thing, of course, for a small group to bring recommendations to the General Synod. It is quite another for those recommendations to be accepted and taken forward in a widespread way. Successive reports on evangelism and mission in the Church of England since 1945 have ended up gathering dust.[6] However, this has not happened to *Mission-shaped Church*. Speakers at the General Synod debate on the report in February 2004 spoke of the need to embrace a *kairos* moment for Church and nation in respect of the report and the action it commended. Undoubtedly the embracing of the report's agenda by the then new Archbishop of Canterbury has been a key factor. His perspective set out in the preface to the report is that the Church of England 'for all the problems which beset it is poised for serious growth and renewal'.[7] The sense that the Church of England is being led and encouraged in the direction of a mixed economy has been hugely helpful particularly in taking forward some of the report's major recommendations.

However, in my judgement, what has most helped to take the momentum forward in dioceses and districts (and more on the Methodist story shortly) is the combined discernment across the churches that in its broadest sense this movement is both a return to gospel principles and absolutely timely for the present context. This is supported by an increasing number of local initiatives of amazing and wonderful creativity, which in their turn are proving extremely fruitful. Something profound and important has been discerned about God's call to mission within our own society and what we need to do to join in.

Four years on from the report's publication it is impossible to track accurately how much is happening in terms of fresh expressions of church. This is partly because there is so much of it and partly because definitions and language are still settling, becoming more widely owned and better understood. In her contribution to this volume, Lynda Barley gives her own perspective on the quantitative research done recently by the Church of England. What is clear, however, is that across both the Church of England and the Methodist Church there is no shortage of stories to be told and good examples to be learned from and engaged with.

In his introduction to a presentation to General Synod in February 2007, the Archbishop of Canterbury said:

> Discovering new expressions of the Church's life has now, rather paradoxically, become part of the blood stream of the traditional, mainstream churches' life. To be, so to speak, an ordinary average Anglican, to be an ordinary average Anglican diocese, to be an ordinary average Anglican bishop, now involves you in thinking about, planning for, and involving yourself in, some quite extraordinary and, on the face of it, sometimes rather unanglican bits of new life. We're rediscovering something about what the Church is, as well as what the Church of England is; rediscovering, to use a favourite metaphor of mine, that the Church is something that happens before it's something that is institutionally organized. It happens when the Good News summons, assembles, people around Jesus Christ. Remember that that is what we're thinking of, not a series of scattered experiments, not a series of enterprises in religious entertainment, not, God forbid, a kind of dumbing down of the historic faith and its requirements so that more people may get vaguely interested.

> The point of fresh expressions is the point of the Church itself, that is to provide a place where Christ is set free in our midst, if one can use such an expression – and I hesitate to, to gather those who want to be in his company. That freedom is always there for our Lord, we can simply try and, as has often been said, join in and not get in the way. So you're going to hear something now about being the Church, and being the Church of England, not about something marginal, something eccentric, but about the very life blood of who we are and what we are.

The Methodist Church contributed a member to the *Mission-shaped Church* working party and approached the Archbishop of Canterbury in early 2004 about a structured partnership in what became the national Fresh Expressions initiative. At the Methodist Conference in 2004 the church adopted a new set of five focus areas including 'the encouragement of fresh ways of being church'. As colleagues and I began to explore what was happening in circuits across the country we have discovered, as with the Church of England, a great deal which is happening already which has been given momentum and encouragement by the wider connexion. The move to develop fresh expressions within Methodism has benefited from committed advocacy by three successive Presidents of Conference, Tom Stuckey, Graham Carter and Martyn Atkins, who has contributed one of the essays in this volume.[8]

In 2006, the church requested a much more complete summary of practice and emerging thinking and a full report, written by my two colleagues, Peter Pillinger and Andrew Roberts, was published and brought to the Conference in 2007.[9] The resolution to Conference which accompanied the report commended what is happening in Districts and Circuits and established a working group to consider and implement structural changes in Methodism to help and encourage this movement, bringing reports back to the Conference on an annual basis for the next six years.

'A principled and careful loosening of structures'[10]

The Church of England has begun the process of implementing the recommendations of the *Mission-shaped Church* report and the revision of the Pastoral Measure which came to the same General Synod meeting in February 2004. This process has resulted in the development of a raft of three key policies at national level to support the development of fresh expressions of church.

The first and possibly the most far reaching are the provisions of the Dioceses, Mission and Pastoral Measure 2007, for the creation of a means to give legal and authorized recognition to a new mission community through the device of a Bishop's Mission Order. This recognition will not be needed where a fresh expression of church is founded within a single parish. However, the Bishop's Mission Order provides a very helpful set of policies for moving forward in mission where the new community is a collaborative venture between several parishes or with ecumenical partners as is often the case. A Code of Practice (in draft form until February, 2008) gives detailed consideration to the way in which an order is made and good practice surrounding fresh expressions of church, which are recognized by this means. We therefore have now built into law a way of granting legal recognition to new and emerging communities which will be a key foundation for future development.[11]

Secondly, the House of Bishops approved a set of guidelines for a new focus of ordained ministry in January 2006 given the designation 'ordained pioneer ministry'.[12] This is not a new kind or order of ordained ministry but a particular focus for some people's gifts and experience around the establishing of new communities: fresh expressions of church. Anyone testing a vocation to ordained ministry in the Church of England can now explore the possibility of ordained pioneer ministry. The criteria for selection are the same as for every ordinand with the one additional set of critera around pioneering gifts. The guidelines introduce the flexibility for ordinands training for this ministry to train primarily in context alongside their leadership of a fresh expression of church. Training is being overseen by existing training institutions with two new centres emerging in London with a major focus on this ministry.[13] The Principal of one of these new centres, Graham Tomlin, has contributed one of the essays to this volume. There are currently around 40 candidates in training for this focus of ministry. The main focus of their title post (curacy) will be the development of one or more fresh expressions of church. We can therefore envisage a small but steady stream of men and women being ordained to stipendiary and self-supporting (non-stipendiary) ministries who have the gifts and expertise to combine ordained ministry with pioneering fresh expressions of church. In Chapter 3, Bishop Lindsay Urwin describes the ordination of someone to this kind of role (though well in advance of the official guidelines).

Finally, and perhaps even more significantly, in January 2007 the House of Bishops approved a parallel set of guidelines for the recognition, training and support of lay pioneer ministry. This pays a particular and due regard to the ministry of Church Army Evangelists. Church Army have increasingly focused their mission and resources in the area of beginning fresh expressions of church and represent a very significant resource and well of expertise for the whole Church in the United Kingdom. Their own selection criteria, training and deployment of new and existing evangelists are all shifting significantly towards the development of fresh expressions of church. The ministry of Church Army Evangelist therefore represents a nationally recognized route to lay pioneer ministry. However, the guidelines also encourage all dioceses to establish and encourage lay people in these ministries in a range of different ways and in particular through the establishing of appropriate training provision. The one-year part-time course, 'Mission Shaped Ministry', initiated by Fresh Expressions and key national partners, is intended to meet this need and is being rolled out across the country over the next two years. We will therefore, as a Church, have the means to encourage and equip teams of lay pioneers in every part of Britain to begin and sustain fresh expressions of church alongside existing and traditional church communities.

For the last century and more the Church of England has largely deployed its self-supporting lay and ordained ministers as support for existing ordained ministry across parishes and benefices (with some honourable exceptions). These two sets of guidelines open up the possibility of the selection, training and deployment of licensed ministers primarily for the creation of new Christian communities: a significant step indeed as we enter the twenty-first century.

Diocesan and district policies and resources

Dioceses and districts are responding in a range of different ways to the challenges and opportunities of developing fresh expression of church. As one would expect, there is a spectrum in respect of accepting and implementing change and some appropriate variation because of social context. At one end are dioceses and districts that are embracing the mixed economy and encouraging fresh expressions of church in a strategic way, embedding the language and ideas into their future vision and policy.[14] At the other are a small number of dioceses or districts where little is happening structurally to engage with this agenda but where there is good evidence of new communities at parish level. In the majority, however, there is evidence of seeking a strategic way forward and embracing the idea of a mixed economy. In a survey carried out in early 2007, all but a handful of dioceses could identify at least one person, and often more, working full time in establishing or leading fresh expressions of church and the number of such posts had increased significantly since the publication of *Mission-shaped Church* in 2004. In a 2006 survey of Methodist ministers' stationing forms, one third of those requesting to move in the following year expressed a desire to be involved in encouraging fresh expressions of church in some way as part of their next post in ministry.

Questions of definition

As policy and resources shifts and funds are made available for local development, the question of a reasonably robust definition of a fresh expression of church becomes more pressing. In my own first year in post, there was a sense of the term being very new and of it being tried on somewhat hesitantly by different sections of the Church. As we have seen, *Mission-shaped Church* does not provide a definition but preserved an intentional ambiguity between the establishing of new communities and existing congregations shaping things differently for the sake of mission.

Once the term began to catch on (which happened with surprising speed) those of us attempting to monitor and reflect on what was happening found it being applied to all kinds of ventures that were not necessarily fresh expressions *of church* (though they may have been quite appropriately fresh expressions of *mission* or *evangelism* or *service* to the wider community). Just occasionally one finds it being applied to something that is not fresh in any sense of the word, although actually I have yet to find an example of a new church notice board being described as a fresh expression. As many people have wisely remarked, if a term can mean anything at all then it quickly becomes meaningless.

We therefore sought in early 2006 to develop with our partner agencies a concise working definition of a fresh expression of church.[15] It was first published in May 2006 and reads:

A fresh expression is a form of church for our changing culture established primarily for the benefit of people who are not yet members of any church.

It will come into being through principles of listening, service, incarnational mission and making disciples.

It will have the potential to become a mature expression of church shaped by the gospel and the enduring marks of the Church and for its cultural context.

- The first part of the definition attempts to catch the truth that what is distinctive about a fresh expression of church is not novelty for its own sake (the word 'new' was dropped after careful discussion) but contextualization of the gospel for the sake of mission. In describing fresh expressions as established 'primarily' for the benefit of those who are not yet members of any church, we wanted to keep the focus of emphasis in the movement as a whole on mission and new communities formed for the sake of the unchurched while not excluding groups formed for those holding onto the existing church, as it were, by their fingertips. Something of the ambiguity present in *Mission-shaped Church* is therefore retained.
- The second sentence attempts to articulate a process by which we observe many fresh expressions come into being. As *Mission-shaped Church* emphasizes, listening to context, culture and gospel is profoundly important as are simple acts of care. My colleague Michael Moynagh has coined the

memorable line that in fresh expressions of church 'loving service will always come before a worship service'. Incarnational mission is engaging in mission after the pattern of the incarnation of Jesus: going to where people are and being with them on their own terms.[16]

● The third sentence contains implicit understanding that fresh expressions of church are defined in part by what they aspire to be (a mature church) rather than what they already are. To some degree that is the case for any Christian community. However, it is particularly the case that something may be appropriately named as a fresh expression of church without that being taken to imply that it has as yet all the essential qualities or marks of a mature Christian community. There is therefore a provisionality about the language of fresh expressions of church which is generally helpful to those engaging in mission in these ways. We had used the language in earlier descriptions of a fresh expression of church not being intended as a stepping stone to some kind of Sunday service and this sense is, we hope, retained in the new and positively framed definition.

Part three of the definition also captures the two poles between which the fresh expression of church must navigate in its journey to maturity. One pole and continual source of inspiration and dialogue is the gospel and the historic marks of the Church – one, holy, catholic and apostolic – (and hence the need for those developing fresh expressions to put down deep roots in this part of the tradition). The other is its own cultural context. New developments in the life of the fresh expression of church will spring out of an authentic and deep dialogue between these two realities.

This working definition of a fresh expression of church is certainly not the last word on the matter. However, it is proving helpful both as a guide to discerning when it is helpful to use the designation and when not (every new entry to our web site directory is measured against it) and as a helpful foundation for teaching and training others. It is now being incorporated into more official documents on policy at diocesan, district and national level.

A spectrum of fresh expressions of church

Within this broad definition it is possible to look at a range of initiatives developing across a diocese or district and see a spectrum emerging at different points in terms of the size and profile of the fresh expression of church.

A spectrum of fresh expressions of church

①

Renewal of existing community through mission and recontextualization

→ *Renewal of all age worship provision*

→ *Rethinking a mid-week service*

②

Reconceiving an existing mission project or service as no longer a stepping stone but 'church'

→ *A youth group grows into a youth congregation*

→ *A lunch club for the elderly adds worship and becomes a midweek congregation and community*

③

A new mission initiative to create a new community within a single parish/circuit; largely lay led; small budget

→ *A midweek after school community meeting for a meal and worship*

→ *An informal service in a local leisure centre*

④

A major mission initiative to create a new community across several parishes/circuits; full time post; recognized by Bishop's Mission Order

→ *A new network church across a city centre*

→ *A home-based church plant in a new housing area*

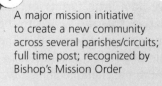

At the lower end of the spectrum (4) are the clearly identified and high-profile initiatives which often have a full- or part-time post attached to them. They may operate across quite a large area and will increasingly, in Anglican terms be recognized by the device of a Bishop's Mission Order. There will normally be just a small number of such projects within an Anglican diocese or Methodist district. Some of the communities formed by this means are quite large; some remain numerically small despite having a full-time person. This kind of project is normally very innovative, acts as a beacon and inspiration across a wider area and plays a role in helping a large number of churches see what it might mean to begin to do church differently for the sake of mission. Examples featured on the Fresh Expressions DVDs would be Legacy XS, a well-established church for the skateboarding community in Benfleet, Tube Station, an innovative church for surfers in Cornwall, or B1, a network church in the centre of Birmingham.[17]

Move up a little on the spectrum (3) and you will find the kind of fresh expression that is led by a team of lay and ordained ministers who are self-supporting or leading this fresh expression as part of their wider ministry. This fresh expression normally operates within a single benefice, parish or circuit and is an additional congregation or community – perhaps on a different day or venue or in a different style as seems most appropriate. In terms of ecclesiology this is not a very big shift from a parish having one kind of service at 8.00 a.m. and another at 10.30 a.m. in a different style. At present, this is probably the numerical centre of the movement. When I look each month at the new projects that have registered in our online directory there will normally be a significant number of this kind of new community. Quite commonly they seem quite quickly to attract a community of around 50 or so people spanning several generations. Examples on the DVDs would include Messy Church[18] in Portsmouth or the Goth Eucharist in Cambridge.

Move up a little further on the spectrum (2) and you will find a group of initiatives that are similar to the second group except that there has been a subtle change of perspective. The initiatives in this group have grown up from something which was previously considered as a mission project or a stepping stone to the church community, but there has been an ecclesiological change of perspective and the venture is now regarded as something which is or has the potential to become church in its own right. Many youth congregations have grown out of youth groups: something that was an add-on for young people has been reframed as church. Examples on the DVD would include The Living Room in Southampton: a thriving Sunday evening community for students, which grew out of an after church gathering and Re:fresh: a fresh expression of church that has grown up from a midweek activity in RAF

Cranfield. Again, this group of examples is numerically quite large and demonstrates very clearly the need for robust thinking and questions around ecclesiology. Sometimes, what is most needed is for an existing congregation and its leadership to see the potential for an existing venture to be or become church. While writing this chapter I had a telephone conversation with a vicar in Yorkshire who has over 100 people coming through the church community centre every week but only ten in his congregation on Sundays. The church he serves has now begun to realize that it needs to recognize the difficulty of encouraging the community into the Sunday service and to begin to explore ways of growing and being church on other days of the week.

Finally, move up a little again on the spectrum and we are in the territory of what *Mission-shaped Church* describes as 'existing churches that are seeking to renew or redirect what they already have'.[19] Where that renewal and redirection leads to the creation of what is effectively a new community (even though it may be meeting in the same building) following exactly the same principles as are followed at other points on the spectrum, it seems legitimate also to call that new community a fresh expression of church. We haven't featured many examples of this in the DVD material, as it's not the centre of the movement – which lies in the new communities. However, one inspiring rural example is the story of the church in Tolland where the church stopped offering a monthly *Book of Common Prayer* Eucharist, reconnected with the tiny hamlet of 30 houses in which it was set and, by a process of double listening, offered a new pattern of worship six times a year, which now engages the majority of the village.

These fresh expressions of church at different points of the spectrum may look very different from one another. What they have in common is not novelty or innovation for its own sake but key principles of mission. They have all taken on board the need to share in the mission of God in new ways; the need for a mixed economy; the need to contextualize the gospel differently for different communities; and the importance of listening. They are all grappling in different ways with what it means to be church and to grow a Christian community to maturity.

Hard questions on mission and church

Given the significant number of diverse fresh expressions of church happening in parishes and circuits, the number of people beginning to engage seriously with this agenda, the resources beginning to move in this direction and the policy shifts to make these things possible, it is no wonder that all kinds of people are asking hard theological questions around fresh expressions of church. To be healthy, any movement needs to be self-critical and a variety of perspectives need to emerge.

The key areas that need serious theological resourcing as these hard questions are asked are in the two areas of reflection on mission on the one hand and on the life of the church, and particularly the interface between the two captured in the report title: *Mission-shaped Church*.

However it is undoubtedly the case that of these two areas, that of mission and missiology is much better resourced than thinking and reflection on church. Although missiology is therefore addressed in this volume of essays, the major emphasis is on our understanding of what it means to be the Church in a changing context and a changing culture.

Both Anglicans and Methodists engaged in fresh expressions of church are drawing on a rich inheritance and understanding when it comes to reflection on mission. The streams that are feeding this movement in terms of missiology include the foundational documents of Methodism and the 'Our Calling' process and the work done in the Anglican Communion on mission over the last generation or so and summarized in the immensely helpful 'Five Marks of Mission'. They also include the magisterial synthesis on mission by David Bosch and the key concept of the mission of God, mentioned and explored in more than one of the essays that follow.[20]

However, I also want to mention and pay tribute to what seems to me to be a very key stream of missionary thinkers – practitioners and theologians – who have spent time engaged in mission to different cultures and have returned to the developed world and then reflected on both that experience of mission and the mission of the Church in their own countries.

Pride of place here must go to Roland Allen (1868–1947), the SPG missionary to China, whose writings remain in print and grow in influence.[21] I scarcely read a book on emerging church[22] or fresh expressions which is not influenced by Allen in some way and you will find several references in this volume to this key thinker. Reading Allen's work was a seminal moment for the life and ministry of Vincent Donovan, an American Jesuit, whose account of his ministry to the Masai, *Christianity Rediscovered*, remains a powerful and moving reflection on mission and church and an inspiration to many who are developing fresh expressions of church today.[23] Lesslie Newbigin spent much of his life in engaging in mission in the Indian subcontinent. On his return to Britain he reflected widely on the current mission of the Church here to its own culture. Again, his books are widely read and remain influential.[24] Finally John V. Taylor served as a missionary in Africa, General Secretary of CMS and Bishop of Winchester. These experiences gave him the ability and the perspective to reflect in a profound and lasting way on the mission of God and the shape of the Church.[25]

The thinking in this volume owes much to these and other writers down the centuries, as will be apparent. However, in each generation it is important to reflect on the wisdom of the past but also to attempt to coin new resources for a new period in God's unchanging yet ever-changing mission. Given this substantive heritage in terms of engagement with mission, the primary theological task in the Hard Questions lecture series and the majority of these chapters is to relate a living stream of reflection on mission to the demanding task of describing and shaping the life of the Church. The hard questions before us at present therefore demand the very best thinking and resources we can bring to support and undergird the energies of those engaged in forming fresh expressions of church for a changing culture.

A note on terminology

The capitalized term 'Fresh Expressions' is used (infrequently) throughout this volume to refer to the national initiative and team, which is a joint Anglican and Methodist venture responsible to the Archbishops and to the Methodist Council.

The lower-case term 'fresh expressions of church' is used (frequently) to refer to the fresh expressions of church as described in this chapter. As these are now accepted and widely used terms in Anglican and Methodist documents, we have avoided (and would encourage others to avoid) surrounding the phrase with inverted commas. We also tend to use the full term fresh expressions of church to make it clear we have in mind the desire and calling to create new Christian communities rather than simply fresh expressions of one or other aspect of Christ's Church.

2

What is the essence of the Church?

Martyn Atkins

Context

The 'What is church?' question is not only a hard question, but a hot question, one asked by a variety of people for a number of important reasons. I think of being invited to preach by the pastor of a student congregation in a university city, loosely affiliated to one of the 'New Church' networks, and doing a fantastic job of growing a vital, healthy congregation, but one without many traditional church trappings in evidence at all. After the meeting, over coffee, he asks of me, the visiting preacher my opinion: 'Martyn is it all right? Is it church?' An affirmative reply is clearly very significant to him. Then I think of a conversation with a young Methodist minister. For a long time I can't work out whether she is asking me to talk her out of or in to leaving her present appointment, ministering to six small traditional chapels in a semi-rural area. All the traditional trappings of church are fixed in place, and seem immovable, and she sighs dejectedly, 'Martyn, I wonder if it's really church at all.'

It is more nuanced than that of course. Some of us will permit fresh expressions if they are episcopally governed and sacramentally ordered in particular ways, otherwise they cannot properly or completely be regarded as 'church'. Some of us require less than that, but believe that a fresh expression must conform to the basic polity and constitution of a parent denomination. Others limit the possibility of 'church' to certain environments and struggle, for example, with church in a pub, while others are perfectly happy with pub-church but struggle with cyberchurch – 'I mean, it doesn't really exist does it?' Still others have a more pragmatic approach, adopting a watching brief on a fast-emerging scene, and, at least for the moment, keeping their powder dry.

The prolific literature about church today is getting better but, as a regular reader of it, there seem to me to be at least two distinct 'groups'. There are those who write about emerging churches, fresh expressions and the like as if the 'What is church?' question has never been asked by anyone before, or if it has, has produced nothing worth recording. Then there are books on ecclesiology that painstakingly outline the nature of the Church without any apparent recognition or awareness that the very ground under our feet is shifting and fresh expressions are bursting forth all over.

I consider the 'What is church?' question to be crucial to the present and future of *both* inherited and emerging expressions of Western churches at this time. It is not a question asked simply by one of the other but by both of each other.

Contours

I want to present a case for the view that the essence of the Church lies in its *derived* nature and, more particularly, its identity as the chosen partner of the Holy Trinity, Father, Son and Holy Spirit, in God's mission. That is, the Church has *no* essence 'in itself' as it were. Rather, its essence necessarily derives from the Christian Godhead, and therefore the nature and life of the Church is created and configured by the life and character of the Christian Godhead. To use theological shorthand, theology – read mainly through the lens of missiology – produces ecclesiology, rather than vice versa.

In the remainder of this chapter my aim is to outline the arguments for such a view of what church is and to begin to engage with some of the questions posed of it.

In the beginning, God . . .[1]

If the essence of the Church does not lie in itself but derives from God's nature and purposes, then we must ask about the nature and purposes of God. How is God known, apprehended and experienced? My response to that is to turn where so many Christians have turned – to the Christian Scriptures, where God is revealed, understood and experienced in terms of Father, Son and Holy Spirit.

Without denying the complexities of the ways in which Scripture is engaged, expounded and applied, I hold to the conviction that the meta-story, the overarching thrust of Scripture can be discerned, is deeply significant, and bears witness to the fundamental character of God, who can legitimately be understood as supreme missionary and evangelist.

In the rich tapestry of the Old Testament is revealed God who creates all things good, who is broken-hearted at the spoiling of creation, and then, even as humankind signs its own death warrant in the garden, begins working for the restoration of everything and everyone, through patriarchs and prophets, matriarchs and messengers, covenants and torah, signs and symbols. God's law is given, and God's people are rescued and led to inherit a land. Time and again they fail but God does not give up on them. A new covenant is made, written on human hearts not on tablets of stone. The means are many and varied and costly, but the overall aim – the mission – is plain.

In the fullness of time God, Father, Son and Holy Spirit, conspires again and the crucial phase of the divine mission takes shape. Christ Jesus, God incarnate, God self-sent as it were, undertakes the missionary task of redeeming all humanity, all creation, through life laid down and resurrection glory. The Son lives out his life making plain the nature and mission of God: teaching, healing, befriending, challenging, and judging. As P. T. Forsyth put it, 'In Christ, God was his own Apostle.'[2] Then God in Christ does what neither the cosmos nor humanity can do for itself: dying he destroys our death and rising he restores our life: sacrificing and saving.

But that is not the end. As fledgling communities of those believing in Jesus Christ are born, God again takes the initiative, and comes as Holy Spirit – a missionary self-sending God in action again. Inside and outside God's new community – the Church – the Spirit comes, making bold, leading outwards, going before, preparing the way 'to Jerusalem, Samaria and to the ends of the earth' (Acts 1.8). As F. F. Bruce used to say about the book of Acts, 'it is as if God drops a pebble into the pool of human history, and we watch the ripples'. The centripetal movement of the Old Testament with its images of nations wending their way to Jerusalem from all directions is reversed as Pentecost becomes the launching of a centrifugal Christian mission as the Spirit impels God's people to join in and move out. The God of the Christian Scriptures – Father, Son and Spirit – is, first to last, a God of mission.

This is not an exercise in poor proof-texting. The meta-story of Scripture reveals what God is *like* by relating what God *does*. God's nature and actions agree and make plain that God is a certain kind of God, a God of mission, and that the people of God are first and foremost the *product* of God's mission, and then *participants* and *partners* in God's mission.

Seeking first the kingdom . . .

What then is the mission of God in which the Church is created to partner?

Mission-shaped Church thinking often presents this rich theme in terms of the pursuit of the kingdom – or reign – of God. For some, 'kingdom' language is problematic for several good reasons: tainted images of patriarchy and power, 'masculine' language, associated too closely to geography or a particular kind of national identity. Consequently, how the New Testament word *basileia* might be properly understood and applied in a globalized, postmodern context is the subject of increasing interest among New Testament scholars and others. Some talk about God's 'reign' or 'rule', which addresses some of the problems of 'kingdom', but not all. Others suggest 'empire' to better articulate the alternative nature of God's new world order implied by *basileia*. For simplicity, I use 'kingdom' here, but mean by it the 'fuller sense' sought by those who seek to use alternative language to describe God's wonderful cosmic desires and designs.

If Christian mission proceeds from the revealed nature of the Trinity, then the *aim* of mission – the 'why we do it' bit, if you like – is shaped by the perceived nature of God's kingdom. Jesus talks often about his 'Father's kingdom', about seeking the kingdom first, and its coming seems to be at the heart of all he says and does. The Holy Spirit enables, inspires and calls forth witnesses to God in Christ, those who live and long for God's kingdom come. The kingdom reign of God is the primary missional perspective of the New Testament.

Then the Church . . .

Such is the symbiotic relationship between God's character, God's reign, God mission and God's Church that it is impossible to narrate the nature of one without reference to the others. But the nature of God and the goal of God's kingdom reign create the proper theological context for a discussion about the essence of the Church. The Church derives its being from the missionary God and is created and shaped to share in the *missio Dei*, the goal of which is the coming of the kingdom. David Bosch writes, 'The classical doctrine of the *missio Dei* as God the Father sending the Son, and God the Father and the Son sending the Spirit was expanded to include yet another "movement": Father, Son and Holy Spirit sending the church into the world.'[3] We see much this same movement in Scripture: 'As the Father has sent me' says Jesus, 'so I send you' (John 20.21). In this way the Christian Church derives its life, nature, mission and ministry from God. Whatever God is perceived to be like, the

Church, if it is true and faithful, will embody and emulate. If God is encountered and experienced as supreme missionary, going before, searching out, inviting and receiving in, abiding with, then those very characteristics will be found in the Church of such a God. If God is known as one who is always self-giving, and urging and bringing *shalom*, then so will the Church be, and so on. The true nature of the Church is determined by its creator. The Church therefore, to quote Paul Stevens who himself borrows from St Augustine, 'does not "have" a mission; it is mission. There is one people, one trinitarian people . . . that reflects the one God who is lover, beloved and love itself . . . one God who is sender, sent and sending.'[4] Church thus becomes the vehicle of God's mission, itself infilled and impelled by the sender sent and sending one.

Consequences

The notion that the essence of the Church is derived from the nature and purposes of a missionary God has consequences – knock-on effects – and I outline some of them here.

Significance

Some will suggest that the Church is relegated in significance when understood in this way. 'Derived' seems to imply 'lesser'. I believe the reverse is true, that the Church only finds its true significance when it understands itself as chosen and sent by God, sharing in God's mission, and without such an understanding the Church lacks ultimate identity, meaning or purpose. There is nothing insignificant about understanding the Church to be divinely created to be the normative partner of a missionary God! So, 'derived' church does not mean 'dispensable' church. We might baulk – as many do – about the seeming non-missionary, un-evangelistic nature of much church as we know it today, of its current nominality and ineffectiveness. We might assert – as many do – that church must change to more closely resemble its role in God's missional intentions. What we cannot do – which some mistakenly attempt to – is to go about the business of mission and ministry as if the Church was some optional extra and can be bypassed. Churchless mission and missionless church are equally unsatisfactory. Whatever works of grace our wonderful God brings about always results in fresh expressions of church. We might remain open to be persuaded about some current expressions of church, but we cannot conceive of the *missio Dei* without 'church'.

Spirit-filled

Nor does the derived essence of church suggest it is lacking spiritual power or authority. Rather, the Church is filled with the Holy Spirit of God as a natural consequence of its derived nature. Without the prevenient, present and permanent work of the Spirit of God, the Church cannot fulfil God's mission. Indeed, the New Testament says at least as much about the Holy Spirit as the fuel and fire of the apostolic people of God in Christ, as it does about the Spirit as the giver of charismatic gifts for the building up of the Church. 'Without the Holy Spirit', Patriarch Athenagoras writes, 'God is far away, Christ remains a figure of the past, the Gospel a dead letter, the Church a mere organization, authority a means to exercise power, mission a propaganda machine, worship becomes outdated and morality the action of slaves.'[5] It is the Spirit who enables the appropriate incarnation and expression of Christianity for each context, place and time.

Human community

Does this focus on church as derived from the perceived nature of *God*, counter or lessen understandings of church as essentially a *human* com-munity? I believe not. It is the Spirit who calls people into ministry and service, and enables them to fulfil their calling. Church understood as the chosen partner of the God of mission always results in a called-out *people*, a *koinonia* community, which articulates and embodies the reign of God. This people of God are the Body of Christ, whom they recognize and gratefully announce to be Saviour of all, regarding themselves as disciples of their Lord, believers in one who is Alpha and Omega, the beginning and the end. They are charged with the Great Commission and engage in the Great Commandment. Dying and rising, and a profound openness to the Spirit of God characterizes their life and their faith. Such a *community*, forged by the *missio Dei*, is the true essence of the Church.

A big map

'Derived' church is essentially focused on God's eternal kingdom reign. This is a rich and varied rather than narrow and shallow mission to participate in. Sharing with God in bringing in the kingdom involves every facet of human life, the whole of life, in all creation. 'Thy kingdom come' may trip off the tongue easily enough, but it is a goal that fills lives and it is the ultimate goal of the Church.

Such a focus rescues the Church from making God's mission too small. Or,

when church falls into that trap – challenges it. God's mission cannot properly be understood in terms of building up the 'interior' life of the Church, much less numerical church growth, getting new people in to 'do the jobs' or perpetuate the internal traditions of local churches. Bishop John Finney once stated 'you cannot sustain a missionary congregation. It's like a ring doughnut, there's nothing at the centre.'[6] This critique is right if being 'mission minded' simply means those 'inside' being obsessed with bringing others inside who become obsessed with bringing others inside. That's less about God's mission and more about exhaustion. But when the mission is partnering God in working for God's kingdom come, being mission minded is the highest and proper calling of the church, and through it the Church finds its best reason for being.

Early warning system

Church understood in this way also serves as an early warning system, or monitor of health. Whenever church seems not to be filled and impelled by the Holy Spirit in the pursuit of God's kingdom come then things can be said to be wrong. It is no accident that the Pentecost event marks not only the 'birthday' of the Church but also the 'birthday' of the Christian mission. So, whenever kingdom mission is relegated or supplanted as the essential defining characteristic of church, things are deemed to be amiss and incomplete. Church defined by the *missio Dei* never finds its true centre by turning in on itself. For example, whenever preoccupation with its own survival takes centre stage then church is deemed to have ceased to live in harmony with its very life-force, to have lost sight of its *raison d'être* and inevitably dysfunction and atrophy set in. Lesslie Newbigin commented, 'When the church ceases to be a mission, then she openly denies the titles by which she is adorned in the New Testament.'[7] Church understood to be essentially the chosen partner of God in the mission of the kingdom therefore implicitly critiques all other understandings of church. Such a view of church is the lens in the camera, no matter what pictures are taken. As such there are implications for all other conceptions and understandings about the nature, life, shape and practices of the Christian Church in the sense that they are evaluated by this primary missiological understanding.

Variety

This missiological approach to the essence of the Church is implicitly *contextual*. It recognizes and welcomes that various forms, structures and expressions of church can and will emerge naturally from essence so defined. But, importantly, the essence is not distilled by boiling down to the lowest

common denominator for all the forms and expressions of church. Rather, that each form and expression imitates its creator God, risen Saviour and infilling Spirit so as to be identifiably, unmistakably church.

The essence of church therefore lies as much in its difference as in its similarity. Not difference for its own sake, but the difference that is a natural consequence of being an incarnational community of the Christian Godhead in a particular time and place and set in a particular context. It is no surprise then that the *Mission-shaped Church* report goes for a simple 'essence' implying church is a community gathered around the risen Jesus.

Helpful historical hints

In support of such a simple essence, we might note three important hints from Christian history. First there has always been a variety of expressions of church, rather than one. Secondly, fresh expressions of church have been a natural consequence of times of renewal or upheaval in the history of the Christian faith, with the most common and repeated factor being a re-discovery of the small group and the quintessential role of the laity in the life of the Church. Thirdly, in every era of Christian history there have always been represented two kinds of expressions of church. The first has been a form of church that adopts an indigenous role in relation to culture, making its home in its native soil in order to truly be church in a missionary sense. The second has been a form of church that adopts a 'pilgrim' role in relation to its surrounding cultural context, identifying itself by distinction from normative cultural themes and values. So, for example, the basilicas of the Holy Roman Empire would belong more to the first group – the 'indigenizers' – and the early monastic orders, whether ascetic or cenobitic, would belong more to the second group – the pilgrim, counter-culturalists.

As our present post-Christian, post-Christendom culture evolves, it will be most surprising then, if fresh expressions of church do *not* appear, and if these are not types tending to *both* indigenous and pilgrim identities. Why? Because this is the required nature of kingdom focus of church created by and configured for the *missio Dei*.

So . . . fresh expressions

Church as the primary partner of the missionary God, then, explains why fresh expressions arise at all. They are not as some assert some aberration or simply an expression of maverick selfishness or discontent. At best they are expressions of a missionary God raising up a people who can effect God's highest intentions and deepest desires for this time and place. Put sharply, if the *missio Dei* in any time and place cannot be pursued with the Church as it is, God raises up a new Church. We might say that 'essence', then, seems only obliquely related to church structures, theological opinions and modes of worship, if only in the sense that a variety of these has existed, and continues to exist today in a collection of entities only very few would challenge as truly church.

'Contributories'

This account of the essence of the Church has not dropped out of heaven! Rather it rests upon and is shaped by themes and theories associated with several theologians whose input, to different degrees, contributes to this missional ecclesiology. The briefest outline of some of these 'contributories' may be helpful.

- A *missio Dei* theological lens, often associated with Karl Barth, but more extensively and explicitly developed by writers of mission theology such as David Bosch[8] and Lesslie Newbigin.[9]
- A dynamic understanding of God working in and beyond human history, particularly related to eschatology and the kingdom of God. This is a key theme in the 'theology of hope' movement, and is developed in the work of Jürgen Moltmann in several places.[10]
- A 'salvation history' understanding of Scripture, 'seeing the Bible whole', permitting an overarching narrative of God's dealings and intentions for humanity and the whole of the cosmos to be discerned.[11]
- Emphasis upon the Holy Trinity, both in terms of 'Persons' with 'roles', partly tending towards modalism in terms of expression, but also Trinity as unity in community and relationality such as themes developed by Miroslav Volf.[12]
- Instincts to hold together the 'this-worldly' purpose and relevance of the Church with its undisputed 'heavenly' derived nature, expressing the conviction that church that is so heavenly as to be no earthly use cannot truly be church.[13]
- A preference for 'bottom-up church of the people' rather than a top down church of ecclesiastical hierarchy is almost instinctive in those who embrace a missiological essence of church.[14]
- An acceptance that 'images' rather than 'definitions' best express the essence of church.[15] Therefore a mixed economy of church, very different in

expression and form, but coherent and unified in its essence is accepted quite naturally.

Continuing conversations

A mixed economy of church, in which fresh expressions take their rightful and crucial role and place, possesses a *number* of understandings about the essence of the Church. Therefore the overtly missiological approach to the essence of the Church I outline here inevitably engages in conversation with other approaches. Here are the beginnings of two of these conversations that need to be had.

The four classic marks: one, holy, catholic and apostolic

It means a lot to me that Christian leaders prayed long and deliberated hard at famous Councils, and came to declare, in a phrase made immortal by the formulations of classic creeds, that the Church was 'One, holy, catholic and apostolic'. Down to today these 'marks' – as they are often known – are taught to those undergoing preparation for confirmation or membership. Any conversation about the essence of the Church needs to include consideration of these classic marks.

Alongside a rightful honouring of these attributes declared to be 'the faith of the Church' is a growing realization that they did not simply drop out of heaven, but rather emerged in a particular context for particular reasons. It was Cyprian, an early Christian leader who, for a number of good local, political and theological reasons, urged their adoption as sound teaching and aspirations for a somewhat fraught local church situation. But what followed is more problematic to many. Applied later by different people in different times and situations 'One, holy, catholic and apostolic' became synonymous with the medieval Western Catholic Church which was itself virtually synonymous with the Holy Roman Empire. This is the era in which Cyprian's famous quotation *extra ecclesiam nulla salus* (outside the Church there is no salvation) became less an incentive to gospel mission and more a threat of the consequences of ecclesiastical exclusion. Liturgically this is marked by prayers for the unsaved changing from expressions that such folk are in *need* of the gospel to assertions that they are in *error* of true faith. As a result, the way the Church understands itself moves away from sober evaluation and towards self-righteous congratulation.

Whether talking to other Christians (particularly those in the East), or arguing with those deemed to be heretics, or contending with Jews and Muslims, the Church based primarily in Rome automatically identified itself as the one, holy, catholic and apostolic Church. 'One' came to mean 'this one' and suffered no real alternatives. This one alone was holy and catholic, nor did any other possess leadership in the true succession of the apostles. What was initially a statement of witness and a challenge to piety became, at its worst, a piece of ecclesiastical apartheid.

None of this makes the four classic marks *wrong* in themselves. But it does mean that these marks have not only been used but also abused. They are not neutral, exhaustive or unquestionably applied in the same way for all time.

Reinterpreting the four marks is not new, of course. The Reformers were almost obsessed with working out the true nature of church and their obsession is understandable. Whether it was deemed possible to part from the body that claims to be the one true Church, to contain its essence, and remain properly church was crucial to the outworking of the nature of the Protestant Reformation. Significantly, they came to decide not to abandon the four marks as 'merely' Roman Catholic. But they also went to great lengths to identify and explain where their interpretation differed from that of the Catholic Church, usually turning to the Scriptures as their guide. This exercise led them to identify new 'marks', which, as far as they were concerned, properly constituted 'church', or even more, were at the essence of church. The word needed to be faithfully preached, (a reduced number of) sacraments had to be rightly administered and 'Godly discipline' had to prevail.

The four classic marks continue to be reworked today, and by those committed to a view of the essence of church much as I outline here. Howard Snyder, for example, retains the four marks but holds alongside them four 'mirror' marks that, though not explicitly found in creeds have always been present in Christianity. Alongside *one* (emphasizing uniformity) the church is *diverse* (emphasizing variety). Alongside *holy* (emphasizing 'apartness') the Church is *charismatic* (emphasizing anointedness). Alongside *catholic* (emphasizing universality) the Church is *local* (emphasizing contextuality). And alongside *apostolic* (emphasizing authority) the Church is *prophetic* (emphasizing 'sentness').[16] Thus, classic marks of the Church are retained but reworked in such a way that church is presented not only as an organized institution but also as an organic movement, this latter being more important to essence than the former. The *Mission-shaped Church* report puts its own reworking more pithily: 'One' focuses 'in', 'holy' focuses 'up', 'catholic' becomes 'of' and 'apostolic' focuses 'out'.[17]

Values, practices and likenesses

The extent to which the essence of church can be articulated as a series of *values* is an important conversation to continue. Many of our mission statements are couched in the language of values rather than 'forms'. Values appear to be, for many of us, an acceptable way of discussing essence in our radically pluralist cultural context. Consequently, terms such as 'incarnational' and 'relational' are becoming popular terms to articulate the essence of the Church, perhaps precisely because they are diffuse rather than definite, and permit many variant expressions, being highly susceptible to contextualizing factors.

It is important, however, that our liking for articulating the essence of church through the language of values does not fall foul of the older distinction, made in cultural modernity, between 'value' and 'fact'. Any understanding of 'values' that can be unrelated to 'fact' is a non-starter today. Yes, church 'is' before it 'does', but today we only know what a thing *is*, in a number of powerful ways, by what it *does* and *how* it does what it does. Today therefore, the essence of church must be more discernibly holistic than modernist distinctions would permit. Our lives and lips must agree.

It follows that the extent to which *lifestyle* and *practices* define the essence of the Church is a necessary continuing conversation. Christianity is closely associated with practices and rituals, some of which are deemed by many to be of the essence of church. Indeed, the nature and identity of many of our historic Christian denominations relate closely to certain traditions and practices. Most Christian groupings still share bread and wine, whether around a common dining table in a 'house church', often at the end of a meal, off paper plates in a café church, or in more traditional settings. Most Christian groupings baptize people in the threefold name, whether they are in the sea, or meeting in the local swimming pool. Nearly all fresh expressions take seriously Christian hospitality as a defining practice.

There seems to be an inevitability that Christian communities that develop defining practices reach a point where these practices are (rightly) challenged by others who argue that these very practices, or the significance now placed on them, cannot legitimately constitute the essence of the Church. This is where some of us are today. The challenge of fresh expressions in a mixed economy for most of us lies not so much in a refusal to inhabit these practices *per se*, but in accurately distinguishing between these practices and the structures and rules in which they take place, especially if they sometimes seem to hamper rather than enable participation in *the missio Dei*.

This conversation is important because I suspect that the more *laissez-faire* attitude inherent within and possibly necessary to fresh expressions of church with respect to some Christian traditions, practices and structures will itself change over the next passage of time. This is not to suggest that all fresh expressions will move naturally to inhabit the structures, polity or practices of their parent inherited denominations, but it is to suggest that structures, traditions and practices of one sort or another seem to be necessary for Christian communities and are not, of themselves, antithetic to being mission-shaped. The mixed economy of practices is therefore, to my mind, both inevitable and welcome. An acceptance of such varieties of practice, together with conversations about their significance in relation to the essence of the Church is a key issue over the next period of time.

Critical to the life of the Church in this land is whether the mixed economy with all its likenesses and differences becomes truly normative and accepted by the gatekeepers of historic denominations. Their non-acceptance will not staunch what many believe to be the impulse of the missionary Spirit, but their acceptance and openness to renewal will free up and speed up what, if it is of God, will be irresistible. For what lies at the heart of the Church – its essence – is a missionary Triune God who calls into being a people with whom to share God's nature and purpose – that people, infused with the Spirit – is the Christian Church.

3

What is the role of sacramental ministry in fresh expressions of church?

Lindsay Urwin OGS

It is still generally the case that sacraments and fresh expressions of the Church are strangers to one another. Why is this? Does it need to be the case? Or is it that sacraments can play a vital role in this potentially exciting and worth-while attempt to connect with a generation that has long since given up much thought to the worship of God, a generation that occasionally comes to itself and longs for something deeper than that which the prevailing culture offers, but looks not to the established churches?

The Church must ever be attending to its stewardship of these mysteries and we all need to recover our love for the sacraments and our belief in them as places of divine encounter. I'm going to be arguing therefore for a fresh approach, and that we need to consider 'chilling out' with regard to the rules and regulations with which we steward them, so that they may be the blessing they truly are.

It is not that sacraments and sacramentals and their potential as symbols to attract have not had advocates in this new movement, but their power has tended to be seen in their use as a technique to attract in a 'more than words' multi-media world, a world where subjective feelings are the test of success, where what 'works' matters more than what is true. Sacraments are only worth celebrating if they draw people into an experience of truth, and for us the ultimate truth is Jesus.

So let me begin, if I may, by reminding you that the Church exists to adore God and to proclaim in word and deed what we know of him. At the heart are the events in the great long Easter weekend and on to Pentecost and the great outpouring – events so charged with divine love that the fortunes of the whole of creation were transformed.

The doing of the Church, and that includes fresh expressions depends on these events. As the Anglican mystic, Evelyn Underhill expressed it:

> Worship is conditioned by a concrete fact; the stooping down of the Absolute ... The primary declaration of Christianity is not 'This do' but 'This happened'.[1]

Worship flows from doctrine, though it also helps us to form it. Those of us charged with leading people in worship must remember the solemn task and responsibility we have, for most people learn or receive their doctrine on their knees. In our worship and the life that flows from it, fresh expressions included, we must ensure that we are introducing people to spiritual experiences that faithfully reflect and present Christian truth as the Church has discerned it.

Of course, all authentic experiences of Christ are the work of the Spirit, who is always the agent of Christ's coming, whether in the overshadowing of Mary, the moving of the stone from the tomb, at work in your faltering declaration of faith, or in the celebration of a sacrament which is my particular theme. Augustine of Hippo says, 'The Word hovers over the elements and a sacrament results.'[2] The Spirit is the agent of the Word.

In an extraordinary sermon from his Anglican days, John Henry Newman speaks of the way Christ continues to come to his world through his Church:

> Christ's priests have no priesthood but His. They are merely his shadows and organs, they are His outward signs; and what they do He does; when they baptize, He is baptizing; when they bless, He is blessing. He is in all acts of His Church, and one of its acts is not more truly His than any other, for all are His ... since historically speaking, time has gone on, and the Holy One is away, certain outward forms are necessary, by way of bringing us again under His shadow; and we enjoy those blessings through a mystery, or sacramentally.[3]

We can say then that sacramental encounter (like preaching) brings us under the shadow of the cross, and to the person on the cross. This is why they both attract and rebuke. It is why they demand so much of the participant. It may be why we shy away from making use of them in evangelism, somehow thinking that 'softer', entertaining services of word and song are more palatable for the 'weaker brethren'. For myself, I cannot accept that authentic Services of the Word are inherently more palatable or accessible than sacramental encounter, for the word is a sword and it convicts, its preaching takes us to the cross. One might even argue that, in a culture saturated with trivial, unmemorable and unreliable words, Christ-filled symbol and action might have *more* chance of breaking through.

Of course, we must approach both word and sacrament with openness, wonder, repentance and with trembling faith but, in the end, both God's word and his sacraments depend wholly on God who instituted them as gift. I would add that I consider it a tragedy that history has left us with a legacy of competition between Bible and sacrament as places of divine encounter. Until they are rediscovered as flowing from the same source we will remain weak.

One of my favourite saints, Ephraem the Syrian, speaks to the Lord:

> In your sacraments we welcome you every day and receive you in our bodies. Make us worthy to experience within us the resurrection for which we hope. By the grace of baptism we conceal within our bodies the treasure of your divine life. This treasure increases as we eat at the table of your sacraments.

He calls the sacraments 'a mirror in which we are able to recognize the resurrection',[4] and so they will have all the mystery of the first experience of resurrection – the joy, the pain of glorious wounds, the wondering, the touching, and the cost.

If all this is true, then sacraments are less an institutional activity, something the Church does, and more something Christ does with and through his people. As I have tried to understand the reasons for the general shyness in making use of sacramental encounter in evangelism and now fresh expressions, I have come to believe that the source of reticence is a wrong-headed notion that sacraments are institutional events. Since we live in a world turned off by institutions we jettison them in order to be free, relaxed, spontaneous and attractive. That is perhaps a bit crass, I know, but I think there is truth in it. What really needs to happen is a rediscovery of the Christ-presentness in the sacraments – that they are a sensuous encounter with him – and their ritual actions de-institutionalized and liberated. This is not as simple as taking off robes! We need to demystify the mystery, making it easier for people to *enter* the mystery, rather than dumb it down!

To make that task seem worth while, we need truly to believe that each sacramental encounter is a fresh touch from Christ, and make it as obviously so as we can. We need to trust that through them we can have a personal encounter with Jesus or, as Newman would say, be brought under his shadow. My own catholic tradition has probably always believed this, but it has over-ritualized sacraments and, in over-analysing the 'how' of them, has hedged them with too many rules and regulations in a desire to ensure they happen correctly and actually. In Anglicanism generally, for which the liturgical *Book of Common Prayer* reflected its doctrine, loyalty to this inheritance has involved declaring obedience to forms of words 'authorized or allowed'. Perhaps more important is a loyalty to the doctrine of the Spirit at work in the encounter.

Some might suggest that only the initiated can recognize or should experience Christ in sacramental encounter. I cannot limit them in this way, for if indeed each sacramental encounter is a fresh touch from Christ, just imbibing the experience, even for the first time, can bring forth the response. I have seen it happen!

For myself, I believe that the Family Service movement, our last foray into fresh expressions, was spectacularly useless in drawing the majority of those who experienced them into long-term commitment, partly because it was almost devoid of the power of sacramental encounter. Services failed to leave people significantly different, and took leave of the truth that Christian worship can never be divorced from sacrifice.

Sacramental encounter

Now let me take you to the theatre of a 2,000-strong Anglican comprehensive school where for some 12 months a 'youth congregation' called Eden has been meeting once a month on a Sunday evening, attracting some 120 people of all ages who are networked between times by small groups and an imaginative blog site. The youth missioner is being ordained priest.

For all the encouragement and strength of Eden there is something lacking in its life and the time had arrived when to hold back would be to give the impression that it is possible to live an authentic Christian life, a life faithful to Scripture without it. What was lacking was sacramental encounter. Eden needed a priest.

I would strongly insist that it would be perfectly possible and appropriate for a brother or sister priest to join the Eden congregation for the specific purpose of presiding at the Eucharist, for relationality in the Body of Christ does not depend on personal knowledge of one another, but on God who is *Our*

Father, and on the unifying, saving work of Jesus. Yet we know in practice the importance of sensitive, connected love, especially when it comes to the challenges of worship with young people and those who are on the edge of faith. Not every priest can witness well to that relationality or has the necessary flexibility and courage to come out of his or her comfort zone. Derek (the youth missioner) had demonstrated to me a growing love – not only of Eden and young people, but for the whole Church – so essential in every minister. I could imagine him ministering in other contexts so felt that I could ordain him safely.

The whole process of organizing this ordination was a journey of discovery! In Chichester deacons are ordained by the diocesan bishop in the cathedral, while priests are ordained by the area bishop, often in the local church where the candidate serves. In Derek's case, his 'local church' was Eden, and so I decided that he should be ordained in that context. As I reflected about how this might affect the way I ordained him, I soon realized I could and should not answer the question alone. I needed the help of the Eden team.

Of course, the local context was not *all* that was important for, however unique Eden is, Derek was to receive essentially the same gift as all the others who were being ordained at the time, indeed they were to receive the Orders given 'from the apostles' time'.[5] Derek was just receiving what everyone else receives: empowerment from above to live the same recognizable life of the presbyterate, in the place where he had been sent. There is, or should be, a sameness about all of us who have received the gift.

All this meant that in the actual planning of the ordination we needed to witness to both the universality, or one might say, the catholic nature of the encounter with Christ that is ordination, and to the particularity of Eden. Actually, this principle should be true for almost everything we do in fresh expressions. The Christian Church should know nothing of novelty,[6] what it must know about is renewal and updating and uncluttering, and the presentation of gospel gifts sensitive to the context. So, alongside the questions about the 'how to' at Eden, we had to ask what was essential to ordination, in order to make it clear that we were doing something that belonged to the whole Church.

As a strong believer in the 'take the risk and, if necessary, apologize afterwards' approach to life, I may have played a little fast and loose with the Canons at this ordination, but have no doubt that had second- or third-century Christians been present (and perhaps they were!) they would have known what we were doing.

Much was planned and delivered by the Eden leadership team. A band played as people arrived, and there was a coffee bar and food. The almost universal tradition that ordination takes place in the context of the Eucharist added a challenge since it would be the first Eucharist at Eden, but the Breaking of Bread was non-negotiable. The Penitential rite included a film clip from *The Mission*. As it happened, because of the screen I had to abandon my well-planned and eminently suitable president's chair for a plastic one! The Gospel reading was done in rap style by the whole Assembly, the text being 'Salt and light'. Although I was wearing my usual chasuble and mitre, Derek began the service as he usually did, wearing jeans and a T-shirt. Only during a haunting musical interlude by a solo flute did he leave and return in a monastic-looking alb, carrying over his shoulder, as all candidates in my episcopal area do, a large self-made wooden cross – in his case made of railway sleepers! As he made his way through the congregation with the heavy cross clunking on each step of the theatre incline, the atmosphere was electric and the shape of his life clear. The sense of wondering among the young people was palpable, all the more so as I called them to prayer and Derek prostrated himself on the floor.

The litany, probably considered by Cranmer (architect of the first Anglican ordinal) to be of great significance as part of the prayer that goes with the laying on of hands to make a valid ordination, was written and sung by young people with a drum and bass track playing (this may be where I strayed from the Canons), and included a presentation on a projection screen. Because I regard the Ordination prayer to be too deep for words, I usually sing it to plainsong. I decided to stick with that, and somehow it didn't jar. Knowing it by heart I prefer to keep my eyes closed. As I laid my hands on Derek I opened my eyes, only to see dozens of young people with their hands outstretched in the act of ordaining! Should I have told them to put their hands down? After all, we want no confusion. You need a bishop to ordain. Only bishops ordain in the Church of England. Or by accident, and through the spontaneity of these young people, who love their pastor and who didn't know the rules, had I rediscovered the important truth so evident in early ordination rites in both the West, and especially the East, in which the prayers of the ordinary people of God invoking the Holy Spirit upon the candidate are as emphasized as the consecrated episcopal hands? Perhaps fresh sacramental expressions are not simply for the sake of making them accessible to the young or the unevangelized but for the rediscovery of their power and importance among those of us who have been hanging around the sanctuary for years. Perhaps this is an unexpected responsibility God is laying upon this movement.

Risky exceptions

It is the tradition at Eden that people feel free to come and go from the main place of action, and the coffee bar remains open throughout the worship. This must have been so, because later, in what was to some extent the holy chaos of the administration of communion, a teenage girl walked past drinking a can of fizzy drink. Was this irreverent? I suspect too, that some received communion who had not yet been baptized, contrary to Christian tradition, at least from the time of Justin Martyr. I content myself, though not easily, that God is well used to people doing things in the wrong order, and it underlines for me the need in sacramental fresh expressions to have a 'lively doctrine of exceptions'.

It is not a question of letting go of appropriate norms in the stewarding of these mysteries, or of any permanent re-ordering, but believing that these gifts are so essential to authentic Christian life, and our duty to offer them so crucial to our own identity and faithfulness, that agreed exceptions on the way are worth the risk. One might even suggest that the naming of exceptions safeguards the norm. Take, for example, the matter of reception of Holy Communion before baptism. The norm is quite properly admission to the Body before receiving the Body. Any exception in an evangelistic context is in the hope that the feeding will lead the person to discover a desire to belong to the Body and seek baptism. It would be a misuse of the exception to suggest the person need not be baptized or fail to seek a timely opportunity to suggest to the person that he or she be baptized.

I suspect that reflection about an agreed doctrine of exceptions is one of the hard questions that we, and especially church, leaders must address. It is surely a question for our Liturgical Commission in consultation with those who are exploring sacramental encounter in the fresh expression context. Perhaps the guardians of the faith, as bishops are sometimes called, are in danger of overprotecting the Lord. Like the disciples with the children we become a stumbling block to an encounter with Jesus.

An inspiring remix

The service didn't end in any formal way, but with praise and dance to a funky and uplifting remix of 'How Great Thou Art' in which I happily joined, mitre and all. What happened during that evening was described in a newspaper article by Danny Baker as a 'huge clash of cultures'. 'The results are inspiring ... as ancient meets post modern.'[7] It was a mingling of the contemporary and transitory youth tradition or 'culture' as expressed by Eden with the abiding tradition, the Christ-given and Christ-filled tradition, which we pray becomes exactly what the Gospel rap expressed – salt and light. It was alive! It was a very different scenario from the norm, yet it was essentially the same thing – a fresh expression of the same thing, so crucial as far as I am concerned to our strategy – a renewed way of presenting the reliable gifts. It was unafraid and trusting, trusting primarily to the greater power of the abiding tradition to break through, to win over, even work through that which is transitory even tawdry and will pass away.

Forgive this long description. It isn't especially unique, but I tell it to underline my strong belief that fresh expressions of the Church are only interesting and will only bring transformation if they are evidently fresh expressions of Christ. Only if they draw people into a personal encounter with the living Christ that is both liberating and costly will they be of abiding significance. Sacraments can do this. Indeed, we have no choice if we are to be obedient to the vision of church life that emerges in Scripture and grew very quickly.

You might suggest to me that this is self-evident, but not necessarily so. A couple of years ago I was asked to chair a working party on teenagers and worship in the Church of England. Among the evidence we gathered was the experience of a fresh expression youth congregation in a large team ministry. It had been in existence for seven or so years, maybe more, and clearly had done great work. But over that time it had celebrated fewer Eucharists than the number of fingers on your hands, and I don't think it had ever presented a candidate for confirmation. This won't do. It cannot be described as an authentic fresh expression of church in terms of the New Testament. I suspect that those who think that to expose new people to the Eucharist is too much too soon might find themselves never getting around to it.

In the New Testament, broadly, but not exclusively in the texts that cover the period from Maundy Thursday to the Ascension, Jesus gently introduces the brethren into the Spirit-infused means by which people will be able to experience him, have fresh expressions of him until he comes again. We need to attend to these, and they need to shape our attempts at fresh expressions. They are not all sacraments, although one might be able to say that they are all sacramental (an outward sign of an inward grace), all sensuous symbols.

The limits of this chapter mean that I cannot write about them all in any depth, but let me mention them briefly. First of all, we see this in the foot washing. As we wash each other's feet and the feet of our local communities we experience Christ. You will remember the text in Matthew (chapter 25) where some are asked at the time of judgement how they had served Christ, visited Christ, fed Christ. Jesus is clear that when you did it to the least of the brethren you did it to him. Don't you see that it is not simply that the poor need us; we need *them* in order to have an experience of Christ? The poor are a fresh expression of Christ. Then, of course, the so-well-known Emmaus story (Luke 24.13-35) speaks of Jesus helping them discover how he can be found in the Scripture. This reflects his teaching in John 5 when he gives the Jews a lesson in exegesis: 'You search the scriptures because you think in them you have eternal life; and it is they that bear witness about me' (John 5.39). People can hear Christ now through their listening with humility to the Scriptures, knowing that they are, as Ephraem the Syrian suggests, like an everlasting fountain, which you can never exhaust and from which you may only draw a little ... but it is a little of Christ. He says the Scriptures can only be consumed little by little, perhaps like Jesus himself, perhaps like the chalice.

Then there is the love of the brethren, which is the essence of life in the Catholic Church, and there is sadly, no room to reflect about the experience Thomas had of the risen Christ in his glorious wounds and what this might say to us about how we live our life as a Church, and the truth that only when people can accept that their name is written on his wounded hands do they know what it cost Jesus, so that they can whisper, 'My Lord and my God'.

It is, of course, in these texts that we find Jesus introducing the supper and then appearing to eat with the disciples after the resurrection, are commanded to baptize and given the promise of the anointing power of the Spirit.

All these ways of having a fresh expression of Christ are primarily his idea and not ours, and are utterly to be relied upon. At their heart is an exchange of love, dependent and flowing from, first and foremost a unique exchange of love that took place within the very being of God on Calvary. Their power flows from that tremendous love. They are key ways in which we can ensure that we are being faithful, that we are offering what he wants us to offer.

The Point

Some years ago now, I heard from two Christians, a priest, Will Kemp, and the well-known Christian song-writer musician Matt Redman. They told me they felt called to set up a network congregation in my episcopal area. I didn't ask them how many other bishops they had spoken to first. By God's grace, we were able to find the money to finance the priest for four years from a newly constituted mission fund, and The Point was born, though not immediately, for the small core leadership team made the wise decision to wait upon the Lord and to pray for six months together, using Acts 2.42-47 as the core text that would shape all that they would do. As I was alongside them in this, I spent some time with them exploring what it might mean – as a fresh expression of the Church seeking to reach out to the uncommitted – to 'break the bread'. This seemed important because it was so clearly central to the life of the first Christians, and there is enough in the early writing of our community that makes it clear that for them, feeding on Christ in the Eucharist drew them into direct communion with him, and strengthened them for the persecutions. Indeed, I think I remember making it clear that in the evolution of this new community, a major step on the road to becoming an authentic expression of resurrection living would be the day we celebrated a baptism, confirmation and Eucharist at The Point. That day came.

I wish I had space to describe fully the testimonies and the total immersion, the immediate pouring of the fragrant oil of chrism on the candidates with laying on of hands in the water as they came 'out of the tomb on the third day'. As it happens The Point meets at a Catholic school that has a central courtyard in the shape of an amphitheatre. It was as if they were entering the arena for death – they were! Spontaneous applause erupted for each candidate, and so many of their non-Christian friends were present to witness the event.

As with the Eden experience, I was confronted as leader of the worship with a series of uncomfortable challenges. Some who had been baptized as infants wanted to get in the water and be immersed. In a culture that tends to think that only the things you remember can really have mattered, and as a genuine response to the new joy they had found in Christ, it was understandable but contrary to sound and well-thought-out church teaching. We found a compromise. They verbally claimed the blessing of their baptism and declared their love for Jesus, took themselves under the water once and were then confirmed. Having said that, I'm not sure how obvious the difference was to many there, and I didn't labour the point at the service (having preached my sermon the previous Wednesday at The Point's evening adult teaching meeting). I have a bit of a suspicion that I confirmed some people who had already received that gift. I live with that. It's not usual or to be encouraged, but I rest content that the Lord knows his own, and what has already happened between him and them.

Then there was the challenge of communion among so many who were unused to the usual liturgy of the Church. Coffee and cake followed the confirmation itself in a large hall set out as a café. A ten-minute address about the fundamental difference between coffee and cake and the bread and wine in the effect it has upon you – cake turns into you, while the latter, the food of the Eucharist, because Christ is the stronger, turns you into him, making you more Christ-like, then a shortened Eucharistic Prayer (probably not quite canonical) with rolls and wine on the tables for folk to share among themselves, passing it to one another. All were invited to share in the gifts if they wished.

I acknowledge that this open table approach is contrary to Anglican teaching. It is an exception, and my fragile judgement on that occasion was that I was not responsible for anyone eating and drinking condemnation to themselves – a serious matter indeed in the writings of Paul. Perhaps I will have the opportunity to baptize someone who received the bread and wine on that day (in the wrong order), just because they had been invited to eat.

I am encouraged in this approach by the feedings of Christ in the New Testament. We know how central eating with people was for Jesus. In breaking all the social and ritual rules that surrounded meals, he turned the social and religious order on their heads. The Jews defined themselves (and they are not alone in this) by who they would or would not eat with.

Jesus was unfussy. Some liturgical scholars point out that eating with Jesus was the initiation rite into life with him before baptism took that role. It is interesting that the teaching in John 6 about eating his flesh and drinking his blood as a required means of sharing in his life – a teaching that surely has sacramental undertones – is preceded by the marvellous feeding on the mountain side. All ate, though none, including the disciples, really knew his true identity. Only Jesus could provide the food, and through his blessing it was magnified beyond measure, magnified with his desire to feed those who needed feeding.

All the apostles could do was gather up the crumbs, which serves as a healthy reminder to those who have the privilege of presiding at the Eucharist that every time we are entirely dependent on the generosity of Christ to make more of the humble bread and wine we place on the table. We stand on tiptoes with breathless expectation that indeed, 'the Spirit will be sent upon the gifts to make them holy'. Of course, these miraculous feedings are not Eucharists as we understand them, in that they are not connected to or dependent on Christ's saving death. Yet I believe that the attitude of heart so evident in the Saviour on these occasions may give us a little licence, a good hope that our exceptions might be acceptable to him, as we seek to introduce folk to the gift of his body and blood. We know that the food was essential to the living of Christian life from the start, and it is nigh on unimaginable to speak of an evangelized person who does not love and share in the sacraments. Risks must be taken.

Talking of gathering up crumbs reminds me that at the café Eucharist there was no strategy for dealing with what we call the ablutions. Such value do we rightly place upon the sacred gifts and the fresh expression of Christ that they are, that in our tradition we attend to the leftovers. This is required. But among those who are not so advanced in their understanding yet want to eat, it would have been meaningless or counterproductive to have made a fuss about collecting it all and consuming it ritually, unless of course we had organized waiters! I would do next time, but this was a time of learning. Some 'higher church' people who attended to observe the celebration were rather perplexed by this. They are not entirely wrong in their anxiety, but I hope they saw the joy and reverence and love among the assembly, which is perhaps more important. In any case I well remember a Catholic theologian when asked about the ablutions and the attention that must be given to their reverent consumption after Communion, suggesting that in the midst of our proper care we can rest on the probability that what God gets into, he can get out of.

Food certainly seems to be a central part of the life of most fresh expressions, but the *agape* is not enough; the laden table of hospitality is not enough. *Alpha* missed a trick, no not a trick, a grace, by not leading people on from the joy of eating supper together to the meal. It led some to want to keep on experiencing *Alpha*, but who did not make the journey to the altar.

And far from being exclusive, the Eucharist is in fact the great leveller. Whether you are the Archbishop of Canterbury, the poorest of the poor, or the Queen of the realm, the headmaster of a school or a snotty boy in the first year, you all receive the same fare – bread and wine. Is not this a wonderful sign to the world of the way God wants his world to live, with an essential equality of provision? That is why a fresh expression of the Church which loads up tables with cakes and goodies to entice the punter and indeed practises hospitality, is not enough of a sign. It is not a true foretaste of the messianic banquet, for there are tables that are empty and some have none.

And there is more. In our Western culture today we have a particular responsibility to bear witness to a different kind of materialism. We must speak to the disease of Affluenza that has struck our land with its obsession with the accruing of more and more and the regular disposal and replacement of possessions. Nothing lasts more than two years. The consequences of that for the planet are now sadly all too obvious. We Christians on the other hand are materialistic in a different way. We reverence matter, we do not worship matter, but we reverence it because, as John Damascene says, 'for our sake, God became material'. The Lord is not done with material things at his ascension. He has embraced the material and will not leave go of it. The sacraments are signs of this with their use of material things to convey the presence of God; a sign of a world charged with the grandeur of God. It is not just people that can reflect the face of God.

There is a desperate need in the fresh expressions movement to nudge the Church, and especially those in leadership, to both rediscover the possibility of an encounter with Jesus in sacramental events and to enable the experience in new ways, for the sake not only of those who do not yet believe, but to rekindle the desire in existing believers. There is a need for de-regulation in evangelistic circumstances, for a proper and agreed doctrine of exceptions as we seek to draw in to life with Christ those who are so far from us and who do not realize the source of their hunger. Jesus has food to give and only he can provide it. We are his providers, and if we fail to feed in his name, we will answer.

4

What is at the heart of a global perspective on the Church?

Tim Dakin

The world's local church

Just suppose you could look down from a satellite on every single expression of church on the face of the globe. As you viewed the earth from space you might look down on house churches in Mongolia, mega-churches in Korea, secret followers of Jesus in the Middle East, or churches on rubbish tips in Brazil. Then imagine zooming in on *your* church – like on 'Google Earth'. Might you see things differently in the light of your 'global perspective'? And if so, how? That's what this chapter is about. It's about how following Jesus implies a global perspective because our discipleship is rooted in God's global mission.

The apostle Paul discerned the vital significance of such a global perspective. In the first two chapters of Ephesians he explores the place of the Church in the mystery of God's mission – its worldwide and even cosmic significance. Paul then identifies his role, as the apostle to the gentiles, directly after which he prays this famous prayer:

> *For this reason* I bow my knees before the Father from whom *every family* in heaven and on earth takes its name. I pray that, according to the riches of his glory, he may grant that you may be strengthened in your inner being with power through his Spirit, and that Christ may dwell in your hearts through faith, as you are rooted and grounded in love. I pray that you may have the power to comprehend, *with all the saints, what is the breadth and length, the height and depth, and to know the love of Christ* that surpasses knowledge, so that you may be filled with the fullness of God.
>
> (Ephesians 3.14-19)

These are not separate issues: Paul knows that unless 'every family' and 'all the saints' enter into, participate in, the vast perspective of God's love, they will not grasp the true relationship between mission and church. God's mission is nothing other than the outworking of God's love for creation: every family in heaven and earth. A certain kind of spirituality, expressed in our praying, is essential to a global perspective on church.

It is all too easy to become focused on our local church and think of God's love in local terms, forgetting how we are enmeshed with 'every family' and 'all the saints'. So, one ingredient in our prayers may be a prayer diary that suggests people, places and projects to pray for in God's mission around the world. And I expect that many of us use 'the Grace' (see 2 Corinthians 13.14) to conclude our prayers. In what follows I relate the four dimensions of God's global mission of love to the four parts of the Grace:

- the grace of our Lord Jesus Christ (height)
- the love of God (depth)
- the fellowship of the Holy Spirit (breadth)
- be with us all for evermore (length).[1]

But first, I begin by exploring the motivational character of this spirituality: what it looks like; and I also offer some initial thoughts on how it affects our perspective on church. Then, in four sections, I look at the dynamics of this spirituality: how it works, fundamentally, in terms of mission. I then review the perspective that has emerged.[2]

Missional spirituality

My way of answering the question about a global perspective on church is to outline the spirituality that creates it. This then defines the Church in terms of the dynamics of spirituality rather than, say, the classic marks of the Church (one, holy, catholic, apostolic). My proposal is that where you find the dynamics of participation in God's mission there you will find the Church – indeed a global perspective on the Church.

Thus God's mission is the 'force field' within which a global perspective on church is developed. God's mission comes first, then the Church. The Church is shaped within the four dimensions of God's global mission: its height, depth, breadth and length. Those caught up in the dynamics of God's mission become the shape and the shapers of the Church. Thus, a global perspective on church is generated by a 'missional'[3] spirituality,[4] this in turn generates a mission-shaped Church – which reinforces a global perspective. Taken together, we have a virtuous circle something like this:

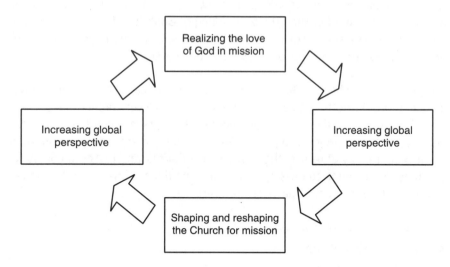

This approach builds on Bevans' and Schroeder's view that: 'mission ... is prior to the church, and is constitutive of its very existence' and then, 'as mission takes shape so does the church'.[5] They illustrate their perspective by rehearsing the breathless – seven – re-shapings of mission and therefore the Church as recorded in Acts: before Pentecost, Pentecost, Stephen, Philip, Cornelius, Antioch, and then Paul![6] Each of these has a profound impact and each is rooted in discovering the height, depth, breadth and length of God's mission.

Fulfilling the gap

Modern examples of how the Church was radically reshaped by missional spirituality include the mission societies that emerged in the eighteenth century. These societies used the model of the overseas trading company, and modern communications, to send missionaries abroad. So the mission societies were largely responsible for generating what we now know as the Anglican Communion, though the local church was largely planted and grown by indigenous leaders.[7] But, significantly, the societies were also fresh expressions of church: Christian communities fired by a missional spirituality that motivated some to offer their lives for the gospel's sake overseas, and motivated others to support them and to live a life of witness. Mission spirituality is not just a viewpoint but a perspective that inspires and motivates Christians to great things.

This missional spirituality led to fresh expressions of church – the mission societies – so that the Church itself became more mission-shaped. This is what the Holy Spirit does: he encourages fresh expressions of a mission-shaped Church by reviving and renewing people in their spirituality. The Spirit draws us into the 'force field' of God's mission. Thus, it was out of the continent-wide European Evangelical Revival that many of the modern mission societies grew. The 'hard question' they addressed was how to relate this new missional spirituality, with its global perspective, to the existing denominational expressions of church. The mission society was the answer.

Andrew Porter outlines four ways in which the mission societies related to the denominations. A society could be voluntary and non-denominational (e.g. London Mission Society); it could be voluntary, denominational but self-governed (e.g. Church Mission Society (CMS) – Anglican, or Baptist Mission Society (BMS)); it could be a formal arm of a denomination subject to that church's leaders (e.g. Society for the Propagation of the Gospel (SPG) – Anglican); or a mission society could be one with the denomination (Wesleyan Mission Society, or indeed like the Protestant Episcopal Church of the USA, which was founded as a mission society).[8]

So, whatever form they take, mission societies remind us that there should always be fresh expressions of mission-shaped church (as proposed in the *Mission-shaped Church* report). But, more importantly, they also remind us of the missional spirituality that generates them: they spring from realizing afresh the height and depth and breadth and length of God's love.

At an earlier period in history, the Protestant reformers had focused the life of the Church on certain key marks: the preaching of the word, the administration of the sacraments and the exercising of discipline. However, their picture of the Church lacked a vital element: there was no goal for the Church beyond the Church itself, i.e. in terms of God's mission. Karl Barth was to call this the 'yawning gap' in Reformation theology and practice.[9] This yawning gap was the lack of *motivation*, a missional spirituality, which generates a global mission-shaped Church. It was this gap that the mission societies were filling. So while the Reformation fathers of the Church of England, as part of the one, holy, catholic and apostolic Church, believed 'they were exploring a *fresh expression* of its particular life and calling',[10] they needed to do more: to shape a church that put missional spirituality into practice.[11]

For these reasons we need to ground our vision for the whole world – for the global – in a vision of the height, depth, length and breadth of the love of God.

It was a renewed vision of God's love for the whole world that encouraged many Anglicans to give their lives in world mission, planting the Church in other countries.

Height: The grace of our Lord Jesus Christ

Any missional spirituality that gives rise to a global perspective on church is going to have at its heart an understanding and expression of the *ultimate significance of Jesus*. The benefits and person of Jesus, 'the grace of our Lord Jesus Christ', is the gospel in a nutshell. People often discover the benefits of grace before they realize the full significance of Jesus. I have been moved by the drug rehabilitation work with which CMS is involved in various parts of the world. Whether it is drug addicts in Pakistan, Russia, or Egypt, it is the persistent love of Christian 'recovering' addicts that helps other addicts to re-evaluate their lives and their worth. They then find out more about the Jesus who loves them, with grace upon grace, as they begin their own recovery.

But how does the ultimate significance of Jesus shape a global perspective on the Church? Christianity began as a renewal movement in Judaism that overflowed its ethnic origins and rediscovered the universal significance of the promises made to Abraham – 'to be a blessing to all nations' (Genesis 12.3). These promises were re-interpreted through Jesus. But the question remained as to how people were to relate to Jesus and to receive the promised blessings. This question opened up the scope of the gospel.

Thus, for Jews, Jesus was the Messiah, 'the Christ', but, for gentiles he was 'the Lord'; yet for Jews and gentiles together Jesus was to *both* groups the Lord Jesus Christ, uniting them in his one Body through the cross. This is how the Church begins to grow and becomes a community that expresses the ultimate significance of Jesus. The more mission happens, the greater Jesus is seen to be – as more and more people discover his ultimate significance. As Paul grappled with his calling to take the gospel to the gentiles, he came to realize who Jesus was and the reality of God's universal Church.

So it is that the Church, for Paul, takes on a global, and even a cosmic, reality. And it is this breakthrough that is celebrated in what Andrew Walls calls 'the Ephesian moment':

> If I understand what Paul says in Ephesians correctly, it is as though Christ himself is growing as the different cultures are brought together. The Ephesian moment – the social coming

together of people of two cultures to experience Christ – was quite brief. In our day the Ephesian moment has come again, and come in a richer mode . . . since the first century. Developments over several centuries . . . mean that we have innumerable cultures in the church.[12]

Roland Allen (a missionary with [U]SPG) believed the same. Writing nearly 100 years ago, he suggests that if only people were open, the Spirit would lead them in a mission that would reveal, 'manifest', Jesus in a new way – this is radical missional spirituality:

Only in the last few years have we begun to grasp what a world-wide communion might mean . . . We begin to understand what the foundation of native Churches in China or in Japan, in India and in Africa may mean for us all, bringing to us new conceptions of the manifold working of the Spirit of Christ . . . we have scarcely begun to see what it is; but we see that it is the manifestation of Christ.[13]

Depth: The love of God

On a recent visit to Eastern Nigeria I experienced again the power of the Ephesian moment. I participated in midweek Cathedral services in Onitsha where 4–5,000 people attended! It was here that the gospel was taken 150 years ago by the first African Anglican bishop, Samuel Ajayi Crowther. And for the Igbo peoples now, in their diocesan missionary areas, Jesus is still the one who breaks the power of the local cults and, in his grace for all, he is the one who includes in his Church the widow otherwise consigned to ignominious poverty. This might be a bit uncomfortable for those from the North, but it brings home afresh the ultimate significance of Jesus.

When Paul spoke to the Athenians at the Council of the Areopagus he talked about the Creator God who made the nations and allotted them their times and places in which to develop their cultures (Acts 17.26). God's love for us, as the Creator, includes the gift of culture. Through culture we develop patterns of living together and ways of making decisions, and so within our culture we search for God and hope to find him.

It is, indeed, in the depths of ourselves in our culture, into our inner persons, that God seeks to penetrate with his converting love. Paul recognizes that this means being strengthened by the power of the Spirit to receive this love of

God (Ephesians 3.16). Yet it is also in the depths of our culture that we find the greatest confusion between what God is and what we are in our cultural selves. It is here, in the depths, that a missional spirituality explores the complexity of inculturation and the challenge of idolatry.

It is in the attempt to share the ultimate significance of Jesus trans-culturally that we sometimes discover our own idolatry: we confuse of our own cultural interpretation of Jesus with what we think others should find of ultimate significance about him. It is here that we make the big mistakes – humiliating mistakes – of trying to colonize others with our culture. The mission societies have often been accused of being the handmaidens of colonialism. Without the strengthening of the Spirit in the inner person it is impossible to address the processes of trans-cultural mission and cultural idolatry. Here we're into the deep love of God's mission and deep church (as C. S. Lewis called it).

The Christian way is not to dominate or subsume other cultures within one institutional monochrome culture – that is, to proselytize. This is not the pattern demonstrated in the incarnation or in the best of Christian mission. Instead, at the heart of the Christian way is a transformation of cultures by the gospel in which they retain their distinctive identities – the process of conversion. The quality and virtue needed for this task is set out by Paul in Philippians 2: at the very heart of the incarnation is the quality of humility.

In a chapter on the Church in his classic book on the Holy Spirit's work in mission, *The Go-Between God*, John V. Taylor (of CMS) writes movingly of the Spirit's humility:[14]

> To be the very power of God yet to wait in frustration and hope until the whole be brought to fulfilment, might be called the kenosis, or self-emptying, of the Holy Spirit. For him it has been so from the beginning. If now we are caught up into his being, we must share his humiliation as well as his power.[15]

We may know that Jesus has ultimate significance for ourselves and believe that he has that significance for all – as does the Holy Spirit! – but we cannot force that truth on others. It is a discovery they make as they receive our cultural testimony to the scriptural truth about Jesus; in the process we may learn about our own cultural limits.

There needs to be a lot of love here. The love of God, known in the grace of the Lord Jesus Christ, is what enables us to come to terms with the humiliation to which Jesus called his disciples: the way of love, the grace of Jesus, is the cross – a daily discipleship!

While we may share Allen's vision of the Anglican Communion as the manifestation of Christ, we still face the challenges of what might be interpreted as a post-colonial critique of the Northern churches. At present, those from the South challenge what they see as the Northern confusion of culture and gospel in the current debate about sexuality: a confusion that some would elevate to the level of idolatry. So this continued diversity and sharp debate is also part of what it means to develop a global perspective on church.[16] Yet God's love reaches deep into culture and creation, as deep as the hell of Holy Saturday, in loving his global Church.

Breadth: The fellowship of the Holy Spirit

We may be asking ourselves, so what's new about cultural diversity, or breadth, in the Church – haven't there always been different cultures and views? It is here that the sacredness of the stranger emerges in the dynamics of missional spirituality.

At a key moment in Israel's history, which most emphasized their particular identity as God's chosen people, we find the stranger, the foreigner, being given special consideration. Even as Solomon dedicates the new temple he asks the Lord to hear the prayers of foreigners when they come to pray, 'so that all the peoples of the earth may know your name' (1 Kings 8.43). The God of Israel is the God of all peoples!

Let us not forget that the term 'foreign mission', which was still in use in the last century, has a double meaning. It implies not only that people take the gospel to 'foreign parts' but also that the gospel has itself come to us, at one time, having been brought by a foreigner. The domestication of Christianity in the European context (especially in the parochial system) obscures the fact that the gospel was brought by foreigners. It was experienced as foreign and as such characterized new believers. In fact, Christians in the Early Church were called 'resident aliens' –the Greek word is *paroikos*, from which we derive the word parish. So one way in which a global perspective on church might change our faith is if we rediscover what it truly means to be a 'parishioner' – a strange foreigner!

The fellowship of the Holy Spirit includes the dynamics of people relating to one another as foreigners, who, because of the gospel, also discover each other as brothers and sisters in the fellowship of the Holy Spirit. This is Paul's point in Ephesians, but it is also the experience of many Christians today. By recognizing those of other cultures as being in Christ, many have also discovered who they are as part of a global Church. This breadth of engagement does not happen quickly or easily, yet as people do enter another culture through language learning, adopting the local ethos and participating in community life, so they are recognized in breadth – they become an insider stranger. As one African proverb puts it: 'A guest remains a stranger until they take a hoe, dig the ground and become a contributing member of the community.'

As we live with others, in this breadth, a profound realization emerges: 'I only know the Jesus I know if I know the Jesus you know.' This breadth of missional spirituality is more than cultural difference; it is also includes the heights and the depths of 'divine foreignness' – the divine mystery who is revealed, but remains a mystery, in Jesus. There is always more of Jesus to know in the lives of others and it is in fellowship with them through the Holy Spirit that this more of Jesus, his fullness, is discovered.

Mission is therefore motivated by the mystery of God: the desire to share with others who Christ is, while recognizing there is always more to discover as his life is made known among more people in their cultures – even in the 'parish'. The creation of cultures was the way in which the divine fullness of Jesus was to be known 'all in all'.

When Max Warren (a former General Secretary of CMS) was speculating about the future of the global Church he suggested that, 'The picture of the future which unfolds is of a continual interchange of men and women between different Churches "making increase of the body unto the edifying of itself in love".'[17] This is a vision for what it means when people *inter-change* with one another their cultural understanding of Jesus. The result is that the global Church is built up and reveals more of Jesus. It is in fact the pattern of interchange that now governs the work of Societies like CMS. The aim is to deepen partnerships beyond the challenges of our neo-colonial relationships, enabling a genuine interchange of people-in-mission, on a long- or short-term basis, between contexts and cultures. Motivating and resourcing this interchange makes real the global nature of the Church that arises from missional spirituality rooted in the breadth of God's love.

John V. Taylor makes a similar point in proposing house groups, 'little congregations', as a fresh expression of church that allow the least possible withdrawal from the life of mission: 'Through the apostolate of a continual *interchange* of persons the separate groups are linked and mutually responsible, being open to the life of the world they find in their mission their meeting place with one another.'[18]

So whether at macro or micro level, it is in the *interchange* of people with one another that the mystery unfolds – so that the height and depth of God's love are discovered in the breadth of the global-local church as people have fellowship in the Holy Spirit.

We might go so far as to say that not only is the Church given to the Spirit for God's mission (as Taylor suggests) but that the Spirit is embodied in the global-local church through the interchange that the Spirit enables (as Taylor implies). David Cunningham says, God was incarnate in Jesus but 'God has also been poured on the world, into the communities of the believers known as Israel and the church; this concrete embodiment of God is called the Holy Spirit.'[19]

Length: Be with us all for evermore

The great promise of the great commission in Matthew (28.16-20) is the ongoing presence of Jesus. This echoes the promise of God's presence to Israel in the Exodus and Exile. It is the presence of this 'God of pilgrimage' that is at the heart of missional spirituality. The perspective on the global Church which this creates is not just the shaping and reshaping of mission, in Exodus and Exile, but also the nature of hope.

The greatest motivation for mission, that generated the global Church, was the hope that Christians had by faith in the love of God. Hope shapes time and gives it meaning. The challenges to mission motivation have changed, but not the response: hope. For the ones who first went as 'foreigners' from the mission societies, it was a question of *missionary survival*; in the decades that followed it was more a matter of *mental strain*, and for many of us today it is now the challenge of *making sense*.

The enervating effects of the Enlightenment, which undermined confidence in knowing God through Jesus, can only be challenged through the power of hope remade. This means rediscovering 'eschatology': a-purpose-for-it-all-perspective.[20] Jesus is the one who reworked the Exodus and Exile into his teaching and his enacting of the kingdom of God. He showed us what it meant for God to be with his people and how this would change our lives. He also gave people hope that this presence of God would recreate the world, and this would happen through him, through his death and resurrection.

The global perspective on the Church is one that comes through looking at the new world that God promises through Jesus. In this hopeful perspective, all nations, tongues and peoples will have found the ultimate significance of Jesus in the depths of their culture and be able to share with each other as they worship God (Revelation 7.9-12).

Such a hope has motivated people and still motivates many today. It is this hope that enables members of the global Church to face global issues: the relationships between the faiths, climate change, poverty and injustice, disease, political ideologies, HIV and AIDS. The (contested) facts of global issues are staggering. For example: up to 10,000 people a day die of AIDS (that's 20 747s crashing daily, or a Boxing Day-like Tsunami every month); the inter-faith relationship between Christians and Muslims in up to 50 countries is not easy so that persecution is a daily experience for many Christians; one in five of us lives on less than $1US a day – about one billion people; a third of the world's population is at war at any time; first world debt is now so big it threatens the global economy; and the consumerism, at root of a global warming created by burning fossil fuels for industry, is now growing rapidly in new areas: Russia, China and India.

But there's a new way that Christians face these issues today. With the growth of the Southern churches there is now, as never before, a truly global expression of the faith. But also now, as never before, the global issues are therefore of daily concern to the *majority* of Christians. The majority world of Christianity is the South, here the Church is the Church *of* the poor not *for* the poor; this is the Church being *damaged* by climate change, and *persecuted* for religious or political reasons. Here God's presence is *the* hope where all there is, is hope – 'hope alone'. The Christian hope is the vision for new heavens and a new earth in which all things are recreated.[21]

This 'hope alone' brings the possibility of change and therefore a future. A global perspective on the Church is one that essentially proclaims the life-changing presence of God. There is a permanent priority of evangelistic mission built into this spirituality. Those who live by this 'hope alone' include the most dis-empowered. For example, the people of Southern Sudan have suffered destruction again and again. Yet in the midst of it all there has been the most extra-ordinary revival in Christian faith. Through this faith people found hope – hope that they can change and can change their context![22]

Christianity was the first form of globalization. It was launched by a small Jewish renewal movement who believed in Jesus' teaching and his enacting of a new way of life called the kingdom of God. Its motivation, its mission, was hope: hope in the transforming reality of Jesus through God's deep love by the Spirit in all cultures.

Yet globalization of another kind is creating a new world order. As Peter Heslam says:

> The processes of transformation are here driven primarily by economic and technological impulses but have an impact on virtually every sphere of life, including politics, culture, education, religion and the family. These processes generate networks of interaction that transcend the previous boundaries between the spheres. The intensification and institutionalisation of global interconnectedness through new global and regional infra-structures of control and communication is unprecedented.[23]

These powerful forces of globalization continue unabated. Christian mission works both *with* these processes and *against* them, pursuing the hope of God's presence in the interchange of Christians within the global Church. Jesus promises, 'I am with you always, to the end of the age.' This promise is what gives people hope for the future.

Conclusion

We should hold to the principle, the possibility and the practice of a global perspective on the Church, and therefore to the hope of the Christian expression of globalization through mission. I have suggested that a contemporary development of a global perspective on church will happen as we are motivated by a missional spirituality based on 'the Grace' – the height, depth and length of the love of God. I've explored what this might mean in terms of the dynamics and challenges of mission today.

Andrew Walls encapsulates what I believe the hope of a global perspective on the Church entails, that was from the beginning and may now be renewed by God's grace:

> Global Christianity is a recent phrase, but not a recent idea. It expresses what has always been the Christian principle. The early church reflected it ... Curiously enough, the conditions of the twentieth and twenty-first centuries have brought about the possibility of renewing both the apostolic model of the church that first arose in Antioch and the catholic model of active participation in a worldwide multicultural church in ante-Nicene times.[24]

5

Is there evidence for fresh expressions of church in the New Testament?

James D. G. Dunn

What is Christianity, in essence? How did it begin? What were the reasons for its early growth and expansion? What lessons for today may be learned from the New Testament records of its beginnings? Is there any support or evidence within the New Testament for seeking fresh expressions of church? To explore these questions we must go right back to the beginnings of the Christian faith.

Christian beginnings

Christianity began as a sect within first-century Judaism, or Second Temple Judaism as it is more satisfactorily referred to. The Acts of the Apostles retains two very early ways of referring to what was perceived as, and what was in fact a new movement within Second Temple Judaism. The first believers were those 'belonging to the *way*, both men and women' (Acts 9.2; also 19.9, 23; 22.4; 24.14, 22), embryonic Christianity understood as a way to be walked, a way of life. They formed 'the *sect* of the Nazarenes' (Acts 24.5, 14; 28.22), a 'sect' within Judaism, that is a 'party', or 'faction', or 'school of thought', just as the Sadducees were a 'sect' (5.17) and the Pharisees were a 'sect' (15.5; 26.5). In all this it must never be forgotten that Jesus was a Jew, and that all his disciples were Jews. Christianity began as a movement within Judaism.

Within Second Temple Judaism infant Christianity was a movement of *renewal*. For Jesus it was primarily a renewal of Israel. He chose twelve disciples, evidently to represent the renewed twelve tribes of Israel. He saw his mission as directed in the first instance to Israel and to the lost sheep of the house of Israel (Matthew 10.5-6; 15.24). He foresaw his death and understood it in terms of the hoped-for renewed covenant between God and Israel (Luke 22.20; 1 Corinthians 11.25). A popular emphasis in contemporary Jesus scholarship is that Jesus looked for the restoration of Israel[1] – an emphasis given a haunting quality by the question that Luke records as the only question put to Jesus during his resurrection appearances: 'Is this the time when you will restore the kingdom to Israel?' (Acts1.6).

At the same time, there were key features of Jesus' mission which make it clear that in his understanding, God's will for Israel was not simply containable within Israel's traditional structures, but required a major transformation. His teaching was outside the recognized authority structures. He subjected the sacred traditions, and traditional interpretations of Scripture to radical critique. He offered God's forgiveness independently of priest, temple and sacrificial cult. He saw his mission as for the benefit not of the righteous but sinners. His table-fellowship with the non-religious and irreligious was notorious. He did not regard the leper's touch or the impurity of blood and death as things to be avoided on religious grounds. The sanctity of the Sabbath was better maintained by doing good than by doing nothing. Above all, perhaps, he preached and taught that the kingdom of God is not simply a distant hope for the future; the kingdom of God was already active and present in the healing of the sick, in the exorcizing of the possessed, and in the bringing of good news to the poor.

What happened after the first Easter, however, was in many ways still more extraordinary. For very soon, within two or three years, the first believers in Jesus as Israel's Messiah began to take the message about Jesus *beyond* Israel, to non-Jews. The amazing character of this turn of events is often missed – particularly since Christianity so quickly became predominantly gentile in composition. But astonishing it was. For Judaism was an ethnic or national religion (the religion of the Judeans). It was not an evangelistic religion. True, Israel had always given sympathetic gentiles a warm welcome when they wished to become proselytes; the story of Ruth was no doubt much prized. There was also a strong hope and expectation that in the last days many gentiles would make a pilgrimage to Zion to worship (Israel's) God for themselves. And the story of Jonah taking his message of judgement to Nineveh was counted among their minor prophets. But prior to the Jesus movement, no sect or faction in Judaism had recognized any call or responsibility to seek to win or to convert gentiles. Theirs was thus a truly astonishing break with the past. Christianity began not simply as a sect within Second Temple Judaism, but as a *missionary* sect. Whereas Pharisees and Essenes drew the boundaries more tightly round Israel, the earliest believers in Jesus began to push the boundaries back.

In summary, we might say that Jesus challenged the boundaries *within* Israel, the boundaries that divided Israelite from Israelite, the boundaries between the 'righteous' and the 'sinner', the boundaries that divided sect from sect, the boundaries formed by the false assumption of the different factions that only they were being faithful to Israel's God. And when the boundaries that *surrounded* Israel became an issue in the earliest Christian mission after Easter, Jesus' disciples simply extended the same theological logic or spiritual insight to these boundaries too.

The boundary consisted primarily of the law, the law of Moses, the statutes and ordinances laid down by Moses. The law functioned, as it had been partly intended, to mark the separation between Israel and the other nations; holiness meant both set-apartness *to* God and set-apartness *from* the other peoples. As one Jewish writer of the period described it, Moses 'surrounded us with unbroken palisades and iron walls to prevent our mixing with any of the other peoples in any matter, being thus kept pure in body and soul' (*Letter of Aristeas* 139). Or in the language of the letter to the Ephesians, the law was a 'dividing wall' whose function in this case was to keep Jew and gentile apart (Ephesians 2.14). It was the law in this separating function that both Jesus and the first Christians put into question.

In particular, the first believers in Jesus dispensed with traditional practices, with scripturally authorized practices, which hitherto had been central to Israel's identity as the people of God – notably circumcision, and the laws of clean and unclean. Peter learned that he must not call any person profane or unclean (Acts 10.28), and controversially ate with and baptized the uncircumcised Cornelius and his gentile friends (Acts 10.44–11.3). Paul insisted that gentile believers should not be required to live like Jews, having learned that God accepts individuals only through faith in Jesus Christ and not by works of the law (Galatians 2.14-16). The dispute as to whether gentile believers should be circumcised and be expected to observe the laws of clean and unclean almost split the infant sect of the Nazarenes. But the policy, the evangelistic thrust which broke through the boundary and insisted that the good news of Jesus was for *all* who believe, without qualification, was what prevailed. Thanks be to God!

What were the characteristics of this new movement as a fresh expression of Israel's traditional religion? Several call for attention.

Eschatological

It was *eschatological* in conviction and character. I apologize for introducing such a technical term here ('eschatological'), but it does sum up the point concisely. The term comes from the Greek, *eschaton*, meaning 'end'. 'Eschatological' refers to that which is expected to happen at the end, as the final stage of God's purpose for his creation and his people. Today we would discuss such subjects as the return of Jesus, the resurrection of the dead and the final judgement under the heading 'eschatology'.

Where Jesus and the first Christians broke new ground was in their preaching that the end was *now*, that what had only been expected in the age to come *was already happening*. The kingdom of God, God's long-hoped-for final rule, was already being exercised and experienced in healings and exorcisms and the good news for the poor (Matthew 11.2-6; 12.28; Luke 6.20). The resurrection of the dead was not simply a hope for a distant future; it had already happened in the resurrection of Jesus; the risen Christ was the first fruits, the first sheaf of the harvest of the dead (1 Corinthians 15.20). The outpouring of the Spirit was not simply something to be longed for with the restoration of Israel; what Joel had prophesied had happened at Pentecost (Acts 2.16-21). Converts were experiencing not simply a fresh expression, but new life; even more, they were experiencing a new creation (2 Corinthians 5.17)!

It is difficult for us now to appreciate this sense of eschatological fulfilment that so marked the first Christians. A whole new epoch had dawned. The story of God's saving purposes had moved on to a new plane. Let us at least try to enter empathetically into their experience and know again something of the excitement and joy and enthusiasm that this new thing they perceived God to be doing inspired in and through them. And let us also note that the first Christians' eschatological enthusiasm was *not* for what was still to come about, so much as for what God had *already* done and was *already* doing through Jesus.

Experiential

The *experiential* character of the new faith and the new life it engendered also needs some emphasis.

The first Christians experienced an *intimacy with Jesus* now risen and exalted which is quite astonishing. They saw it as a reflection or extension of Jesus' own intimacy with God as Father, 'Abba' (Romans 8.16-17; Galatians 4.6-7). They experienced and expressed it as being part of a new family: God as Father, Jesus as eldest brother, fellow-believers as sisters and brothers. Paul spoke of it characteristically and consistently as being 'in Christ', as acting 'in the Lord'. John's Gospel envisaged it in terms of mutual indwelling – 'On that day you will know that I am in my Father, and you in me, and I in you' (John 14.20). We should hardly be surprised, then, when the experience of new life today in Christian circles so often focuses on the intimacies of relationship with Jesus.

Still more noticeable is the experiential character of the earliest Christian understanding of the *Spirit*. As Eduard Schweizer noted, 'Long before the Spirit was a theme of doctrine, he was a fact in the experience of the community.'[2] What needs to be remembered here above all is that the great, the amazing breakthrough of taking the gospel to uncircumcised gentiles, is attributed in our texts entirely to the work of the Spirit. For all Peter's loyalty to traditional Jewish practices and attitudes, it was the manifest fact that the Spirit had been poured out on Cornelius and his friends which convinced Peter that God had accepted them, and that they should be baptized forthwith (Acts 10.44-48). And the proof of the Spirit was so strong that it convinced even traditionalist James of Jerusalem (11.3-18; 15.14-18). Paul's account of the breakthrough is to similar effect. When at the Jerusalem conference, the pillar apostles, James, Peter and John, saw that the grace of God had been so fully and freely given to gentiles through the mission of Paul and Barnabas, they agreed that God no longer required gentile believers to be circumcised (Galatians 2.6-9) – a hitherto unheard of step. The terms of Paul's report of his evangelistic success are indicated in his questions to his gentile Galatian converts: 'How did you receive the Spirit? By works of the law, or by hearing with faith?' (Galatians 3.2). In both versions of the great breakthrough the key factor is the same. In both accounts it was the experience of the Spirit, the manifest fact that non-Jews were receiving the Spirit of God without becoming proselytes, which convinced even traditional Jewish believers in Jesus that it was now God's will to dispense with the scriptural requirement of circumcision.

Integral, then, to the understanding of earliest Christianity as a fresh expression is the recognition that mission was not conceived as taking the Spirit into new territory, so much as following where the Spirit was leading the way. It was openness to the Spirit moving in unexpected ways that was the key. Not just openness to the possibility that the Spirit might do so, but recognition that the Spirit was already doing so. Christianity as a fresh expression is primarily a matter of keeping up with the Spirit, of following the Spirit's lead.

Questioning tradition

A third important feature of earliest Christianity was its *readiness to question tradition and traditional practices*, and if the new situation demanded it, to move on from them.

Jesus famously referred to (some of) the traditions of the elders, that is, religious traditions, which obscured the will of God and encouraged merely lip-service to God (Mark 7.6-8). He would presumably have reacted similarly to the box-ticking mentality that now smothers so much of the integrity of our professional services! The traditions of the Sabbath had begun to endanger the Sabbath by stifling and preventing what was good (Mark 2.23-3.5). The point of the commandments forbidding adultery and murder could be missed and lost when treated merely on the surface (Matthew 5.21-30). The social conventions, religious conventions, restricting and preventing human contact with those suffering from contagious skin disease, blood disorder, or lax in their observance of the laws of tithing and such like, he disregarded as inhibiting the primary commandment to love God above all else and one's neighbour as oneself. Such putting love above religious tradition was no doubt one of the major reasons why the religious authorities found him such a threat. Observing tradition as the first priority is always safer than following the impulses of sacrificial love.

Likewise, it was the going beyond what tradition prescribed and allowed that marked the outreach of the first Christians. We should never forget that the requirement of circumcision was a scriptural injunction that dated back to the time of Abraham (Genesis 17.9-14). We should never forget that the laws of clean and unclean had been sanctified by the blood of martyrs (1 Maccabees 1.62-63). Scriptural warrant, the practice of the founding fathers, and the blood of martyrs: these provide three of the most persuasive factors demanding loyalty to ancient traditions. But the reason why Christianity grew beyond being simply a sect of Second Temple Judaism was that just these traditions were now seen to be restricting and preventing the grace of God in its full expression. It was no easy decision they made. The pages of the New Testament bear witness to the agonized debate that was involved. Some Jewish believers in Messiah Jesus were never reconciled to the decision. But it was precisely that willingness to question, to challenge and to change tradition if necessary which marked and made Christianity what it is.

We should not exaggerate or overstate the point. By no means all law and tradition was challenged and moved beyond by Jesus and the first Christians. Jesus still expected the Sabbath to be observed; the question was rather *how* it should be observed. He looked for a purity that required much more than the washing of hands. He pressed beneath the commands against murder and adultery to the more profound subject of personal relationships, inner attitudes and motivations. Likewise, Paul did not abandon the law as such; his main objection to the law was to its function of separating gentile from Jew and from the covenant grace of God. He denied that circumcision was necessary for believers in Jesus, for, as with Jesus, the circumcision of the heart was more fundamental (Romans 2.28-29; Philippians 3.3). In the same spirit, he taught that nothing was unclean in itself (Romans 14.14; echoing Mark 7.15). But he also insisted that Christians as much as Jews should avoid idolatry and sexual licence (e.g. 1 Corinthians 6.18; 10.14). And the traditional Jewish concern for the poor was still one of his chief concerns (Galatians 2.10; Romans 15.26). Not least, of course, we should never forget how both Jesus and Paul depended on and drew from Scripture and the promises to Israel's patriarchs. So it was not simply a matter of ignoring or riding roughshod over tradition in general.

The key probably is to realize that both Jesus and the first Christians were in dynamic dialogue and interaction with Scripture and tradition. Christian liberty was experienced and expressed in honouring both Scripture as a fundamental principle and tradition in general; but also in the recognition that some tradition had completed its function, and that some Scriptures were no longer the word of God to the present. It is worth noting that Paul's own treatment of the tradition of Jesus' teaching which he explicitly quotes manifests a similar attitude. He recalls that Jesus had clear teaching both on divorce and on the financial support that those who proclaimed the gospel should be given (1 Corinthians 7.10-11; 9.14). But immediately he moves on from the one, in the light of the new situation which confronted the church in Corinth (1 Corinthians 7.12-16), and indicates his resolve to ignore the other (1 Corinthians 9.15-18). Christian liberty lives and is most itself when it lives on the cusp of respect for tradition in general and willingness to question tradition in particular. Without such a critical respect for Scripture and tradition Christian liberty cannot survive. Christianity thrives when it thinks of revelation not simply as limited to the past but as an active possibility and reality in the present. The third article in our confession of the triune God is, 'I believe in the Holy Spirit', not 'I believe in the Holy Book' or 'I believe in the Holy Tradition' – not even, 'I believe in the Holy Church'!

Not tied to buildings

A fourth feature of Christianity's beginnings worth noting is that at no point was it tied to particular buildings. The term 'church' was much used, of course.

But the Greek term *ekklēsia* denoted the 'assembly', the 'gathering' – the people who gathered, not the place where they gathered. They chose the term *ekklēsia* rather than its near synonym *synagōgē*, no doubt partly because 'synagogue' was already in use quite often to refer to a building where Jews living in Mediterranean cities came together. *Ekklēsia* simply denoted the people of God gathered together in the service of God.

The only building in question for the first Christians was the temple in Jerusalem. Jesus came to Jerusalem to attend at least one of the pilgrim festivals in its courts and in his final week he regularly taught there. But he also is remembered as expressing Isaiah's hope as his own, that the temple should be 'a house of prayer for all nations' (Mark 11.17). It is also true that the first disciples used to meet in the courts of the Jerusalem temple (Acts 2.46; 5.12). But part of the move to push out the boundaries of Judaism was a move away from the Jerusalem temple. In the first instance by the Hellenists of Acts 6–7, in the person of Stephen, who turned away from the temple, on the grounds, it would appear, that 'the Most High does not dwell in houses made with human hands' (Acts 7.48). Luke tells us that it was precisely those who were driven out from Jerusalem following Stephen's lynch-mob execution who first took the gospel beyond Judea (Acts 8) and who first preached to gentiles (Acts 11.19-26). And in the subsequently wider gentile mission, Paul reinforced the switch away in focus from the Jerusalem temple. In his letter to the Galatians he made a point of contrasting the earthly Jerusalem with the heavenly Jerusalem of God's plan (Galatians 4.25-26). And, writing to the Corinthians, the temple that counted is the temple of their bodies indwelt by the Spirit (1 Corinthians 3.16; 6.19). 'The Church of God' is people not a building.

The actual meeting places of the first Christians were in almost all cases their own homes or apartments. We should not deduce from the few explicit mentions of 'the church in someone's house' (Romans 16.5; 1 Corinthians 16.19; Colossians 4.15; Philemon 2) that these refer to house groups, only part of larger congregations. The only churches were house churches. Apart from some gatherings in the open, the only Christian gatherings were gatherings in the homes of individual Christians. Nor should we assume that all the houses where Christians gathered were large villa-type dwellings. Such an impression can easily be given by some textbooks, which have looked only at the still visible remains of such houses at Pompeii and other archaeological sites. But by far the majority of the first Christians were poor, and even the better off, like Prisca and Aquila could probably afford no more than the ground floor apartment of one of the many tenements that provided the bulk of housing in the Mediterranean cities. The church in the house of Prisca and Aquila may only have been able to accommodate about 12 people. And even when the small minority of well-to-do Christians could provide hospitality for 'the whole church', as was the case with Gaius in Corinth (Romans 16.23), such a house would have been hard pressed to host more than about 40, and probably spread between two rooms (triclinium and atrium) at that.

This is a sobering piece of data which is too little considered. Modern denominations tend to think of any congregation less than 100 as failing, and to despair over chapels with membership of less than 20. But the congregations in the beginnings of Christianity were mostly as small, and even when the whole church in a city like Corinth could assemble in one house, they can only have been about 40 strong. Presumably the smallness of the assembly helped promote the features mentioned earlier – the sense of family intimacy not least. Where *we* think of congregations as too small, perhaps the real danger is that they are too *large*! And the rediscovery of the reality of the house church has been too long in coming.

Non-religious

An important fifth characteristic should not go unmentioned – that is, the *non-religious character* of these early Christian assemblies. John the Baptist, whom the Gospels recall as the beginning of what became Christianity, had offered forgiveness to those who repented, quite independently of priest and temple and sacrificial cult (Mark 1.4). Jesus had done the same; forgiveness was offered to repentance without reference to the ordinances and rituals designed to provide the pathway for forgiveness (Mark 2.5; Luke 7.48). And when the first Christians met for their worship or their shared meal, there was no priest without whom the ritual would be invalid, there was no orientation to Jerusalem, there was no sacrifice or libation as when other voluntary associations met in the Mediterranean world. The earliest house churches were not religious by any measure of religion that was then applicable.

Of course, Paul did not avoid the concept and language of priesthood. But he used it for his own work in the service of the gospel (Romans 15.16; Philippians 2.17). He used it for the kindly ministry of Epaphroditus in bringing financial aid to Paul in prison (Philippians 2.25). The sacrifices he wanted to see offered were the sacrifices made in committed social relationships on behalf of others (Romans 12.1-2). 1 Peter follows suit, in reviving the old ideal of the people of God as a priestly people, offering spiritual sacrifices acceptable to God through Jesus Christ (1 Peter 2.5). The Revelation of John echoes the same characterization of believers in general and as a whole as 'priests to God' (Revelation 1.6). And Hebrews drives the point home by portraying Christ as the only priest and by insisting that the tradition of a special order of priests within the people of God belongs to the old age and no longer applies for Christians.

The more powerful image used by Paul was of the Church, the assembled believers in any place, as the Body of Christ (particularly Romans 12.3-8; 1 Corinthians 12–14). The image was drawn from the political philosophy of the time: the city or state as a body made up of many different ethnic and religious, trade and interest groups. Paul wholly shared the point that the unity of the body is a unity in diversity, a unity which functions because the diverse members recognize their common interest and work together for the common good. For him too the most striking feature of the body was the mutual interdependence of its members. However, he qualified the common use of the image in two ways. One is that the Church is the Body of *Christ*. It takes its identity from him alone. It is how Christ is present and acts in the world. That which identifies Christianity as Christianity is Christ – not some buildings, or some traditions, or some hierarchy, or some rituals, but Christ. The other is that the life force of the Church is the *Spirit*. The oneness of the body is possible because 'we were all baptized in one Spirit into one body' (1 Corinthians 12.13). The functions of the body, Paul says, are the charisms of the Spirit (Romans 12.4), that which discloses the Spirit, brings grace to concrete expression (1 Corinthians 12.4-7). The life force of the Church is most evident in the words and actions inspired by the Spirit, which constitute the movements of the body. Without the Spirit, the body is dead.

Here indeed is a new way of being church, of being the people of God, of being the presence of Christ in the world.

Conclusion

So much for historical analysis. Three further points need to be brought out by way of conclusion.

In the light of the above, the Christianity which began to emerge within first-century Judaism is appropriately characterized as a fresh expression of the religion of Israel – a fresh, an eschatological expression of the faith and practice of the patriarchs, of Moses and the prophets, of David and the sages of Jewish wisdom. That continuity with earlier Israel is at the heart of Christianity, a key defining marker of Christianity, integral to its identity as Christianity. So to recognize the importance of Christianity's continuity with

Israel, that Christianity was taking up Israel's obligation to be a light to the gentiles, is also to affirm the character of Jesus' own mission as aimed at the restoration of Israel, and to affirm also Paul's insistence that the word of God in regard to Israel has not failed (Romans 9.6; 11.25-29). A Christianity, two-thirds of whose Scriptures are the Scriptures of Israel, can never be content with a theology which regards Israel as wholly superseded by the Church. The tension between an understanding of Israel as the chosen people and an understanding of the call of God as embracing gentile as well as Jew remains a defining characteristic of the Christianity which defines itself from Scripture. The dialogue between Paul the Jew and Paul the Christian, which was largely overtaken in subsequent centuries by a growing Christian anti-Semitism, has to be revived if Christianity is to be true to its heritage and to itself.

Secondly, what has been described is not just the history of earliest Christianity – a history that might be interesting but is long behind us and of little relevance to today. For this history has become Christian Scripture. The character of Christianity as a fresh expression is enshrined in our sacred texts. These are the texts which define Christianity more clearly and definitively than any other writings. And the Christianity they define is a movement with the five characteristics already documented:

- A Christianity that has lost all sense of newness, of what had only been hoped for being now realized, is no longer Christianity as defined by the New Testament.
- A Christianity that cherishes no sense of intimate relation with God through Christ, that regards the Spirit as effectively shut up in the Bible or confined to the Church, and that treats the experience of the Spirit as essentially threatening, is no longer Christianity as defined by the New Testament.
- A Christianity that regards the maintenance of and faithfulness to tradition as its highest responsibility is no longer Christianity as defined by the New Testament.
- A Christianity that can think of church only as building and not as people, and that is not seeking new ways to be the people of God, to be church, is no longer Christianity as defined by the New Testament.
- A Christianity that defines itself less in terms of Christ and more in terms of ecclesiastical hierarchy and liturgically correct forms is no longer Christianity as defined by the New Testament.

In short, canonical Christianity is Christianity ever open to the Spirit bubbling up in Easter new life and Pentecost fresh expression.

As a practising Methodist I cannot resist a third and final parting observation. For anyone who is familiar with the beginnings of Methodism will be well aware that they reflect several if not all of the five characteristics of primitive Christianity highlighted above. Methodism is a classic example of a renewal movement within Christianity, a fresh expression of Christianity, which was frozen out by the rigidity of ecclesiastical structures and the unbendingness of tradition. Their enthusiasm reflected the earliest post-Pentecost enthusiasm of the first believers. Their sense of intimacy with Christ was a trait they learned from the Moravians. The experience of assurance, of assurance as a feeling and not just a conviction is imprinted on their hymns. Disowned by the established Church they found a reality and vitality of church in their home-based 'societies'; they rediscovered the house church. And their insistence that there should be no order of priesthood distinct from the priestly ministry of the whole people of God encouraged a growth and diversity of ministry that brought the gospel to generations overlooked by those who insisted on traditional forms and hierarchy. Methodism reminds us that fresh expressions are not only the way in which Christianity began but also the way in which Christianity will be revived.

6

Can we develop churches that can transform the culture?

Graham Tomlin

Twenty-first century Britain is a place of many cultures. No longer is there one overriding, predominantly white, English-speaking way of life, but a number of quite distinct cultural groupings exist alongside one another, sometimes uncomfortably, in cities, towns and rural areas across the country. These cultures find their predominant identity in shared consumer choices, religion, allegiance to football clubs, hobbies, language and many more instances of distinction. This recognition, that British culture is increasingly fragmented, and that no longer does one message in exactly the same form reach all types of people, lies behind much of the impulse towards fresh expressions of church. Because cultures are different, different approaches are needed to express the life of Christ in those cultures, and to do church in those very distinct social groupings, many of which are located more in networks than in geography.

So, culture is a strong driving force in the fresh expressions movement, and perhaps even more so in the 'emerging Church' discussions that continue throughout different denominations and outside them. Yet one anxiety held by some critics of these movements is that they fly a little too close to culture. If a church makes such an effort to attune itself to a particular culture, does it simply pander to transient and ephemeral societal moods? If it adjusts its styles of communication, meeting times, forms of music, venue and even the content of what is proclaimed (if it is proclaimed at all), has it not sold out on the gospel to cave into consumerism, individualism and a culture of choice?

A short satirical video on the popular web site 'YouTube' advertises '*MeChurch: where it's all about You*'. 'Imagine a church' it starts, 'where every member is wholeheartedly, passionately and recklessly ... calling the shots.' This is a church that caters for busy people, so it only starts whenever people happen to show up, where babies are allowed to cry so the parents don't feel bad, where attendees can have their cars waxed and cleaned during the service and free tickets to sports events are offered. It is a church led by consumer demand.[1] A church that bends over backwards to fit the expectations and needs of a particular culture is always open to the charge of soft-selling the challenge of the gospel.

A further question arises. If such churches have adapted themselves so fully to particular cultures, can they at the same time transform those cultures? There comes a point at which camouflage becomes dissolution – blending into a particular context becomes so complete that it becomes very hard to recognize anything that is different from the surroundings. Are fresh expressions so concerned to contextualize that they lose the ability to transform?

Church and the transformation of culture?

There is, however, a prior question to be asked before addressing these concerns, and that is whether church should be trying to transform the culture anyway? It is often assumed in both liberal and some more conservative circles that that is exactly what church does – church exists to exercise a benign influence on society, adding an extra religious or spiritual dimension to life, seeking to make society more equitable, just or, simply, more Christian. It often thinks nostalgically about the era of Christendom when faith was central to European society and wishes those days were here again.

This way of thinking frequently refers back to the seminal work of Richard Niebuhr, who published a highly influential work in 1951 called *Christ and Culture*.[2] The book proposed five different models of relationship between Christian faith and culture, from 'Christ against Culture' to 'Christ of Culture'. The book was presented as a straightforward account of the five types, but Niebuhr's own preference was fairly clear, advocating a position of 'Christ transforming culture' – the idea that faith is critical of culture, yet engages with a particular context to transform and change it. Since Niebuhr's book appeared, however, a critique of his position has emerged from various other American theologians and ethicists, in particular, John Howard Yoder[3] and Stanley Hauerwas. For these thinkers, the Church is not there to transform culture but cheerfully to build its own. The Church is seduced into irrelevance when it tries to change anything outside itself. Its main focus is not to transform cultures that couldn't care less about Jesus, but to bear witness to the kingdom of Christ that lies beyond the structures of human society. The Church's task is to bear faithful witness to its own vision of life, and not worry about the culture. As Hauerwas argues: 'Christians must again understand that their first task in the world is not to make the world better or more just, but to recognise what the world is and why it is that it understands the political task as it does.'[4]

In the contemporary context it is difficult not to have some sympathy with the views of Hauerwas and others, for at least two main reasons. One is that we live in an era that is very wary of imperialistic Christian visions of the restoration of religious hegemony. Critics of religion in general and Christianity in particular, such as Richard Dawkins, Philip Pullman and Christopher Hitchens argue that when Christians held the upper hand, they abused their power and persecuted all those who didn't agree with them. This is just the sharp end of a culture that is nervous about a Church that has designs on controlling society and culture. The political philosopher John Gray argues that these liberal humanists are no better, as most of them still adopt a secular version of Christian eschatology, believing in the idea of progress towards a better world. What he likes about Christianity is not its eschatological hope (which he thinks is misplaced) but its pessimism about human nature: 'In traditional Christianity the apocalyptic impulse was restrained by the insight that human beings were ineradicably flawed. In the secular religions that flowed from Christianity, this insight was lost.'[5] He suggests that a Christianity that still aims to transform culture has lost its own sense of the fallenness of humankind. If the Church does not have a great record in wielding the political and cultural upper hand, then maybe it should be cautious about trying to regain it.

There is another reason to question the instinct towards the transformation of culture: that is, the command of Jesus. The first call of the risen Christ to the Church was not to transform culture but to bear witness to himself. The Spirit was given at Pentecost precisely for the task of witness: 'But you will receive power when the Holy Spirit comes upon you and you will be my witnesses in Jerusalem, and in all Judea and Samaria and to the ends of the earth' (Acts 1.8 NIV). The task is not to change the world, but to bear witness in both life and words to a kingdom that is essentially beyond this world. It is a calling not to create a particular social order but to point to a different one that is yet to come, which lies in the hands of God and to be brought into being one day. As Hauerwas puts it: 'The service that Christians are called upon to provide does not have as its aim to make the world better, but to demonstrate that Jesus has made possible a new world, a new social order.'[6]

For this line of thinking, the Church can only ever be understood eschatologically, as a sign of something yet to come, although experienced in part now. It is vital as we think about church, not to get ahead of ourselves (literally!). We always misunderstand the Church if we forget its future orientation as a sign, of course often a muddled and imperfect one, but a sign nonetheless of the coming new heaven and new earth that God will bring to pass one day. Many in our culture are suspicious of a Church that thinks it can bring about heaven on earth. Maybe God is too.

So church exists to point creation towards a new culture, a new order of things where crime, injustice, poverty, boredom, despair – these endemic facts of life in our present experience of life – are no more. Church is intended to be a place in which we can catch an echo, a glimpse of the kingdom of God, in which God really gets his way. Church, of course, is not the same as the kingdom, but it is to point to it, to embody it, to identify it, and to demonstrate it for anyone to see.

The culture of church?

Now if this is true, then we might expect church to have its own culture, quite distinct from any geographical or communal cultural expression. If church is oriented not primarily towards the world but towards the kingdom of God, then a crucial task will be ask first of all the question of how it can exhibit the patterns of behaviour, values, expectations and practices of the culture of that kingdom rather than the culture of twenty-first secular middle-class urban life, or leather-clad bikers or Bangladeshi immigrants to the United Kingdom. Naturally, church will seek to inculturate itself in those subcultures, but that is a second-order rather than a first-order question. Church will inevitably have its own culture that makes it different from other cultures around it. The question is: What are the practices, expectations and values that express that culture of the kingdom? What is the culture of church that we expect people to learn to adopt?

Very often, people experience 'church culture' as a particular form of discourse, artistic forms or formats, styles of music or architecture. To join church you have to learn the language. Depending on which church you happen to turn up in, this might be sonorous spoken liturgy, hymns, organ music, incense, pews and robes or, elsewhere, a repertoire of praise songs, open prayer and informal clothes or, alternatively, bean bags, candles and Taizé chants. Now the problem of these is not the usual charge that they are imposing a 'Christian culture' on prospective believers. As we have seen, to an extent it is inevitable that church will have a different culture from the culture outside, and that culture will have to be learnt and accepted. Christian culture is inevitable and a good thing. The problem comes in identifying what that culture consists of.

To the great frustration of liturgists everywhere, the New Testament shows comparatively little interest in matters of form, style and manner of Christian worship. We get little direction on precise forms of liturgy, styles of music, prescriptive orders of worship (except where things have gone a little wrong as they did in Corinth). We have to go beyond the canon into other first- and second-century literature, such as the *Didache* or the works of the early apologists to find such instruction. But that is not to say that the New Testament does not give us a culture to be cultivated, taught and encouraged in church. The key point, however, is that the main characteristics of that culture seem to be primarily moral rather than liturgical. The New Testament presents for us a new way of living, relating and behaving, a way of life that echoes the life of the kingdom of heaven. A characteristic passage is this one:

> Put on the new self, created to be like God in true righteousness and holiness. Put off falsehood and speak truthfully to your neighbour, for we are all members of one body. 'In your anger do not sin.' Do not let the sun go down while you are still angry, and do not give the devil a foothold. He who has been stealing must steal no longer, but must work, doing something useful with his own hands, that he may have something to share with those in need. Do not let any unwholesome talk come out of your mouths, but only what is helpful for building others up according to their needs, that it may benefit those who listen. Get rid of all bitterness, rage and anger, brawling and slander, along with every form of malice. Be kind and compassionate to one another, forgiving each other, just as in Christ God forgave you.
>
> (Ephesians 4.24-32 NIV)

This is the new culture we are introduced to when we join church. It is a culture that reflects the nature and character of the God of Jesus Christ (the new kind of person it describes is 'created to be like God'). It is a culture that has very definite expectations of behaviour, language, values and attitude. Truthfulness, generosity, encouragement, compassion, forgiveness are highly valued. Anger, theft, deception, gossip, bitterness, malice are frowned upon. The qualities that are most highly valued seem to be the ones that build relationship and community. The ones that are shunned are those that build personal empires and conflict. Church is a community in which people learn patterns of behaviour that create community and reflect the nature of God.

They also learn to avoid patterns of behaviour that destroy relationships and fail to exhibit the purpose of our creation as humankind: to reflect the image of God on earth.

These highly cherished characteristics are not necessarily virtues in other ethical traditions. Humility, forgiveness, love for enemies, regard for the poor, sacrifice and chastity are distinctive Christian virtues that are not held universally. Humility was definitely not a virtue for the Greeks, chastity is not highly prized in contemporary Western European life, and love for enemies is held hardly anywhere as an ideal outside of the Christian Church. Yet this is the culture we are to learn; this is the culture of church. Church is intended to be a place in which we learn how to keep our promises, love our enemies, be faithful to our wives and husbands, provide for the poor, and suffer loss for the sake of doing what is right. Church is a community of people created by God, filled with the Spirit, learning to live the life of Christ.

Transforming culture?

This then perhaps gives us a lead as to how the Church does go about exercising a transforming influence on culture, especially bearing in mind the critique of too quick an adoption of Niebuhr's optimism about the Church's mandate to change society.

Stanley Hauerwas puts it like this:

> The most important social task of Christians is to be nothing less than a community capable of forming people with virtues sufficient to witness to God's truth in the world.[7]

> Insofar as the church can reclaim its integrity as a community of virtue, it can be of great service in liberal societies.[8]

> The most important service the church does for any society is to be a community capable of developing people of virtue.[9]

In 2007 Britain celebrated one of the most remarkable times when the Church 'transformed culture' in commemorating the two-hundredth anniversary of the passing of the Abolition of Slavery Act in 1807. This victory was largely due to the efforts of William Wilberforce and a coalition of friends motivated largely by a passionate Christian faith, rooted in a local church at Holy Trinity, Clapham in London. Was this an instance of the Church transforming culture, or was it the effect of the work of a few individuals who happened to be Christians? The question is irrelevant, because the point is that the nineteenth-century British Church, for all its faults, was a community capable of producing people like William Wilberforce, James Stephen, Hannah More, Henry Thornton, Henry Venn and the rest, whose faith taught them the moral vision to discern the evil of slavery at a time when it was not at all obvious to everyone, and the perseverance to carry the task through to its conclusion.

Holy Trinity Clapham, and churches like it, presented a pattern of worship, study, relational interaction and devotion that shaped the life and motivations of Wilberforce and his friends. They fought for the abolition of slavery not because they thought they could bring about heaven on earth (they were, after all, evangelicals with a deep sense of the enduring fallen sinfulness of humankind), but because they believed that slavery was incompatible with Christian faith, an affront to God, which needed eliminating. The fact that human trafficking is still rife across the world is an enduring reminder that even heroic triumphs like the abolition of slavery are always imperfect and that the Church's true identity is found eschatologically not historically. However, if the Church can continue to produce people like William Wilberforce it can continue to exercise a transforming influence on society and culture.

It is a reminder that the way the Church exercises a transforming influence on culture is not primarily through Acts of Synod or official pronouncements (Who really listens to Acts of Synod except the Church itself?) but through Christians who are shaped by their Christian faith more than they are by the media, living out Christian lives in shops, schools, businesses, neighbourhoods, offices and parliaments. The culture of church is one that teaches, enables and encourages a certain, distinct and not uncontested way of life. It is a way of life that will often seem strange to the culture around it, yet it might also hold a strange attraction to that culture. If the Church can focus on bearing witness to the kingdom of God in its own life and community, if it can discover and embody that kind of culture, the kind of culture that produces people of virtue, then it might as a by-product, make quite a difference to the cultures and societies in which it is placed.

Fresh expressions, virtue and transformation

There is a challenge for fresh expressions of church in all of this. As important as it is to respond to particular cultural forms, they will need to pay close, if not closer attention to putting in place the proper culture of church, thinking about how to create communities in different social or cultural contexts that are capable of producing 'people of virtue'. Beyond the task of changing times and spaces for meeting to fit in with particular ways of life, over and above the need to find forms of worship that express the faith in different settings, or the need to communicate the faith in culturally relevant ways, is the need to establish a true ecclesial culture that is focused upon the cultivation of certain habits of life, what some moral traditions would call virtue, or what the New Testament might call the fruits of the Spirit. How then can this be done? Here are four aspects to be considered.

Identifying virtues

If a church is serious about expressing the life of the kingdom of God within a particular culture, it will need to go beyond asking about forms of communication that will be effective in that culture. It will also need to ask what particular virtues need cultivating in that particular context to exhibit the kingdom of God in its sharpest and most distinctive form. If the surrounding community is one marked by greed, acquisitiveness or conspicuous over-consumption, it may be that radical, sacrificial generosity, contentment or simplicity of life are the characteristics that would most effectively bear witness to the kingdom of God in that area. If it is a culture of high family breakdown, then faithfulness to promises or forgiveness might be the main focus. If a culture of violence and aggression predominates, church might need to focus on being a place where love for enemies, peaceableness or patience can be learnt. If there is a mood of boredom, futility and frustration, then perhaps a new kind of passion (what the New Testament calls 'zeal') for goals that are of enduring worth and value need to be the focus. This kind of exercise needs a high degree of contextual and social awareness, a knowledge of the environment in which a church is placed, so that its precise characteristics, temptations and character can be discerned. It also needs a wise knowledge of the shape of Christian moral life, so that the connections can be made between culture and character, the quirks of a local community and the corresponding qualities that will give people the distinct taste of the kingdom of God in that place.

Introducing disciplines

The next question concerns the spiritual disciplines necessary to cultivate those qualities. Dallas Willard argues persuasively that spiritual formation is vital not just for leadership but for discipleship and mission in the contemporary Church. In fact his verdict is blunt: 'In its current and recent forms, Christianity has not been imparting effectual answers to the vital questions of human existence.'[10] The reason is that it rarely goes beyond a general aspiration to live the Christian life, to putting in place the disciplines needed to develop that life. Disciplines build a steady, regular quality of life rather than isolated but rare self-conscious instances of heroic behaviour, much as physical training produces a level of fitness that enables a person to run, bend over, play tennis with unnoticed ease, rather than the painful exertion involved when a patently unfit person tries out such actions.[11] Willard calls the spiritual disciplines the 'time-tested activities consciously undertaken . . . to allow our spirit ever-increasing sway over our embodied selves'.[12] So if a church, whether fresh expression or not, is to express the culture of the kingdom through the exercise of particular virtues, it may need to ask what are the particular disciplines needed to help these virtues or characteristics to grow in this specific context.

So, for example, in an area where busyness, work and achievement are the predominant idols, and the chief qualities needing to be learnt are contentment or simplicity, a church might begin a special focus on learning to keep Sabbath, a day a week of little productive activity, time for relationships and family not money and work. If the quality needed is faithfulness to promises then it might be valuable to introduce a voluntary structure of accountability, even perhaps the discipline of regular confession to help encourage and enable the keeping of promises.

Setting expectations

There is a third, less precise and definable aspect to this, and that is the setting of expectations in the Church, the creation of an atmosphere that gently encourages goodness and discourages deviousness, deceit or divisiveness. An example of this comes in Ephesians 5.3-4 (NIV), a passage that seems, at first sight, to be an instance of rather prudish huffiness by St Paul:

> But among you there must not be even a hint of sexual immorality, or of any kind of impurity, or of greed, because these are improper for God's holy people. Nor should there be obscenity, foolish talk or coarse joking, which are out of place, but rather thanksgiving.

We are not to imagine this said with a frown, a legalistic, Victorian sense of disgust. Instead, the point of such instruction is the desire to create a space in which a life of chastity, sexual restraint and control can realistically be lived. In the culture of first-century Mediterranean cities, where sexual imagery, literature and allusions were common (just like twenty-first century Britain) it could (and can) be hard to live lives of sexual self-control. If every second advert on the billboards sells something through the use of sex, if TV schedules and Internet sites leave sexual temptation one tantalizing remote control switch or mouse click away, if conversation at work or among friends is laced with sexual innuendo, jokes or expectation, it can be very hard for someone conscious of their vulnerability in this area, who wants to live a different kind of life, a life of sexual restraint. In that context, the words of the letter to the Christians in Ephesus strike a different note. They urge that church to create an atmosphere of a healthy respect ('thanksgiving') for sex, but where it is not the constant topic of conversation, and not the subject of constant reference and humour. In a space where the focus in relationships is elsewhere, it becomes possible to create a community where men and women can relate in a way that has sex in a sense off the agenda, where the question of infidelity or sexual incontinence is just not an issue. As a result, it becomes easier for non-married men and women to relate in normal, natural paths of friendship and mutual love.

The same can be true of other virtues. To cultivate a culture of generosity or humility requires an intentional focus that is as much to do with example and expectation as it is with explicit teaching or programmes. A church leader who often criticizes other churches or groups or denominations should not be surprised if his or her church develops a critical or judgemental spirit, some of that criticism being directed back towards the leader him- or herself![13] On the other hand, leaders who set a tone of positive affirmation towards other Christians will often find a much more positive and affirming atmosphere developing in their own church community. Expectations are set by example; they are also set by discipline. Discipline is probably the last thing on the mind of a fresh expression or a new church plant just setting out, but it is a vital issue in the arena of setting expectations. If greed, lying, rage or drunkenness in the church, especially when exhibited by leaders, goes unremarked upon, uncensored and implicitly accepted, then the expectation is set that that kind of behaviour is just fine and perfectly acceptable. Of course, discipline is hard to exercise and appropriate, gentle ways need to be found in putting it into practice, but some way of showing what kind of behaviour is to be encouraged and what is not to be tolerated is needed if a church is to be serious about creating a space in which the relevant kingdom-reflecting virtues can be learnt.

Of course, all this can slip into legalism, or a harsh, heavy atmosphere of judgement. It does not, if a spirit and theology founded on grace underpins everything. Establishing such a culture in church is not a matter of salvation but rather a matter of mission. We do not cultivate such a culture because by living in such a way we can make God approve of us more. We do it in order to express his life, his character to the world around. That distinction is vital. An atmosphere of generous-hearted, warm, accepting grace, a tone of encouragement rather than criticism, a positive enactment of the very virtues we have discussed (generosity, patience, kindness, humility etc.) sets the context in which destructive behaviour can be dealt with and discouraged.

Cultivating a different life

The final step is putting in place the specific means of teaching and encouraging such a culture. How do you teach generosity? Not just by doing Bible studies, or preaching sermons on it, but by teaching people how to practise it. On several occasions I have taught a small 'Generosity Class', an experiment in this kind of teaching. The aim is not to discuss generosity or understand it, but to practise it. Each class contains some theological teaching, perhaps on living in a world that constantly exhibits the generosity of God at every corner; or the radical teaching of Jesus that a Christian does not 'own' anything – all we 'possess' is really entrusted to us to use wisely for his kingdom and the benefit of others; or the beauty and attractiveness of a generous spirit. The classes include exercises in prayer, and always include 'homework' – not books to read or essays to write, but practices to try out. These are in the form of suggested actions to do before next time – buy a cup of coffee and a takeaway for a homeless person before being asked; invite a neighbour for a lavish meal; give away any clothes you have not worn for several years. The aim is to cultivate generosity as a habit of life by reflecting on a God who is so radically generous to us and by practising generosity so that it becomes a natural habit of life rather than a rare and occasional gesture.

A church needs to be able to say to people in its local area something like this: 'We can teach you the things you need to be able to do to survive and thrive in living a human life – not necessarily the things you think you need, but certainly the qualities that will enable you to build healthy long-term relationships, maintain families, bring up children and contribute to an enjoyable, worth-while community life. We can teach you to forgive, to be kind, to be patient and to trust, because we believe in a God who is forgiving, kind, patient and faithful. By coming into relationship with this God you can learn these vital qualities that will enable you to live a better and more positive life, and we will show you how. Church has been doing this for 2,000 years, so we have a decent track record and some experience in this area!'

Fresh expressions of church are well placed to do this kind of work, because they tend to be communities of Christians well attuned to the culture of their target audience. But if they are to transform the cultures which they are trying to reach, they will need to be as attentive, if not more so, to the question of how they express the culture of the kingdom as they are to the question of how they relate to their target culture. If they fail to ask this question, they will tend to blend into the culture so much that they will become indistinguishable. It then becomes hard to see the point of joining a community that is just a religious version of the surrounding culture. If, however, they can embody and cultivate the true culture of church, the life of the Spirit in a way that shows particular cultures exactly what they are missing, they can have an exciting future.

7

What questions does Catholic ecclesiology pose for contemporary mission and fresh expressions?

Angela Tilby

The fresh expressions movement is a rather painful wake-up call for Catholic-minded Anglicans like myself. Difficult though it is to admit it, our current record on mission is pretty dreadful. We have taken comfort in the argument that our real strengths lie elsewhere. It is true that we are often good at producing imaginative, well-ordered liturgy. We are frequently good at sustaining a life of prayer. We are sometimes good at offering costly service in the community. But when it comes to 'naming the Name', to giving 'reasons for the hope that is in us' (1 Peter 3.15) we become very reticent and unsure of our ground. The things I associate with the Catholic movement in the Church of England – confident and intelligent theology, a readiness to engage with the whole person and with the whole of society, pastoral patience, fun and good humour – have turned inward as Catholics continue to bicker about women, or dissolve into a vapid liberalism, or become sniffily defensive of particular practices and territory.

Dealing with history

In these failures we are guilty as charged. But having confessed our sins, let me offer a question in response to fresh expressions. How do we know when a church is a church? What does a fresh expression have to be or do if it wants to *be or become* part of the Church, which we believe to be apostolic?

The question behind the question is how we deal with history. Most Catholics would distance themselves from one contemporary view (shared by some Anglicans) that history is like a theme park or antique shop. You wander round, you pick and choose the pieces that attract; a bit of Celtic here, a bit of Syrian Orthodox there; *ancient is awesome.* Some will come to see that this is not an entirely rational way to behave. The logical outcome for them is to submit to the weightiest tradition available. So we can understand the move some have made from charismatic evangelicalism to Roman Catholicism without ever really passing through the Anglicanism they apparently started from.

In this chapter I want to argue against the idea that history exists for us as a kind of simultaneous present from which we can construct whatever patterns we like or find meaningful. My key point is that the identity of the Church is constituted by the fact that it lives in time. In a very real sense the Church *is* its history. The DNA of the Church is the gospel of Jesus Christ, the historical figure of Nazareth whose divine mission is continued through the apostles: 'As the Father has sent me, so I send you' (John 20.21).

So Catholics will want to say that history, Church and mission go together. Where there is no history there can be no Church and no mission. Or as Clement of Rome put it in about AD 96:

> The Apostles received the Gospel for our sakes from the Lord
> Jesus Christ; Jesus the Christ was sent from God. Christ
> therefore is from God, and the Apostles are to do God's will ...
> They (the Apostles) went out in the confidence of the Holy Spirit,
> preaching the Gospel, that the kingdom of God was about to
> come. So, preaching in country and city, they appointed their
> firstfruits, having tested them by the Spirit, to be bishops and
> deacons of those who should believe.[1]

Whatever we make of the details of this, the implication is that mission is part of the hierarchy of grace and flows from the nature of God. As God sends the Lord Jesus Christ, so the Lord sends the apostles, and so the apostles commission ministers – bishops – to serve, shepherd and send out those who believe. When Irenaeus (c. AD130–200) faces the question of what constitutes the Church, one of his answers is to give a list of named bishops.[2] He does this to show that the Church is not an abstract entity; it is not an experience or an idea, it is not simply an *agency* of God's missionary purpose that can change its shapes and structures at will; it is rather an organic reality, a 'Body' whose life is passed on from person to person. Irenaeus *knows* these people, he knows their names, where they came from and what they did.

The Church, then, simply as the Church is the mission of God extending through time. The Church is not the origin of its mission, but nor is it merely an accidental instrument of God's wider mission to the world. The Church is the part of the God-loved world that is already in some sense transformed by the gospel of grace and is therefore commissioned to live, act and speak that grace in the world.

Those involved with fresh expressions thinking do, in fact, appeal to history and specifically to the values and tenets of the Anglican Communion as summarized from what has become known as the Chicago–Lambeth Quadrilateral. This identifies as hallmarks of Anglicanism, Scripture, the Apostles' and Nicene Creeds, the dominical sacraments and the historic episcopate. It was the Protestant Episcopal Church's House of Bishops that produced the Quadrelateral in Chicago in 1886. The Quadrilateral was adopted by the Lambeth Conference in 1888. The original context was ecumenical concern; the American bishops in particular wanted to ensure that other churches did not regard Anglicans as 'predatory'. They were offered at Lambeth as a contribution to the wider ecumenical debate.

The Quadrilateral is invoked today in the context of fresh expressions thinking[3] both to persuade the wider Church that a loosening of the structures does not involve a loss of historical continuity, and also to warn practitioners that *some* continuity is important. The critical question is, how much?

So far there has been little engagement with how these hallmarks might be mediated in such a way as to form long-lasting communities of faith. However much we may say we adhere to these principles, unless we can demonstrate it, our adherence remains a pious hope. So how does church become church? The typical Anglican answer is that the Body of Christ is formed in its belief, commitment and devotion by what it actually does and says, in other words, by its liturgy. The shape of the Body in Anglican ecclesiology is in essence a liturgical shape.

The significance of liturgy

Public worship provides the Catholic strand in Anglican spirituality, which complements the more evangelical strand that is nourished on private prayer and Bible reading. It was absolutely essential for Richard Hooker, perhaps the greatest Anglican theologian, that the Church was grounded in a reality that was both corporate and scriptural. Thomas Cranmer gave expression to both the corporate and the scriptural dimensions of Church life in the liturgies he created. In this, Cranmer and Hooker were in tune with both the Western and

Eastern liturgical traditions, and this can be traced back through Augustine in the West and Pseudo-Denys in the East. For both Cranmer and Hooker, worship is essentially (and not accidentally) corporate. Liturgical worship highlights what it means to be a Christian in the world. It forces Christians to make a stand, to be distinct. It confers an identity that is orientated more widely than to the merely local and congregational. This saves the Church from sectarianism and frees it for missionary engagement with the whole of society. Habits of virtue are to be cultivated within the corporate, repeated offering of thanks and praise. Cranmer and Hooker assumed that the point of worship is not only to tell God how we are feeling and what we want, but to have our desires and affections transformed by what we hear, say and do together. A Scripture-based liturgy used over time actually forms our thoughts and affections on a Christian template, it does not just express the inspiration, or otherwise, of the moment.

How much of this corporate, liturgical worship is necessarily sacramental? The Reformation was at least in part an attempt to re-appropriate the Lord's Supper for the Lord's people, at a time when it had become so terrifying and inaccessible that many people preferred not to participate at all. In this attempt, the Reformation largely failed. Like many other Reformed Christians, Church of England worshippers took part in the Eucharist three or four times a year. But even if people communicated infrequently, the retention of the Church Year and a lectionary that increasingly came to mirror the liturgical cycle, pointed implicitly towards the Eucharist. I was brought up on Mattins but I knew the Eucharist was important. Like Christmas and Easter, the incarnation, and the paschal mystery, the Eucharist is the point of departure and return because this is where the central reality of the gospel is discovered afresh and shown forth to and within the community.

Some current writing, which is proving influential among those involved in the fresh expressions movement, seeks an answer about the identity of the Church, not from its liturgy but from social observation. We saw sociological analysis being used in *Mission-shaped Church*, and, though it painted a recognizable picture, it seemed to me to provide only a limited diagnosis of the cultural context in which the Church now operates. Such analysis does not answer the question of how the Church should respond to this context without losing its identity. I can't see any Catholic answer to the question of *How do we know when a church is a church* other than the answer that says, when it conforms to the given nature of the Church as the Body of Christ in time, united with him through word, sacrament and the recognition of the threefold orders of ministry. This is, of course what is implied by the Chicago–Lambeth Quadrilateral.

In other parts of the Anglican Communion it is the principles of liturgical life that make Anglicanism recognizable and distinctive. To go back to the context in which the Chicago–Lambeth Quadrilateral emerged, the four-point statement is an important factor in the already-existing, but imperfect, communion with the wider Church. It strikes me that fresh expressions thinking sometimes ignores or undercuts a significant amount of ecumenical consensus on ecclesiology, liturgy and worship, and the formation of the people of God. We can think of ARCIC,[4] the *Baptism, Ministry and Eucharist* document[5] and others.

Yet the constant cry of those involved in fresh expressions is for even greater freedom, even less constraint than what is allowed by canon. In support of greater freedom, it is often argued that the Church's mission has required a benign development from the use of common texts, to common structures, and finally, to common values. The problem is that the appeal to common values is like a resolution against sin, we can all sign up to it, but it does not achieve very much. What are these common values? Are they the ones we can agree about? If so they are likely to be so bland or petty that they are irrelevant. The values that are really important are patently the ones we can't agree about. It may sound rather cynical but I think the reason the Church of England held on to its Prayer Book with such insistence in the sixteenth and seventeenth centuries was because of a realistic recognition that the one thing such a Church could not rely on was any real sense of common values. We do not all think the same thing, emphasize the same doctrines, value the same approaches – and the Anglican Reformers knew that better than almost any other group of people! Common texts and structures gave us a way of negotiating this chaos and keeping our tempers with each other in the process. I think those involved in fresh expressions need to examine their attitudes to liturgy from a much more self-critical perspective. Otherwise they risk losing the very flexibility they desires to promote. We have already virtually lost the Psalms as corporate texts for prayer and praise and by doing so have totally alienated ourselves from the vast majority of historic liturgies, and risk separating ourselves from our origins in the people of the Hebrew Bible. This can lead to all sorts of subtle and not so subtle heresies. It also puts at risk that very important Anglican principle of *lex orandi lex credendi* (how the Church prays and worships tells us what it believes). Until quite recently we have always been able to say that if you want to know what Anglicans *believe* take part in our liturgical worship. I am not sure that all fresh expressions initiatives would permit that discernment to be made.

The principle of flexibility

That does not, of course, mean that the liturgies of word and sacrament have to be inflexible. Anyone ministering in the armed services, in schools or prisons or hospitals will have adapted and worked on liturgical forms to make them accessible and relevant to their particular pastoral contexts. That principle of pastoral flexibility is well understood in *The Book of Common Prayer* where the wisdom of the Church of England is found in keeping the mean in public liturgy 'from too much stiffness in refusing, and of too much easiness in admitting any variation from it'. There is nothing new about relying on a fair degree of ministerial discretion about the way liturgical rules are applied. There never has been uniformity, nor should there be.

In fact, Christian history has many examples of different kinds of ecclesial community living alongside one another; often, unfortunately with considerable tension and mutual suspicion. The 'mixed economy' Church is nothing new, though I would prefer the phrase 'mixed ecology' as it does at least suggest that new movements might be a manifestation of the work of the Creator rather than a spiritual counterpart to the enterprise culture.

In the late second century there were many attempts to diversify the ways in which Christ might be encountered. These initiatives drew in large numbers of people whose spirituality was marked by what E. R. Dodds called 'an age of anxiety'.[6] What we might call astrology, mysticism, speculative cosmology and psychology were all part of the mix that we now call Gnosticism. Christian Gospels emerged, which claimed to be authentic, often in the form of persuasive spiritual instruction. A good example would be the Gospel of Thomas. If the enormous number of scraps of copies of this alternative Gospel found in the deserts of Egypt is anything to go by, the Gospel of Thomas seems to have been regarded as virtual Scripture by vast numbers of Christians. The sayings and parables of the Gospel of Thomas overlap those of the canonical Gospels, but there is a particular skewing of the material to suit the spiritual needs of those for whom it was designed. It is teasingly obscure, elitist, intimate and conspiratorial in tone. Attractively presented and well in tune with the various strands of spirituality prevailing in the ancient world, the Gospel of Thomas and the other alternative Gospels posed a real issue for the Church; were their extra revelations to be received or not?

The crises posed by Gnostic expressions of Christianity led to the emergence of what we would now call orthodoxy. This was not so much a rejection of the prevailing culture as a critical sifting of it, which involved the setting of limits both in terms of agreeing the canon of Scripture and in the way authority was handed on, person to person, as I have already suggested. The challenge of Gnosticism forced the Church to discern afresh the DNA of the gospel; and make judgements about which developments were in continuity with the Jesus of history and therefore to be judged as the work of the Holy Spirit, renewing the tradition, and which were destructive of faith and unity.

There are movements in society and Church at the moment that might be thought to echo the Gnostic heresy. It is not always easy for the Church of England to recognize these. When a bishop can suggest, as one did in my presence, that the Church might produce a calendar for Sunday worship based on the signs of the zodiac, I do begin to wonder what is going on! Bishops are not infallible, of course, and we do not have a Magisterium. Nor do we have an agreed confessional statement. We don't even have, as our Methodist colleagues do, a prophetic founder who might give a particular shape to our quest for holiness. What keeps our new movements potentially orthodox is our liturgy. Once that is abandoned – either by imposing upon them ideological 'corrections' which are foreign to Scripture, or by the over-encouragement of extempore worship at the expense of the more formative – we lose all capacity to orient ourselves within orthodoxy.

Christianity has always been in the business of both confronting and creating culture. Converting the powers meant a concern not only for individuals but for the deep structures that permeate society. By the middle of the third century Christianity had become more of a real threat to the Roman empire than it was in the second or the first because Christians taught people to read and thus produced literate young men from non-aristocratic backgrounds who were capable of entering the imperial civil service. Of course there are interesting problems of interpreting the gospel in terms of particular cultures. Christ is portrayed in fifth- and sixth-century iconography in imperial purple, and for some that will be a valid translation of the gospel into imperial culture and for others a betrayal of the historical truth about Jesus of Nazareth.

It is because of our propensity for turning the gospel into something rather agreeable that we should be aware of times when Christian authenticity has required a disengagement with culture, a disengagement that has resulted in extraordinary missionary expansion. With the accession of Constantine the Church became, for the first time, free from the threat of persecution. The growing respectability of the Church under Constantine and his successors gave rise to opposition from within in the form of the monastic and ascetic movements which have been so vital to the development of Christian spirituality. These movements comprised a form of alternative church. They were often deeply unpopular and controversial because they challenged a

Church that was coming to a comfortable accommodation with its new cultural context.

The monks were often rude about bishops, shunned ordained ministry, sometimes neglected the sacraments or the Bible or both. Bishops fought back. They were robust in their attacks on those who used the language of special vocation to disguise self-indulgence and indiscipline. After a very considerable period of testing and sifting, the ascetics became the missionary vanguard of the Church particularly as the movement spread Westward through John Cassian and others. We all know of the missionaries inspired by monasticism. Palladius went from France to Ireland, Patrick and Columba from Ireland to Iona. These evangelical monks knew that the gospel was not a merely private matter. It was the *culture* that needed converting to Christ as well as the people. So they addressed kings and rulers, they interfered with politics, they held out a vision of society derived from and dependent on the gospel.

The medieval and Reformation periods saw other developments in the Catholic Church of what one might call a mixed economy Church shaped towards mission. These, again, arose out of new forms of monastic life, focused on poverty and simplicity. The Dominicans and Franciscans came out of the monasteries to preach, persuade, convert and revive, transforming the rules of monastic life and requiring a new accommodation with the rest of the Church who grumbled, of course, that the friars were too radical, too ignorant, too lazy, too disruptive. Recognition was given but not always easily or without struggle. Perhaps the most significant of these new movements was the founding of the Society of Jesus in the sixteenth century, culminating in its acquisition of papal approval in 1540. The *Jesuit Constitutions* required what for some was a terrifying abandonment of the normal rules of monastic life, alongside a dangerous encouragement of personal discernment in relation to Scripture. A new flexibility was built into the individual's Rule of Life alongside the encouragement of imagination and initiative in missionary endeavours.

In a much later period, the early Jesuit missionaries in Asia were deeply concerned about how they might penetrate ancient cultures that had no former knowledge of Christianity or Judaism, but did have their own philosophical and religious traditions. How far could a gospel that had come from the European world be translated into the world of Confucius and Lao-Tse? The question was raised in a constant stream of correspondence between the missionaries and with Europe, with Rome, with university life in Paris and elsewhere. Liturgical and doctrinal innovations required papal authorization and did not always get it. Back home the question was 'Has X, in his zeal for souls, gone native?'

The impulse to test the boundaries continues in Roman Catholic Church life. There are new orders, new institutions, new experiments with ecclesial life. Some last, some fail. *Opus Dei* is one manifestation. The *New Catechumenate* is another. *Chemin Neuf* in France would be yet a third. Some are treated with suspicion and hostility by bishops and parochial clergy; others are welcomed. They all challenge the culture out of which they have arisen in various ways, and no doubt will continue to do so. What all of them have in common is a love for Jesus Christ, which is expressed not only in proclamation but in lifestyle; prayer and detachment from the world, certainly, but also poverty, chastity, obedience, which are after all the practical living out of the baptismal promises. Purity of heart is what keeps the missionary safe from merely baptizing everything in sight or by being seduced by that which he or she is commissioned to convert.

The question of asceticism

At this point I would like to throw in the question to those involved in fresh expressions thinking: *What is your asceticism?* What is your personal and corporate discipline? What of your life in the world have you given up to make you safe for mission to that world? And how does this asceticism play out in commitment to the poor and the marginalized? Will churches based on networks of the like-minded ever be able to engage with issues like dustbin collections, education and crime rates? The monastic movements began in a fierce rejection of the world and its dominant culture. There was no easy appeal to an incarnational theology to justify an accommodation with a culture judged to be sinful. Antony and Columba were able (too able, perhaps) to reject the world. Their passion for God and the gospel was coming from somewhere other than this world and they knew it.

But this model of Christian mission confronting a culture that is strange to it cannot easily be applied to our own situation. We are not confronting a non-Christian culture, or even in a straightforward sense, a post-Christian culture. We exist in a cultural world, which is an amalgam of Christian memories and secularism that is stirred by the arrival of other articulate faiths and a new, confident atheism. Our society values choice and seeks meaning and fulfilment in the accumulation of possessions and experiences. Christian believers no longer come to church because they have absorbed a particular view of personal freedom that does not require them to express their faith in this way unless they spontaneously happen to want to. We have become radically disassociated from inhabiting what we claim to be, from developing Christian habits of body and mind.

We are all tempted to assume that church is a choice, to only go where we 'feel' we can agree with what is offered and we are going to get something out it. It must be a joy; it has failed us if it is merely a duty. Missionary-minded Christians have become adept at reading this culture and understanding the way it works.

But am I wrong sometimes to discern in fresh expressions thinking an itchy restlessness which may itself be a product of our media-saturated consumerist culture? This restlessness is sometimes turned against the rest of the Church, in a tone and language that is sometimes aggressively dismissive of more traditional ways of being church. I am worried that fresh expressions practitioners read too well and too uncritically the concern for comfort, gratification and instant comprehension that our culture endorses. Have we just become too good at identifying people's needs and producing a version of the gospel that apparently meets the need, but fails to transform it?

I have suggested that the authenticity of our approach to culture could be focused by the question of asceticism. To reach to the margins means living on the margins, and where the margins are is not always easy to discern in the current climate. Fresh expressions thinking has been embraced very thoroughly and very quickly by the Church. Practitioners have been very adept at seeking episcopal authorization for new initiatives. They have ensured that a focus on mission is one of the criteria for selecting future ministers, and has even encouraged the development of special tracks for the training of pioneer ministers. In the light of all this it can hardly claim that the mission agenda is now a voice *from* the margins. And yet, when I look at the question which John Drane addresses – How does a fresh expression come to maturity? – I wonder whether one of the problems we are facing is the difficulty of finding the time to allow maturity to happen. It may be that more time on the margins, at the edge, worrying away at the Church from this uncomfortable place of testing is really what is needed. Has the movement become Establishment too quickly?

If you will forgive one last glance at the Christian history it is striking that the Early Church did not allow people to become Christians easily. Baptism was once for all. As for the Eucharist, this was the mystery in which the baptized were incorporated – HAGIA HAGIOIS: 'Holy things for the holy'. Mission on the margins depended on there being a firm boundary beyond which the general enquirer or fellow traveller could not go without a personal willingness to submit to the disciplines of the life of the Body itself. Of course, there was a place in early Christian communities for enquirers and fellow travellers. Augustine listened to the preaching of Ambrose, Bishop of Milan, for some time before he made the momentous decision to seek baptism. Candidates for adult baptism attended the start of the Eucharist but were dismissed before the Great Thanksgiving. They could not be present at that point because at this stage they were not part of the Body of the Church. We too, need pre-Eucharistic assemblies (and we have them). The question is whether they are, want to be, and should be regarded as churches. I have suggested that this might happen, but not before the point when the DNA of the gospel working through a common set liturgy to form individuals into the Body requires them to celebrate the Eucharist together. It is clear that not all wish to. Some practitioners speak of being 'bored' with the Eucharist, which, from a Catholic point of view suggests either that the Eucharist has not really been understood or that the community concerned are not ready to celebrate it.

Conclusion

So how to summarize and conclude? My chief concern has been with how the Church as part of the *missio Dei* retains its continuity as it moves through time. However this is answered, the central point is that the Church does not exist for itself but for the transformation of the world of which it is a part. In Anglicanism, continuity, and therefore authenticity is expressed largely through the Church's scriptural liturgy and its sacramental life, both of which *form* Christians and *inform* their engagements and disengagements with culture.

From the point of view of Catholic ecclesiology many, though not all, fresh expressions initiatives are perhaps best understood as bridges between a culture increasingly detached from its Christian roots and the Church which connects human beings with Jesus of Nazareth. They operate on the margins of Church life and their purpose is to make a bridge where Church and culture engage with one another. Out of the conversations I have had with fresh expressions practitioners, I would like to suggest three particular things that these initiatives should be offering:

- The first is an opportunity for dialogue and self-expression around some critical issues of desire and identity that are not addressed by secular culture and not well-handled in conventional church settings.

- The second is safe space for experimenting with a Christian identity within particular familiar peer and interest groups.
- The third is a chance to experience some of the elements of Christian worship either in an unstructured way, or in a way that begins to develop form and structure.

But the fact remains, a bridge is a bridge that serves its purpose if it effectively crosses a chasm. Fresh expressions is a gift to the Church, but its practitioners need to recognize the limitations of what they can offer and not encourage a premature integration with a Church they do not really wish ('we are bored with the Eucharist') to be part of.[7]

8

What does maturity in the emerging Church look like?

John Drane

Introduction

The title of this chapter is arguably the most ambiguous in the entire book, for almost every word in it is contested in one way or another. The lecture in which it originated was, of course, initiated by Fresh Expressions – but not every fresh expression would qualify as an emerging church, and not every emerging church would regard itself as a fresh expression in the sense of being a form of church that is identified with the Fresh Expressions initiative of the Anglican and Methodist churches in England. Far from being a distinctively English phenomenon, the emerging church is a worldwide movement that can be found in various guises in many different countries. In sociological terms it is perhaps best described as a meta-network, or network of networks, and certainly has no overarching organizational structure to compare with Fresh Expressions. Even the terminology is not fixed, with some preferring the word 'emergent' rather than 'emerging', though I have never quite grasped what the difference is supposed to be.[1] Trying to define the emerging church is therefore like wrestling with the proverbial jelly. At the same time, it is worth attempting some sort of definition of it at the outset here, if only to clarify my own use of the term.

Emerging

As of now, we can clearly identify at least three ways in which the terminology is being used.[2] In some circles, the language of 'emerging church' amounts to nothing more than an exercise in advertising: a way of repackaging an existing product in order to present it to a new generation. This repackaging manifests itself in various forms, some of which can appear to offer a flexible space for spiritual exploration, but in the end of the day it is about adapting an old product to new markets. There is nothing intrinsically wrong with doing this, of course, but by attaching the label of 'emerging church' to what is in effect just a variant form of traditional church the usefulness of the terminology is diminished.

Alongside this, though by no means identical with it, the desire to create 'emerging church' can also begin from dissatisfaction with existing churches, with a mixture of sad and angry people who are predominantly alienated from what Alan Jamieson and Steve Taylor have called the EPC end of the theological spectrum (Evangelical – Pentecostal – Charismatic).[3] This is the phenomenon that first came to prominence through Dave Tomlinson's book *The Post-Evangelical* and it largely consists of individuals who abandon their previous allegiances in favour of their own independent movements.[4] Their mantra tends to be, 'we'll show them how to do it right', and the creation of emerging churches on this model then inevitably becomes a way of holding two fingers up to the establishment. As a rough rule of thumb it is not too inaccurate to say that they tend to be more prevalent in north America than in England, or for that matter Australia and New Zealand.[5]

In addition to these two, however, there is another form of emerging church that consists of creative groups who in different ways are still embedded within the tradition and heritage of historic Christianity, and who might well have been both encouraged and empowered from within the tradition to ask radical questions about the nature of church in the context of our ever-changing culture.[6]

Because of these multiple ways in which the term 'emerging church' is used, whenever I meet a particular example of it, I invariably ask a further question: Emerging from what? For there is a world of difference between those groups that are emerging out of a fundamentalist-evangelical sub-culture that tends to set the agenda, and those that are emerging from a three-way, missiologically intentional conversation between gospel, tradition and culture. The one tends to define itself by reference to what it is not, whereas the other is engaged in a more open-ended exploration of key questions, such as:

● How might we follow Jesus faithfully in today's postmodern culture?
● What might new wineskins for new circumstances look like?
● How can gospel and culture be brought into a creative dialogue that will affirm and challenge both of those conversation partners?

In reflecting on the 'emerging church', it is this third type that I have in mind here.

Maturity

'Emerging church' is not the only contested term in our title, however. There is a corresponding ambiguity in the notion of 'looking for maturity'. For it all depends on who is doing the looking, where they are looking from, and what they consider maturity to be. Maturity is not some self-defining objective reality, but is a culturally determined category, and it is arguable that the understandings of maturity which we tend to take for granted belong to a cultural matrix that no longer exists. Personal maturity is often assumed to consist of the sort of intellectual and emotional development that has traditionally been associated with adulthood, with the accompanying assumption that life consists of a series of linear and progressive changes that automatically lead from the naïveté of childhood to the wisdom of old age.[7] Undergirding that is the expectation that change itself is always measured, gradual, and controllable. In today's world, this is no longer the case, not even in terms of human development. We live in an age when adolescence can begin at the age of eight or nine and for some people can last well into their thirties, while it is not at all uncommon to find people in their fifties and sixties reverting to teenage behaviour in response to the fragmentation of their intimate relationships. If by 'maturity' we mean the wisdom that will allow us both to survive and to thrive, then it is becoming increasingly obvious that the tried and tested wisdom of the past is often incapable of dealing with the challenges that we now all face. As a consequence, in the wider culture the nature of maturity (along with many other things) is being reconfigured.

Historically, maturity was always defined in relation to the past, as one generation grew into and inherited both the positions and the wisdom of those who preceded them. Today, organizations and individuals that look exclusively to the past are struggling, while those that thrive are the ones that look to the future. In the process, many of the categories that once seemed fixed are now being re-imagined. The reason for this is that the nature of change itself has changed, and instead of being gradual and predictable it is now random, rapid and unpredictable. Within this frame of reference, the nature of maturity is being redefined as a quality that will enable us to live in the future rather than the past. The old maturity was characterized by nostalgia; the new maturity is marked by innovation. The old maturity valued tradition and rationality; the new maturity centres around imagination and creativity. The old maturity found a home in religious performance; the new maturity prioritizes values and spirituality. This might sound like a novel and challenging concept, though the idea that spiritual maturity should have an eschatological, future-oriented core is deeply grounded in the biblical tradition.[8] It does, however, raise a serious question for the Church. We know how to do history – especially in England – but are we now going to take the risk of becoming partners in building the future?

Running in parallel with this theological perspective, there is an expanding body of sociological research suggesting that the key to the future is in the hands of what is being called 'the creative class'.[9] This is how Paul Ray and Sherry Ruth Anderson describe those whom they identify as the cultural creatives:

> 'At times the journey feels awkward or perilous: you're asking questions that everyone wishes would go away; you don't know how to put into words what you're searching for; you're wondering just how big an idiot you really are for leaving what felt sure and safe and comfortable' – though all this is tempered by 'the freshness and exhilaration of setting out for new territory'.[10]

Anyone who has ever connected with the emerging Church will identify with those sentiments, and it is not coincidental that the emerging Church has an abundance of people who exactly match the profile of the creative class.[11] If maturity is about developing our innate human potential – or in theological terms, fulfilling the promise of the *imago Dei* (Genesis 1.27) – then we will find it among those groups who look forward rather than backward, and who themselves actually become an embodiment of the future by taking responsibility for their role in shaping that future for all the world's peoples. At the lecture on which this chapter is based, my mention of the creative class proved to be rather contentious, with some attendees claiming that this merely confirmed their perception that the emerging Church is an exclusively white, middle-class movement. But creativity is the one capacity that depends on neither background nor education, but is an intrinsic quality of being human. Creative imagination is not limited by class or social circumstance – which is exactly what we would expect, given that the first page of the Bible identifies the whole of humankind ('male and female', Genesis 1.27) as co-creators with God, by virtue of being made in the divine image. Nor, significantly, is creativity age related, which helps to explain the presence of older people even in emerging congregations with a predominance of twenty- and thirty-somethings. As I compare what we know of the Church in previous generations with what we see today, I cannot help but conclude that over the years we have lost touch with creative people – of all sorts – in a way that is now threatening the future of the institution itself. From the Hebrew prophets to Martin Luther King Jr – and with many others since – every significant renewal movement of the past has been initiated by courageous and creative individuals, who have been prepared to step outside the recognized constraints of tradition and convention in the effort to create a new future, their understanding of maturity exemplified by the home-spun wisdom that was made famous by Robert Kennedy: 'Some people see things as they are, and ask why? I see things as they might be, and ask why not?'[12]

Marks of maturity

With all this in mind, then, what might some of the marks of emerging maturity consist of?

Concern for an organic way of being

The emerging church is firmly rooted in the realities of a globalized culture, and recognizes that it is no longer possible for any one group to live within its own isolated cultural bubble. In the 1998 movie, *The Truman Show*, Jim Carrey plays a character who is an archetype of traditional Western institutions of all sorts – living in an imaginary world of their own creation, but believing that it is the real world.[13] This is how emerging church people tend to see the fragmented forms of Christianity handed on from the past. At a time when institutions are generally distrusted just because they are institutions, it is inevitable that the inherited forms of church should be subjected to the same scrutiny. Many wonder why they should be anything other than 'Christian'. What point is there in adopting labels such as Anglican, or Methodist, Roman or Pentecostal, Baptist or Reformed, evangelical or liberal, when a reading of Church history seems to show that such sectarian fragmentation, if not actually part of the problem, has certainly not turned out to be much of a solution? A majority of emerging church people – especially those who come into faith from no previous church background – have no interest in such matters, and simply take it for granted that there is a fundamental unity among Christians of all sorts, regardless of how they might express it. If they think about it at all, they might speculate that the traditional divisions, with their diverse styles of worship and governance, have more to do with the preferences of different personality types than with any significant issues of belief.

When emerging churches reflect on the wider Christian tradition, they tend to identify with models that pre-date the Reformation, whether in medieval monasticism or the missional spirituality of the Celtic saints. Of course, the further back we place our focus, the less certain we can be of what we are focusing on, particularly in the case of Celtic Christianity. From a purist historical perspective, I can sympathize with those scholars who argue that what we know about such ancient times is too insubstantial to bear the weighty reconstructions of Christian spirituality that are now being placed upon it.[14] But, from a missiological point of view, these arguments entirely miss the point. For when a culture finds that the meta-narrative that it once took for granted is either untrue, or merely unserviceable in changed circumstances, it is natural that we look back into our own story in the effort to identify new paradigms that might inspire us for the future. Faced with the diminishing prospects of the people of God, the Hebrew prophets repeatedly looked back to more ancient times and reinterpreted an old story (usually the exodus narrative) for new circumstances. The historical knowledge of the exodus available to Isaiah or Jeremiah must have been just as flimsy as our certain knowledge of the Celtic era, but that never stopped them reshaping the story. In a different way, and on the basis of more certain historical knowledge, the New Testament evangelists did something similar with the stories of Jesus. When the emerging Church looks to ancient times for patterns of organic spirituality and then remodels them in the light of new circumstances, this is just the latest phase in a very old story.

Accompanying this (and often inspired by the past) is a concern for social justice and environmental care, as well as an intentional effort to ensure that worship is relationally interactive, and that teaching and learning incorporates multi-sensory ways of knowing – not as a way of supplanting the importance of written texts and rational reflection, but as a pathway of obedience inspired by biblical exhortations to love God with heart, soul, mind, and strength (Mark 12.29–30). There is a challenge here for both emerging and traditional church. The challenge for those emerging churches that see little value in the wider tradition is to understand that, whether they like it or not, being Christian by any definition does place you within a story stretching back over two millennia. Recognizing that, and being able to live within the reality of it, is surely going to be a key marker of spiritual maturity. For those at the traditional end of the ecclesiastical trajectory, though, there is a different challenge – to recognize that an organic way of being is unlikely to be a structural thing, or even a theological thing. It is, on the contrary, a human thing, as people who follow Jesus find themselves journeying with others who also follow Jesus – and recognizing that the Church's wholeness, within itself and with the rest of humanity and the cosmos, is guaranteed only in so far as it walks alongside the founder.

Recognizing the spiritual in all things

Being faithful has often been understood as separation from the prevailing culture. The Catholic tradition has emphasized the exclusivity of sacred space, while evangelicals have tended to focus on an internalized personal ethical space. When projected into the philosophical space of modernity, both these outlooks led to a privatization of faith, with a consequent division between the sacred and the secular and the implication that we are unlikely to encounter God in the events of everyday life. This has arguably been one of the most damaging effects of recent Western thinking on the mission of the Church, especially in the pietist version that required Christians to withdraw from engagement with the wider culture in order to be fully Christian.[15]

It was Karl Barth who in 1932 first proposed that mission should be understood as an activity of God, rather than as a church programme, though it was the mid-twentieth century before the term *missio Dei* ('mission of God') was coined as a way of describing this reality.[16] Today, it would be hard to imagine the emerging church without some reference to this concept. The notion that this is indeed God's world, that God is at work in it, and that being the Church involves a call to discern where God is at work and to be intentionally aligned with that, is fundamental to much emerging thinking. It is this concept that has enabled emerging congregations to be established in locations that previous generations would have considered off-limits for the Church and its worship – places like night clubs, bars, health clubs, or (worst of all) ground occupied by the proponents of other spiritualities. The recognition that no place can be designated as a no-go area for God has opened up significant spaces for emerging churches to occupy.[17]

Here, then, is a second sign of maturity towards which the emerging church is pointing: the challenge to look beyond ourselves and our own internal affairs, to grasp the bigger picture of what God is doing, and to choose to get alongside God, no matter how strange the territory might seem to be. This is something on which many of us talk a good talk, but struggle to grasp the radical reality to which we are being called. A fair number of emerging groups are inwardly focused, offering a form of spiritual therapy for their own members, rather than opening themselves to the missional activity of God. But then, much of traditional church operates in the same way, with sermons that are little more than personal anecdotes, tuneless songs that are devoid of any meaning beyond the personal angst of those who write and sing them, and an assumption that real church can only happen within the four walls of our buildings. Frustrated clergy find themselves running a spiritual hospice while all the time God is moving the waters in the birthing pool. At a recent diocesan retreat, one priest, who was clearly frustrated by his lack of missional appeal, asked me, 'How can we get the people to come to the altar?' When I turned the question on its head, by asking 'How can we take the altar to the people?' he was dumbstruck. The notion that the spiritual could possibly be encountered anywhere except in a church building at a certain time of day formed no part of his world view. The emerging church would never think like that.

Working towards an inclusive community

Inclusive is the one adjective that can probably be applied to most manifestations of emerging church. One of England's longest-established emerging churches describes its world view in the following terms:

> We believe that God is already in the world and working in the world. We recognize God's indefinable presence in music, film, arts and other key areas of contemporary culture. We wish to affirm and enjoy the parts of our culture that give a voice to one of the many voices of God and challenge any areas that deafen the call of God and hence constrain human freedom.[18]

This is inclusivity with a vengeance. Unlike most church statements about inclusivity, it makes no mention of sexuality. But neither does it mention the Church! Instead, building on the notion of the *missio Dei*, it offers an understanding of inclusivity that embraces and incorporates whatever God may be doing, wherever that may be taking place. Moreover, it takes for granted that God may be found in what many people would regard as unlikely places. At the same time, it is certainly not uncritical and could never be accused of advocating the sort of uncritical inclusivity in which 'anything goes'. On the contrary, there is a strong emphasis on the need for discernment and a call to be appropriately challenging those aspects of the culture that undermine the purposes of God. This statement could never be misconstrued as an invitation to syncretism, but at the same time it is all a very long way from the categories in which Richard Niebuhr taught us to think of Christ and culture.[19] It does, however, have strong biblical roots in a creation-centred spirituality, and in the teaching of Jesus about the kingdom of God. Even if it does not always know the answers to its own questions, the emerging church is at this level engaging with some of the key issues of our day by insisting that God is not limited to the religious world, let alone the church world, but may be encountered literally everywhere. It takes as its text Mark 9.40, 'whoever is not against us is for us', and is actively engaged in exploring both the extent and the limits of that sort of inclusive embrace.

Discernment, inspired by a vision of the kingdom, is absolutely central to this outlook. For if our cultural context is the source of the alienation and discontinuity with which people struggle in their everyday lives,[20] it can never be good news merely to affirm the culture without further qualification. Doing that has led numerous congregations in directions that actually undermine their missional calling, as they continually reorganize themselves in line with the latest trendy insights from the business community, and all too easily end up with a religious version of those oppressive McDonaldized systems that are the very antithesis of the gospel.[21] At the same time, what may need to be challenged today will not be the same as the dehumanizing trends that characterized Western culture 50 or 100 years ago. If the temptation of syncretism and cultural integration is a challenge for the emerging church, the challenge of addressing the culture as it is, rather than as it once was, is a matter requiring urgent attention in more traditional churches.

This sign of maturity frequently manifests itself as an intentional hospitality, and the sharing of food is a central aspect of worship within many emerging churches. We live in a society full of lonely people, in which we are scared of making the very connections that we know we need. Our inner lives might be collapsing, yet we construct impenetrable legal barriers to protect ourselves from others![22] But the kind of suspicion that the culture applauds is actually contrary to the gospel. The emerging church knows that, and challenges it: welcoming the stranger is not just a social need, it is also a biblical principle, and it is one factor that connects emerging church with a much bigger frame of reference, by drawing on the insights of emergence theory. Originating in geometry and chaos theory, this identifies the phenomenon whereby a complex organization comes into being not as a result of a grand design promoted by a leader, but as a consequence of the collective actions of its relatively humble members.[23] In church terms, this kind of socialized enterprise invariably develops when the people of God are empowered to imagine their own future from below, rather than accepting the cascaded (and truncated) responsibility that is handed down from on high. That sense of empowerment always begins with people's personal stories being taken seriously.

Living in the story

In a day when both the power and relevance of abstract reasoning is questioned, story is re-emerging as a form of discourse in which we can speak of ultimate realities without implying any universal claims. Story creates a space within which we can reflect with others on our own personal stories, while understanding the shared cultural story into which we are born. Theologically, this can become a space in which we allow ourselves to be caught up into the all-embracing narrative of the divine story. In his book *A Whole New Mind*, Daniel Pink suggests that what we need today are 'creators and empathizers, pattern recognizers, and meaning makers ... artists, storytellers, caregivers, consolers, big picture thinkers'.[24] The emerging church lives happily within this paradigm.

For generations brought up in the traditions of Cartesian rationalism, the preferred model of theological reflection was located in the sort of analytical presentations of Christian faith that can be found in embryonic form in St Paul, and in the highly developed systems of philosophical speculation that came to define the meaning of faith for centuries after that. There were good contextual reasons for this, as our forebears struggled to make sense of Jesus in the conceptual categories of their day. The emerging church is not uninterested in St Paul, though it certainly tends to be much more interested in Jesus – but in Jesus as a person to be followed rather than Jesus as an object of belief to be dissected and analysed. William Bausch expresses the difference well:

> Propositions are statements on a page; stories are events in a life. Doctrine is the material of texts; story is the stuff of life ... Theology is a secondhand reflection of [the Christ] event; story is the unspeakable event's first voice.[25]

Starting with the stories of Jesus not only informs emerging understandings of mission, but also of the nature of the Church. Whenever we define the Church from within our inherited ecclesiologies, we will always get a Christendom-shaped Church, because the inherited theological patterns are themselves a manifestation of Constantinianism, and in many cases their structures are all but identical to the governance of the political systems of the age in which they came to birth. This is most obviously the case with those traditions that have taken over the structures of the Roman empire itself.[26] But it is just as true for the inherited ecclesiology of the Free Churches, modelled in its Reformed versions on the governance of sixteenth-century Switzerland and Holland, and in its Baptistic versions owing more than a little to Cromwellian notions of republicanism.[27] If, as is now widely recognized, the contextualization of the gospel represented by Christendom is no longer an appropriate vehicle for the good news, that must be taken into account in any discussion of what it means for the Church to be both emerging and incarnational. Both these terms imply a bottom-up rather than a top-down process, and whenever people and their stories are taken seriously as vehicles for the transcendent, then, by definition, we end up with something very different from the sort of generic Church with which we are all familiar. At its best, the emerging church creates space for stories to be heard, shared, and acted upon – but only when it has authentic leaders who are willing to acknowledge their own struggles and weaknesses as well as their strengths.[28]

This is one point at which many emerging churches have some way to go to achieve maturity, for some of them continue to perpetuate patterns that look suspiciously like Christendom, even while they speak the language of the kingdom. Nowhere is this more obvious than in their leadership structures. For whether by design or historical accident, the vast majority of emerging churches – on any of the definitions offered at the start of this chapter – are bastions of male leadership.[29] It would require further research to tease out the reasons for this, though I suspect it may have something to do with the blog culture within which a majority of discussions about the emerging church take place, and which tends to be dominated by men. They are not all chauvinists, of course, but some of the more prolific bloggers belong to my second type of emerging church (angry ex-fundamentalists), or are funded by conservative organizations, and bring that baggage into the conversation in ways that others (being less familiar with the Bible and Church history) find hard to resist or disagree with. On the other hand, the relative paucity of women leaders in the emerging church might also be related to our understanding of the nature of leadership, something that is a cultural problem and not just an emerging church issue. Though great strides have been made in recognizing the need for many voices and stories to be heard, it is still the case that most Western institutions (including churches that ordain women) operate with structures and processes that reflect the preferences of white males, and others who are either unable or unwilling to operate within this culture (whether male or female) find themselves marginalized.

Conclusion

One of the things that can surprise newcomers to the emerging conversation is its fascination with ancient forms of Christian spirituality, whether that be through the adoption of traditional rituals or the creation of new ones that may indeed be newly minted, but which turn out to bear more than a passing resemblance to practices that were embedded in the earliest days of the Christian story. This is a manifestation of a wider trend within the culture of postmodernity. Our dissatisfaction with modernity has created a spiritual vacuum that we are more than ready to fill with ancient nostrums that our grandparents would have dismissed without a second thought. In the effort to make sense of our present predicament, we are quite happy to jump backwards to what we imagine was a simpler time imbued with spiritual wisdom of the sort that rationalism and materialism dismissed too readily. How else can you explain our fascination with the mystical and the numinous, with angels and tarot cards, with holistic healing therapies and guidance from spirits? It is as if we have come to regard anything recent and Cartesian (rational and scientific) as the source of all our troubles, and therefore anything that is ancient and non-Cartesian will be the solution to them. Robert Webber has aptly called this the ancient-future axis of the emerging church.[30] It also takes our quest for maturity in the emerging church back to an unexpected starting point. In the Nicene Creed, we affirm our belief in a Church that is 'one, holy, catholic and apostolic'. Is that just another way of speaking of a Church that is organic, that finds the spiritual in everything, while being inclusive and living within the story?

These wise words from Gert Rüppell seem to summarize much of what we must now contend with:

> I think we are back to what is called 'square one'. We may timidly admit that we are living in 'apostolic times', in times where the cloth is being woven. A risky time in apostolic mission, where we have to tell one another the basis of our hope, join with each other in the expression of the strength of our faith, telling one another the questions we have in order to find together the answers that the world, the people, are expecting from us as disciples of Christ.[31]

The image of weaving the cloth is a powerful metaphor for today's Church. So much of what we have inherited is like a comfortable sweater that is now unravelling around the edges. We can do one of two things with that sort of sweater: either we patch it up, to try and make it last a bit longer, or we pull at the loose ends to see what happens, with a view to taking the wool, washing it, and knitting it into a garment that will be fit for a new generation. No one could possibly deny that the unravelling is happening. It is the creative spirits of the emerging church who are acting with missional intentionality to imagine, and then to create, unfamiliar shapes and patterns of faithful discipleship that are both old and new (Matthew 13.52).

9

What are the lessons from evangelism and apologetics for new communities?

David Wilkinson

Introduction

If the movement of fresh expressions has a missiological motive and context, then it seems quite odd to explore the challenge of apologetics and evangelism for these new communities. After all, many fresh expressions of church arise out of a deep commitment to apologetics and evangelism, the community shaped in large part by the perceived need of the 'outsider' or 'enquirer'. It might be argued that apologetics and evangelism are far more of a challenge to the more traditional churches in the mixed economy, where the challenge is either completely ignored or the source of guilt, despair and recurring study commissions.

Nevertheless, there is great value in bringing the hard questions of apologetics and evangelism into conversation with fresh expressions. Evangelism and apologetics are areas of much current thinking and discussion in the light of contemporary culture and a failing Church in Europe. Evangelism is 'spreading the good news that in Jesus Christ God is establishing a new order and calling people to renounce all alternatives and embrace this reality'.[1] Some argue that we must rediscover and regain confidence in traditional forms of evangelism[2] while others argue that the context means that we need completely new models.[3] At the same time apologetics has been undergoing a similar transformation. The old model of answering intellectual problem questions about the Christian faith does not work if no one is asking the questions. Apologetics in a post-Christian culture is more about building bridges of relevance.[4] As Alister McGrath writes, 'The chief goal of Christian apologetics is to create an intellectual and imaginative climate conducive to the birth and nurture of faith.'[5] While evangelism may involve the proclamation of and response to the good news, apologetics has become increasingly important in providing the theological foundations of reading, understanding and creating links with contemporary culture. This transformation of evangelism and apologetics is important as any renewal of the Church has to be linked to a rediscovery of the mission of God.[6]

If, evangelism and apologetics are undergoing considered renewal, we need to ask the same hard questions about the fresh expressions movement. We need to ask one very hard question: Are some fresh expressions really missiologically driven? Are they simply new expressions of church for those with faith who are bored and unfulfilled by traditional church? We know that it is often easier to populate new churches with dechurched rather than unchurched people.

I know this from my own experience of leading a very middle-of-the-road Methodist Church in Liverpool in the 1990s. Well before the language of fresh expressions, we had new initiatives in contemporary worship, alternative worship, midweek all-age worship and planted a new congregation into Liverpool city centre. We developed the use of video in worship, greater congregational participation in learning in sermons, and initiatives in liturgy, music and drama. Some of it worked and some of it failed. We grew as a congregation, but our growth was at times more in drawing disaffected Christians back to church than in drawing new people into their first experience of the risen Jesus. Whatever our 'success' I found myself having to ask hard questions of our evangelism and apologetics.

So, I want to reflect on the challenges faced by apologetics and evangelism in post-Christian Britain and apply those questions as appropriate for fresh expressions. I have picked out five key challenges of apologetics and evangelism for new communities:

- affirming passion
- deepening theological foundations
- living with risk
- developing diversity in ministry
- being local in a global context.

Affirming passion

Evangelism and apologetics have often been viewed with either a lack of passion or fear of passion. The minister proclaims loudly at the end of the Eucharist that people should go into all the world to love and serve the Lord.

Very few will respond with any passion to talk with their work colleagues about what they did on Sunday morning, never mind saying hello to the visitor who is sitting in the same pew. At the same time, there are those who fear passion. They worry that those interested in evangelism and apologetics have too much enthusiasm and are rather naïve. As Rob Frost has written, evangelists are often seen as 'oddballs, extremists and off the wall'.[7] It is this lack of passion and fear of passion, which is part of the reason why so many gifted individuals, passionate about apologetics and evangelism, have moved their base out of the local church into para-church organizations. These become the vehicles of new work rather than the local churches.

I rejoice as I listen to or read stories of many involved in fresh expressions, who are people with passion – passion for new church life and relationships, and passion for Goths, the homeless and families. I do not believe that as a church community our challenge is to create passion. Our challenge is how we recognize, affirm and not stand in the way of genuine passion for Jesus and the kingdom.

For example, how do we affirm passion in training for church leadership? This operates at selection, training and giving responsibility. When we attempt to discern vocation and call to leadership, do we look for theological knowledge and pastoral gifts, rather than vision and energy? Too often in assessing a call to ordination or lay leadership we prefer safety to passion. It needs a wise and secure leader to recognize and liberate people of passion and not see them as a threat that needs to be controlled. Then in the training of leaders, our philosophies of training and formation, if not explicitly, affirm talk about making a person a 'safe pair of hands', or someone who is proficient in all ministerial functions. Affirming passion is about giving flexibility and diversity in training for students to develop specific skills and charisms. To affirm passion is also to see ministry as a joint activity where people lead within the context of the Body of Christ, putting their passion and gifts alongside other passions and gifts. Finally, in stationing people to specific posts, we need to be careful that we do not shape senior leadership posts in the Church to be only for those of academic qualifications and pastoral gifts. Many evangelists and apologists have found themselves unable to enrich their churches or denominations at senior levels of leadership and having to express their passion outside of the Church. While fresh expressions and pioneer ministry do give new contexts for people with passion, it would be a shame if they simply become a convenient niche for people that the Church cannot affirm adequately. Both in the local church and nationally, let us affirm the young convert, the older person with the new lease of life, the initiator of projects and the imaginative artist with support and opportunity.

At the same time, there needs to be something more than passion in those involved in apologetics, evangelism and indeed fresh expressions. Albert Outler, the Methodist historian, suggests that the key point for Wesley in his evangelistic ministry was when 'his passion for truth had been transformed into compassion for persons'.[8] Part of the affirming of passion is to develop it in the context of compassion. The danger of passion divorced from compassion is often manifested in the growing of a new church community in order to validate the ministry of a particular leader. It begins to use other people to reach a goal, rather than serving others and looking to their needs. In a context where we talk about the importance of fresh expressions, those involved in such work will be under immense pressure to deliver numbers, value for money, and indeed demonstrate just how fresh their expression is. We must be careful not to lose a sense of compassion for people.

Where does this movement from passion to compassion come from? Both passion and compassion come from a deep encounter with the Lord Jesus and an experience of his ministry in our own lives. As Matthew speaks of Jesus, 'When he saw the crowds he had compassion for them because they were lost and helpless like sheep without a shepherd' (Matthew 9.36). Kenda Creasey Dean points out theological resonances between the passion of Christ and adolescents' experience of passion, in order to argue for a passionate church.[9] Thus, prayer, encounter with the Scriptures and worship that regularly focuses on the death and resurrection of Christ is crucial to any fresh expression of church that affirms passion and gives it a context of compassion.

Deepening the theological foundations

Our common experience of apologetics and evangelism in Britain today is that it is a very difficult and dispiriting activity. The cultural context is such that people are not flocking into evangelistic meetings and they are not battering down the doors of the church wanting to ask questions. As John Drane has often indicated, there may be a spiritual hunger in our country but the last place that people will find a good meal seems to be the Church.[10]

In a post-Christian culture, where the Christian message is often ignored and indeed often lampooned, the temptation in evangelism has been to look around for some new programme whether *Alpha*, Seeker Services or Purpose Driven Church, which, by its very newness, gives us some hope that it will work. This is the particular temptation for those who hear that a particular programme is working in one place and immediately try to transplant it into a different cultural setting. It is interesting that in a short space of time many involved want to ask theological questions of such programmes, not least about the content of the gospel.[11] In a similar way, one of the current initiatives in apologetics is to build bridges through pop culture, whether it is music, film or literature.[12] However, such initiatives mean a new theological understanding of God at work in the world, the nature of media culture and the role of the imagination.[13]

This need to deepen the theological foundations is essential to sustain a difficult and risky new movement. The Methodist leader Donald English, a regular contributor to BBC Radio 4's 'Thought for the Day', was once asked where his confidence to do such work came from. His answer was, 'My confidence comes from John 1, Colossians 1 and Hebrews 1.' This understanding of Jesus as the source and sustainer of all creation means that wherever you start with contemporary culture, there is a natural path to Jesus. It may take you a little bit of time to find it but it is there. When apologetics is difficult, this gives you hope.

Richard Lovelace, commenting on the history of movements of the Spirit within the Great Awakenings, writes, 'The purity of a revival is intimately related to its theological substance. Unless revival involves and issues in theological reformation its energy will be contained and its fruit will not last.'[14] What are the questions of theological reformation posed by fresh expressions? While questions of ecclesiology and authority are obvious, the question of discernment of the Spirit seems key. As my colleague, Roger Walton, the Director of the Wesley Study Centre asks, in all the diversity of fresh expressions, 'Where is Jesus in all this and how do we recognize him? How do we identify the same living Christ?'

We need to take these theological questions a step further. Graham Cray characterizes theology as the 'daughter of the church's mission', or 'missionary thinking for missionary action'.[15] While *Mission-shaped Church* highlighted the theological foundations of the mission of God, mission after the pattern of Christ, the community of the Spirit, the Church as a community created to reproduce, and classic marks of the Church according to the Nicene Creed, I would want to push further the place of Scripture within this emerging movement. How is Scripture involved in missionary thinking for missionary action?

Western apologetics has traditionally owed more to Greek philosophy than to biblical narrative. The development of the design argument stemming from the scientific revolution saw a decisive shift from revelation to reason as the basis of Christian faith. Intelligent design is a move back to such a decisive shift, with a form of rational argument that ignores Jesus and biblical revelation.[16] The danger is to adopt a strategy that bears short-term fruit but forget the nature of being a community formed by the biblical story. In evangelism many practitioners deal with a distilled gospel rather than immersing the hearers in the whole biblical narrative. Even in models of evangelism it is important to develop these in a serious conversation with Scripture.

Take, for example, the parable of the Prodigal Son (Luke 15.11-32). I have heard many evangelistic sermons or indeed missiological expositions of this passage. On the basis of this, some argue that the missional model is one of God/the Church/the evangelist waiting and giving space to the world/the culture/the non-believer to return, just like the waiting Father. Churches of all kinds in the mixed economy must be set up to make easy this return. However, Luke 15 contains two other parables – the lost sheep (Luke 15.3-7) and the lost coin (Luke 15.8-9). Whether you believe that Jesus put these three parables together, or whether this is Luke's editorial arrangement, it is important to recognize that these three parables need to be read together. The first two parables convey a picture of God who seeks, who initiates and who pursues. Taking them all together, we get a picture of God who is both the one who seeks and the one who waits. This biblical tension, or even paradox, critiques our models of mission against a model that is completely based on dragging people into the kingdom, and against a model that is happy to let the Prodigal be at home in the pig sty. It is only by taking the whole of Scripture seriously that we begin to tease out some of these fundamental issues.

The great New Testament scholar C. K. Barrett once said: 'A church however well-organized, learned and ecumenical is dying if it has lost the power to read, understand and preach the Bible.' Initiatives in apologetics, evangelism and fresh expressions need to hear this challenge. Traditionally, many churches have encountered the whole sweep of the Scriptures in liturgy, in preaching and in personal Bible reading.

Writing from the Hungarian context, Lovas argues that 'context-shaped liturgy does not shape missional people'.[17] He sees the danger in new church movements of shaping the message and liturgy for best results. Agreeing with Newbigin and Wright, he argues that liturgy must assist God's missional people to indwell the gospel story. In our concern for fresh expressions of church, a missional community can only be sustained if formal or informal events of worship allow us to enter the biblical story. Michael Quicke makes a similar point concerning preaching. Preaching Scripture sustains the essential tasks of confronting culture about godlessness, confronting the Church about its worldliness and challenging the Church to model a new identity as a missional people for its cultural context.[18] Whether Scripture is encountered in a traditional sermon form, or whether there are fresh expressions of encounter through discussion, drama, the senses or the imagination, fresh expressions will be kept vital by a regular and serious engagement with the whole of the Bible.

Living with risk

The experience of those involved in evangelism and apologetics is that it is a risky business – clearly these are pertinent lessons for a new and creative movement. In Acts 17.16-34 Paul engages with people in the Athenian market, which leads to an invitation from the Epicurean and Stoic philosophers to hear more. At this point it is easy to imagine Paul as a kind of Arnold Schwarzenegger who strides up to the Areopagus ready for some Greek philosophers to 'make my day'. However, Luke is very clear that Paul was extremely vulnerable in this situation. In fact, some of the philosophers had already snidely asked what this gutter-snipe was trying to get out of his mouth (v. 18) – not something that would have given Paul confidence! In addition, here Paul goes into debate by himself, whereas for most of his evangelistic ministry he worked as part of a team.

If he felt vulnerable before the philosophers, he may have also felt vulnerable to condemnation from his own community. It is interesting that Luke just notes the comment: 'Now all the Athenians and the foreigners living there would spend their time in nothing but telling or hearing something new' (v. 21). You can imagine one or two in the Early Church saying, 'Paul, don't devalue the gospel by taking it into these philosophical circles and debating at their level, you need to stand apart and proclaim to them the gospel.' However, Paul engages with the Epicureans and Stoics in their territory and in their language, is clear about proclaiming Jesus, and ends with a very strong call to repentance.

Luke presents the response in far from overwhelming terms. Some scoffed and some of them joined him (vv. 32-34). A few commentators have used this to say that as Paul failed in Athens, he then decided to return to the simple gospel, preaching Christ crucified in his next stop in Corinth. This, of course, does not do justice to the way that Paul contextualizes the gospel in Acts. Yet we do well to notice there was a mixed response in Athens, and it was not an overwhelming success. And Luke is to be commended for being honest about it.

The risk involved in evangelism and apologetics is huge, and not least the risk of failure. Many of us know the planning, investment, prayer and commitment that leads to very little fruit in terms of our attempted evangelistic and apologetic attempts. However, we are not good at being honest with one another when we fail. Lack of attendance at meetings or lack of fruit can all be justified away in spiritual language. Yet we only begin to learn and grow when we are prepared to be honest with one another, acknowledging our failures and also acknowledging what a hard task this is in a post-Christian culture.

Of course, for many churches in the mixed economy the first step to fresh expressions is recognition of failure. It is vital to be honest together that we no longer live in Christendom and many of our efforts have previously failed. That same willingness to be honest needs also to be encountered in assessing fresh expressions. Fresh expressions is a risky business and sometimes will fail. A willingness to be honest about our numbers, what we have and have not been able to achieve seems to me to be important to the health of the ongoing process. In promoting fresh expressions and its inherent risk, we need to be authentic in presenting stories of both success and failure.

My own experience back in the 1990s in Liverpool is instructive. We were able to plant a new congregation in the upper room of a pub in the city centre. Its growth was steady but not dramatic. New forms of worship were developed. It attracted into its life a number of individuals who have later gone on to work in more traditional churches and indeed into church leadership within the Methodist denomination. The experience for the young team, of planting such a church, was invaluable. However, due to problems in leadership and lack of support from the wider Church it eventually had to close. It was an attempt that did not live up to the dreams we had of it, and we need to be honest about its successes and its failures.

It is at this point that the theological understanding of the gospel becomes so important. As Christians, who believe in death and resurrection, we need to tell these stories of success, failure and risk. In the cross we see a God who risks the vulnerability of human death and offers forgiveness for those who have failed. After such death there is resurrection. As Moltmann comments, 'Faith in the resurrection is the faith in God of lovers and the dying, the suffering and the grieving. It is the great hope which consoles us and gives us new courage.'[19]

Developing diversity in ministry

In a much-quoted passage, Newbigin set out what has become a key understanding for many involved in fresh expressions:

> How is it possible that the gospel should be credible, that people should come to believe that the power which has the last word in human affairs is represented by a man hanging on a cross? I am suggesting that the only answer, the only hermeneutic of the gospel, is a congregation of men and women who believe it and live by it.[20]

This understanding of the community as the hermeneutic of the gospel raises the important question of just how much diversity is expressed within the leadership and ministries of fresh expressions. *Mission-shaped Church* recognized that diversity is practically important and theologically grounded in the nature of God.[21] The Trinity models diversity as well as unity, and election and incarnation 'reveal God daring to be culturally specific within diverse contexts'.

Western apologetics and evangelism have been too often dominated by 'the ministry of experts'. It has been seen to be the domain of the C. S. Lewis or Billy Graham. The perception for many has been that this ministry is only for males, with certain intellectual backgrounds, and certain evangelistic gifts. If the hermeneutic of the gospel is the community, then how do we move away from the ministry of experts to releasing the whole people of God?

Roland Allen (1868–1947), the Anglican missionary to China, as a result of his experience in the Boxer rebellion and his encounter with the Chinese belief that Christianity was foreign-led, began to think about what it means to move to a ministry of the whole people of God and the importance of indigenous church. Fundamental to his developing view was that Paul endowed the earliest Christians with spiritual authority. In fact we can see this in Acts 20.28 where Paul at the heart of his farewell speech to the Ephesian elders says, 'Keep watch over yourselves and over all the flock of which the Holy Spirit has made you overseers, to shepherd the Church of God.' C. K. Barrett, in commenting on this passage, sees Paul boldly using the same language to describe these young church leaders in the same way that he would describe his own call. It was this understanding of the call of young Christians that allowed Allen in his 1927 book, *The Spontaneous Expansion of the Church: And the causes which hinder it*, to argue that new churches could cast off paternalism and that spontaneity and simplicity were the marks of authentic Christianity.[22]

As Verkuyl has pointed out, the problem in such analysis was that it made the Church, not the kingdom, central. In fact the same problem has been raised for fresh expressions, that is, should we be talking about fresh expressions of the kingdom rather than fresh expressions of church?[23] Nevertheless, Allen's analysis can be applied to the fresh expressions movement of today. That is, how do we broaden diversity in leadership and ministry? Does the very language of fresh expressions or the forms of structure that we adopt, mean that older or younger people are favoured in the giving of opportunities and resources? Do we need to look especially at the question of gender? In fact, is there an argument to say that women are better able to initiate fresh expressions than men, or the forms of fresh expressions leading from the leadership of women are different from those of the leadership of men? Yet are women given enough opportunities compared to men? It is undeniable that the parent structures of the Church of England and the Methodist Church have few women in senior positions. Is this 'genetic defect' passed on to fresh expressions?

Apologetics and evangelism have been greatly impoverished by denying opportunities and mentoring to women compared to men. It is to be hoped that this will not be the same with fresh expressions. In order for this to happen we need to have a biblical understanding of call, and for those already in power to be prepared to make space for others to lead and grow very different kinds of congregations.

Being local in a global context

Mortimer Arias has argued that mission, while being contextualized, has to be global in its vision, its strategy and its content.[24] Without that we do not reflect the nature of God, the kingdom or the missionary mandate. This global vision is particularly important for evangelism and apologetics. Within evangelism it continually calls the wealthy or successful mission fields to look beyond themselves to the more closed cultures and unreached people groups. Within apologetics, it is a reminder that the questions of Western philosophy are not the only challenges or opportunities in building bridges for the gospel.

Fresh expressions recognizes the needs, problems and opportunities of the immediate locality. Yet we need to remember that the local is not the whole Church or indeed kingdom. This is important for a number of reasons.

First, a global vision leads to a sense of perspective for leaders and congregations. Too often we can be blinkered by our own experience, of either difficulty or blessing. A new project can see itself out of all proportion in terms of its importance. Many years ago Jonathan Edwards, in a section in his classic work on the spiritual dynamics of the revival in New England,[25] pointed out the danger of pride in church leadership in the midst of new movements of God's spirit. Pride clogs and hinders the work of God; it magnifies what we have achieved and finds faults with others. It is only by reflecting on God's global work that we find ourselves in our rightful place.

Secondly, the global context is a reminder of our sense of responsibility. When we talk about fresh expressions how do we see fresh expressions mixing into the economy of church? How do we see the growth and nurture of leaders within fresh expressions, feeding into God's purposes, not just in the mixed economy in this country but into God's purposes worldwide?

Thirdly, the global context raises the question of how do we in fresh expressions reflect the value of larger structures to something that is created in response to a local need? How do we represent our part of a world communion, the whole Body of Christ? In the nineteenth century the Anglican Henry Venn (1796–1873), Secretary of the Church Missionary Society, and the Congregationalist Rufus Anderson (1796–1880) considered the question of how young churches become independent. They were both concerned about the missionary context and how young churches funded in developing nations are able to move away from the paternalistic control through finance and leadership of parent churches. This led to the three-self formula as a long-term vision or strategy of church planting. That is, the chief goal was to build churches that are self-supporting, self-governing and self-propagating. This was an important corrective to the paternalism associated with the giving initially of finance and leadership from parent churches. Such thinking has become important in considering the question of how fresh expressions of church move to maturity. Lings has suggested, however, that the three-self formula does have its limitations. He suggests that Venn, in particular, looked for progression from disabling dependence, through independence into interdependence in the Anglican family.[26]

Verkuyl pushes the critique further. He argues that the three-self formula was important for its time but that self-support is not a distinguishing mark of a true church.[27] He points out that the New Testament is very clear that prosperous churches should aid the poorer churches (2 Corinthians 9.1–15), and this is part of a theological understanding that the local church is inextricably bound to the global Church. In fact, the three-self formula pushed too far led to huge financial burdens on the young churches inhibiting growth and the dismantling of long-term relationships within worldwide communions. How do we work with fresh expressions and other churches in the mixed economy to foster interdependence in the larger structures of church worldwide? Leaders at both local level and international level will need humility and a very strong global experience and commitment.

Excited by the challenge of the Spirit?

I have explored five challenges of apologetics and evangelism for new communities: affirming passion and moving to compassion, deepening theological foundations, living with risk, developing diversity in ministry and being local in a global context. There is a wealth of literature and experience in evangelism and apologetics to inspire and support the leaders of fresh expressions in addressing these challenges. These are challenges to be faced by any movement of the Spirit and are challenges related to how we understand the work of the Spirit. I am excited by seeing the Spirit at work in fresh expressions. Theology is not just about missionary thinking for missionary action. It is about discerning, understanding and getting alongside what God is doing through his Son and by his Spirit.

10

Mission-shaped and kingdom focused?

John M. Hull

Introduction

The difference between a Church-shaped mission and a mission-shaped Church is crucial, and I concluded my pamphlet *Mission Shaped Church: A theological response*[1] by making this distinction. This refers to the difference between a mission that is essentially shaped by the interests and concerns of the Christian churches and a Church that, forgetful of itself, is ready to perceive and respond to the mission of God. The expression 'kingdom focused' refers to the focus of the Church's activity as being not upon itself but upon the coming of the kingdom of God. The expression 'kingdom of God' refers to that heavenly and earthly reality in which the purposes of God are realized. It also refers to the teaching of Jesus himself, the proclamation of the Early Church, and it is also a symbol of the utopian future. Christian faith is best understood in its messianic aspect as an agent of the now and future kingdom, and church as an agent of Christian faith for the same ultimate purpose. In this sequence, only the kingdom of God, which is the object of the mission of God, is self-authenticating; both Christian faith and church are instrumental to kingdom.

In the present statement I shall try to clarify this distinction and support it biblically and theologically.

The problem

Let us start with the notion that Christian faith invites us into a double relationship, one vertical and the other horizontal. The vertical is said to be our individual or collective relationship to God while the horizontal is said to represent our relationship with each other.[2] It is sometimes said that the vertical empowers the horizontal, or motivates it, as is suggested by the expression 'social responsibility', which indicates that the Church in its vertical relation to God must not forget that it also has a responsibility to others. I have even heard preachers use the shape of the cross to illustrate this idea. The vertical arm, it is said, points heavenward while the outstretched arms embrace all humanity. It is something like this that stands behind the concept of a Church-shaped mission, where the Church has become the location for a vertical transcendence, or the guardian of an other-worldly revelation, so that the horizontal dimension becomes an extra, albeit a necessary one.[3] I shall offer a reconstruction of this duality in order to provide a more secure focus upon the kingdom of God leading to a genuinely mission-shaped Church.

Knowledge of God in the Bible

The biblical revelation announces the good news that the vertical has been collapsed into the horizontal. In other words, biblical faith in its prophetic form, that tradition which is most significant for the mission of God, transforms the experience of transcendence from the remote to the near, from the abstract to the concrete.

We may distinguish between three kinds of transcendence: vertical transcendence, horizontal transcendence and future transcendence. Vertical transcendence is hierarchical. Like Jack's beanstalk or Jacob's ladder it creates two worlds, an earthly one and a superior, spiritual one. Horizontal transcendence means that we are confronted by absolute otherness, by the presence of the other person, the fellow human being, whose need places upon me an unqualified demand such that in that demand I find myself in the presence of God. The third kind, the transcendence of futurity, means that beyond the need of the brother or sister before whom I stand there lies, outside my reach, beyond my grasp, the brothers of that brother, and the sisters of that sister, stretching out to the whole of humanity and indeed to all creation now and to come. In this understanding of future transcendence, God is the lure of history, the one who calls to me from the far side of the horizon. I shall argue that the Bible tells the story of the God who came down to earth, the one who became God-with-us, in such a way that the transcendence of height has become transmuted into that of presence, in horizontality, and into the extension of the horizontal into the horizon, the future of the coming kingdom of God.

The Great Commandment

I shall commence my exposition of the biblical foundations of this theology by drawing your attention to the answer given by Jesus to the question about which was the greatest commandment:

> Jesus replied, ' "You must love the Lord your God with all your heart, all your soul, and all your mind." This is the first and greatest commandment. A second is equally important: "Love your neighbour as yourself." '
>
> (Matthew 22.37-39 NLT)

Most of the English translations render verse 39 as 'the second is like it'. The word translated 'equally important' or 'alongside it'[4] is *homoia*. This is the word attributed to John the Baptist when he said that the person who had two tunics should share with the person who had none and the one who has food should do 'the same'. The first husband of the woman referred to in Matthew 22.23-33 died and the second, third and all the rest did 'the same'. This is the paradox of the two great commandments, one is 'greatest' yet the other is 'the same'. How can this paradox be resolved?

Perhaps someone might wonder why the text does not read *homooia* (of the same substance), bearing in mind the distinction between *homoousion* and *homoiousion*, which became so significant in the fourth century. At that time, in the debate between Arianism and what was becoming orthodoxy, *homoousion* came to mean that which is numerically or ontologically identical, whereas *homoiousion* was regarded as meaning only similar. This is why *homoousion* emerged as the orthodox description of the relation between the Son and the Father. But this distinction only emerged in the course of the controversy, to meet a particular conceptual crisis; before this, the two words were virtually identical in their meaning.[5]

The word *homoousia* is not found in the New Testament, and it would have made no sense to have used it in the later meaning it came to have, in any of the passages we are discussing.[6] The lawyer who was told to go and do *homoia*, the same kind of thing, could not do exactly the same unless he waited by the Jericho road for a Samaritan to be mugged in identical circumstances. The third brother could not die with exactly the same death as the second simply because he was the third and not the second. But they both died and their deaths were the same. If we introduce the later distinction, we may say that the love of the transcendent is not ontologically identical with the love of the immediate, just as the love of ultimacy is not identical with the love of penultimacy but since one is the way to the other, since one is fulfilled in the other they are tantamount to the same thing. In practice, for all intents and purposes, they are the same.[7]

Thus the paradox is resolved: the first commandment is ultimately the greatest, but for all practical purposes, the second is the same. The vertical has no independent existence as far as human beings are concerned; it has conceptual but not practical independence. Indeed it is only approached by that which is similar to it. Nevertheless, the ultimate remains greatest.[8]

The origins of the prophetic tradition

In this teaching Jesus stands squarely in the prophetic tradition. In the Hebrew Bible there is to be no image or likeness made of God (Exodus 20.4) and yet God made human beings in God's own image and likeness (Genesis 1.27). Does this mean that human beings are to be worshipped as God? Or that images of the human may be objects of worship? Certainly not! Then how are we to explain the paradox? There could be no independent image of God precisely because the revelation of God came only through the human other.[9] Nor could images of the human be made for worship, for what had become holy was not the image of the human but the image of God in the human such that God was available in no other form or image save through God's image in the human. God had become present only through inter-subjectivity, and through inter-subjectivity qualified in a particular manner, the way of justice.

Thus, over and over again, the God of the Bible is described as the God who loves justice:

> The Lord is known by his justice.
>
> > (Psalm 9.16 NIV)

> The Lord is righteous; he loves justice.
>
> > (Psalm 11.7 NIV)

> The Lord works righteousness and justice for all that are oppressed.
>
> > (Psalm 103.6 NIV)

The references to God as the God of justice not only refer to the character of God but to what God does and thus to where and how God is to be served and found. The Bible does not merely announce an abstract ethical quality in God but reveals a God who executes justice and who requires justice.

It is sometimes said that the first part of the Decalogue (Exodus 20.3-11) represents the human duty towards God while the second part (Exodus 20.12-17) is duty to our fellow humans. But this must surely be to divide where no division is to be found. The whole of the Two Tables is based upon its preface, in which God is the redeeming and liberating Saviour, who brought Israel up out of Egypt, out of slavery (Exodus 20.2). It is as the emancipator of slaves that God graciously gives the covenant.[10]

The popular impression that the Ten Commandments are a series of abstract demands rather than a consequence of the mercy of the liberating God may have been effected by the fact that in the 1662 *Book of Common Prayer* the text is introduced by the words 'God spake these words, and said, I am the Lord thy God: Thou shalt have no other gods but me', thus omitting the crucial words 'who brought thee up out of Egypt, out of the house of bondage'.[11]

In the Deuteronomic version of the origin of the Decalogue its ethical foundation is emphasized. This is done through declaring the character of God as the lover of foreigners:

> For the Lord your God is God of gods and Lord of lords, the great God, mighty and awesome, who shows no partiality and accepts no bribes. He defends the cause of the fatherless and the widow, and loves the alien, giving him food and clothing. And you are to love those who are aliens, for you yourselves were aliens in Egypt.
>
> (Deuteronomy 10.17-19 NIV)

The implication of our own liberation is to set others free; indeed, it is through recognizing the demand of the oppressed other that God, the great God, is both recognized and obeyed. If God is not worshipped in this way, God becomes just another religious idol, but God is to be worshipped in this way and thus there can be no making of graven images.

The prophets of Israel

Whenever the cult of worship and sacrifice tried to approach God without passing through the demand of the other for justice, it was regarded by the prophets as being blasphemous and an insult to God:

I can't stand your religious meetings.
　　I'm fed up with your conferences and conventions.
I want nothing to do with your religion projects,
　　your pretentious slogans and goals.
I'm sick of your fund-raising schemes,
　　your public relations and image making.
I've had all I can take of your noisy ego-music.
　　When was the last time you sang to me?
Do you know what I want?
　　I want justice – oceans of it.
I want fairness – rivers of it.
That's what I want. That's all I want.

(Amos 5.21-24 The Message)

Isaiah shows us that when the vertical is honoured apart from the horizontal, it becomes trivial and corrupt:

'The multitude of your sacrifices –
what are they to me?' says the Lord.
'I have more than enough of burnt offerings,
of rams and the fat of fattened animals;
I have no pleasure
in the blood of bulls and lambs and goats.

When you come to appear before me,
who has asked this of you,
this trampling of my courts?

Stop bringing meaningless offerings!
Your incense is detestable to me.
New Moons, Sabbaths and convocations –
I cannot bear your evil assemblies.

Your New Moon festivals and your appointed feasts
my soul hates.
They have become a burden to me;
I am weary of bearing them.

When you spread out your hands in prayer,
I will hide my eyes from you;
even if you offer many prayers,
I will not listen.
Your hands are full of blood;

> wash and make yourselves clean.
> Take your evil deeds
> out of my sight!
> Stop doing wrong,
>
> learn to do right!
> Seek justice,
> encourage the oppressed.
> Defend the cause of the fatherless,
> plead the case of the widow.'
>
> (Isaiah 1.11-17 NIV)

In Hosea we find the same bold affirmation. Reading the book as a whole, it could be said that Hosea teaches that the vertical has become corrupt because the horizontal has been ignored; it could also be said that the way to the vertical has been blocked by failure to observe justice in the horizontal. Israel has become faithless in her religious life in that the character of the covenant God has not been acknowledged:

> For I desire mercy, not sacrifice,
> and acknowledgment of God rather than burnt offerings.
>
> (Hosea 6.6 NIV)

> They will not pour out wine offerings to the Lord,
> nor will their sacrifices please him.
> Such sacrifices will be to them like the bread of mourners;
> all who eat them will be unclean.
> This food will be for themselves;
> it will not come into the temple of the Lord.
>
> (Hosea 9.4 NIV)

> Sow for yourselves righteousness,
> reap the fruit of unfailing love,
> and break up your unploughed ground;
> for it is time to seek the Lord,
> until he comes
> and showers righteousness on you.
>
> (Hosea 10.12 NIV)

It might appear that the teaching of the prophets was no more than the demand for a balance between the vertical and the horizontal and a claim that without a just dealing with the horizontal the vertical would be imperfect. The truth of inter-subjective transcendence, however, is more radical:

The rubric of covenant thus requires a departure from the more conventional philosophical categories of immanence and transcendence and the entire Cartesian temptation to dualism, for covenant is not balancing of transcendence and immanence, but is a complete rejection of a dualism that is too tidy and free of risk.[12]

One of the clearest statements of the knowledge of God in the whole Bible is in Jeremiah 22.15,16. The prophet is attacking the luxurious lifestyle of the king, and comparing him unfavourably with his father, the great and good king Josiah:

> 'Does it make you a king
> to have more and more cedar?
> Did not your father have food and drink?
> He did what was right and just,
> so all went well with him.
>
> He defended the cause of the poor and needy,
> and so all went well.
> Is that not what it means to know me?'
> declares the Lord. (NIV)

This, the prophet says, is what it is to know God: to defend the oppressed and the helpless:

> Note well these lines do not say that judging the poor and needy is the cause and knowing Yahweh the consequence; nor, conversely, that judging the poor and needy is the consequence and knowing Yahweh the cause. Rather the two are equated.[13]

We may conclude that the prophetic tradition attacked a religion-shaped mission in the name of a mission-shaped, or a kingdom-of-God-shaped religion.

Jesus and the prophetic tradition

The same teaching is typical of Jesus. Access to the vertical is impossible unless the horizontal is first recognized:

> Therefore, if you are offering your gift at the altar and there remember that your brother has something against you, leave

your gift there in front of the altar. First go and be reconciled to
your brother; then come and offer your gift.

(Matthew 5.23, 24 NIV)

There is no point in worshipping God if you are not at peace with your brother
or sister. Human reconciliation is a condition of access to the divine. There is no
point in praying for forgiveness unless we forgive others.

Forgive us our debts,
as we also have forgiven our debtors.

(Matthew 6.12 NIV)

This is how my heavenly Father will treat each of you unless you
forgive your brother from your heart.

(Matthew 18.35 NIV)

There is a precise reciprocity between the human and the divine. Forgive us as
we forgive. Of course, God remains God, and sometimes the ultimate breaks
through disregarding the failure of the penultimate. Jesus prayed that God
would forgive those who nailed him to the cross, not because they had forgiven
him but because they did not know what they were doing. But in all ordinary
human relations, divine/human similarity is the rule of grace.

It is through the demand for justice that the kingdom is declared (Luke
4.18-19). The central theme of the teaching of Jesus, the great reversal,
announces the blessing upon the poor and the disaster to fall upon the rich
(Luke 6.20-26). He fulfilled the spirit of what Mary had sung about, by casting
down the mighty from their seats, filling the hungry with good things, and
sending the rich empty away (Luke 1.52-53). Jesus interpreted the meaning of
following him as consisting of a life lived within the sphere of the great
reversal, the demand for justice in inter-human relations. The rich young ruler
went away sorrowful when Jesus invited him to get rid of his possessions in
favour of the poor (Luke 18.18-26), Jesus makes radical and concrete the
commandments of the law and then interprets their meaning as relationship
to himself, but only when the demands of inter-subjectivity have been
recognized. In the same way, Zacchaeus, confronted by the gracious
acceptance of Jesus, put right the injustices that he had carried out in his
professional conduct (Luke 19.1-10). There is a contrast between the man
who brought Jesus to his home having recognized his social obligations and
the man who went away sorrowful to his own home, not able to accept the
demands of radical discipleship.

Typical of the prophetic understanding of God was the scribe of Mark 12.32-33 who responded to the reply of Jesus about the greatest commandment who said:

> 'Well said, teacher,' the man replied. 'You are right in saying that God is one and there is no other but him. To love him with all your heart, with all your understanding and with all your strength, and to love your neighbour as yourself is more important than all burnt offerings and sacrifices.'
>
> (Mark 12.32-33 NIV)

In Matthew's Gospel, the prophetic principle that mercy is better than sacrifice is twice referred to. In Matt. 9.17 Jesus defends his ministry to the marginalized by referring to it and in and in Matthew 12.7 he defends his disciples against the demands of religious legalism.

The absence of Jesus and the presence of other people

In discussing the God of the Hebrew Bible, we saw how in the absence of God, justice, extended to the image of God in the other person, became the way of God. At first, in the garden of Eden, God came visiting like a friend, but after the murder of Cain the resumption of human trust became the principal direction of the will of God and this, as we have seen, implied the absence of the explicit image of God. So it is in the New Testament as well. The truth that the biblical God is known in inter-subjectivity reaches its fulfilment in the person of Jesus Christ, in relation with whom, his first followers found God (John 20.28; 1.1; Mark 1.1). When God was found in the face of Jesus Christ it was not the supreme anomaly of biblical religion but its epitome, it encapsulates all the other tendencies.

In the absence of Jesus, he is to be found through the open acceptance and reception of others:

> And whoever welcomes a little child like this in my name welcomes me.
>
> (Matthew 18.5 NIV)

The way to Jesus Christ is through an open reception offered to children, and the whole logic of the inter-subjective structure is brought out clearly in the parallel in Mark and Luke:

> Whoever welcomes one of these little children in my name

> welcomes me; and whoever welcomes me, welcomes not me but
> the one who sent me.
>
> (Mark 9.37 NIV)

In Luke 10.16 the logic is the same although the interpersonal direction is reversed, now the reference is not to receiving but to being received:

> He who listens to you listens to me; he who rejects you rejects
> me; but he who rejects me rejects him who sent me. (NIV)

In Matthew 18.10 an additional mediation is introduced, that of the angel who represents the child before God, but the logic is the same, since God remains the Father of Jesus, and access is through a child:

> See that you do not look down on one of these little ones. For I
> tell you that their angels in heaven always see the face of my
> Father in heaven. (NIV)

The disciples of Jesus are to find him again and again in the face of human deprivation and poverty, wherever there is human loneliness or sickness, there he is to be found (Matthew 25.37–40). The remarkable thing about this last saying is that access to Jesus Christ is secure through the needy other even in ignorance, thus the cognitive aspect of recognition is transmuted into ethical action.

This is the essential message of the Minjung theology of South Korea. As Professor Kim of the South Korean church said to a group of people invited to meet him in Birmingham some years ago, 'This is the teaching of the Minjung theology: Jesus Christ was born among the poor. If you would find him, there you must seek him.'

This meaning of the absence and the presence of Jesus continues throughout the rest of the New Testament. Examples may be found in 1 John 3.17, 18; 4.20-21; James 1.27; 2.14-16; 3.9; 5.4. It is worth pointing out that in James 2.8 the commandment which Jesus described as being equivalent to the love of God is described as 'the royal law' and that this central tradition of the New Testament is squarely in the prophetic tradition is illustrated by the anti-iconic reference in James 3.9.

The transcendence of otherness

Let us return for a moment to the saying by Jesus about the greatest commandment and the one like it. Jesus says that we are to love our neighbour not as the neighbour loves us but as we love ourselves. The relationship between love of self and love of neighbour is not reciprocal but parallel, nor does the text say that we are to love our neighbour in so far as our neighbour loves God, nor in so far as we ourselves love God. The commandment places upon each one of us an unqualified, one-directional, non-theological obligation. It is in these characteristics that transcendence is to be found. Emmanuel Levinas puts it like this: 'the idea-of-the-Infinite-in-me or my relation to God – comes to me in the concreteness of my relation to the other . . . in the sociality which is my responsibility for the neighbour'.[14]

Levinas goes on to say that we certainly will not discover it by looking upon the human face as some kind of emblem or picture of divine creativity. Nevertheless, it is when I contemplate the origin of this that 'the word God comes to the tip of my tongue' and it is in this sense that the idea of the infinite is placed within me as a prophetic event, that is, because my responsibility to the other is unqualified and is not reciprocal.[15] Levinas concludes 'responsibility for the other is transcendence'.[16]

Because I am placed under the command of the infinite, which comes to me through otherness, I am not free to decide whether or not I shall respond. Responsibility for the other is not a product of my freedom. I am thus hostage to the other. In the same way, we are not to have the luxury of choice as to which neighbour we will select for the exercise of our responsibility. I do not designate the neighbour for whom I will be responsible but I say 'Here I am.'[17]

This, of course, is not a proof of God's existence. It is not a proof of anything. It is a trace of ultimacy found in the penultimate. 'Our relation to God is itself real only as it shows itself in relation to our neighbours.'[18]

Modernity and the loss of biblical otherness

It is easy to see why the significance of this biblical tradition has been so misunderstood and minimized in our culture. Possessive individualism,[19] which has been the central characteristic of the Western world view since the seventeenth century, tends to exaggerate the character of human beings as consuming units, and the place of mutuality has been overtaken by an emphasis upon the interior life, heightened by the continually growing expectation of freedom and multiple choice.

It is true that the modern status of human rights has been enormously important in the protection of the vulnerable, and of all citizens in the presence of the state and other powers, but this theology of the covenant does not refer to the other as having rights but to myself as placed under a responsibility of guardianship for my fellow human being. True, conservative newspapers are fond of saying, rather resentfully, that we have emphasized rights at the expense of responsibilities but they are always speaking of the responsibilities of the other upon whom rights have been conferred, not of my unqualified responsibility to the other in a realm which transcends rights. Levinas sums this up by saying in this way I am 'ousted from my interiority as an ego'.[20] Is it any surprise that in a society built upon the stimulation of the consuming ego, such an ethic is seldom heard? In such an ethic the identity of the self does not reside in possessions.

> Then he said to them, 'Watch out! Be on your guard against all kinds of greed; life does not consist in an abundance of possessions.'
>
> (Luke 12.15 NIV)

So, Levinas remarks, to listen to the cry of the desolate is to 'walk among reasons that reason does not know'.[21] I am torn out of my habitat, stripped of my comfort zone by the fact that I am not innocent of what happens to my neighbour.

The intention of the word 'God'

We see then that the logic of the word 'God' implies ethical intentionality on my part. This is not in the first place an intention to worship God because one must resort 'to the notion of a horizontal religion, abiding on man's earth, and which ought to be substituted for the vertical one which departs for the Heavens in order to refer to the world'.[22]

It is important to recognize that in this relationship, the space between, or the distance, is always preserved. If I love myself in the neighbour this distance disappears. The parallelism implies relationship not fusion. This has the effect of making religion objective. After all, interiority can only be memory, given the 'darkness of the lived moment'[23] and if I live for my inner Christian experience I am involved in a kind of religious memorial reconstruction but if I acknowledge the intentionality of faith in God towards the human other, I am dragged out of my feelings and memories, out of the salvation of my soul into my love for my brother and sister. Moreover, to realize the full force of this it is necessary to grasp the fact that it goes beyond dialogue.[24] I am responsible for the other whether or not the other is interested in or capable of dialogue with me. This is clearly evident in the Christian concept of love, and at this point I may perhaps part company with Levinas, whose concept of love seems to be embedded within friendship, with associations of fecundity and the erotic. The divine love, which was poured out upon us in that while we were still sinners Christ died for us, is not a matter of friendship but of the God who loves even when love is not returned (Romans 5.8; 1 John 4.10).[25]

The mission of God distorted when its agent becomes its objective

The mission of God is therefore to restore the brokenness of the body of humanity and to renew the face of the earth. Of this mission Israel was to be an agent, a chosen vessel, to be a light to the nations. Again and again, however, Israel assumed that it was the object of God's mission. This is why the Deuteronomist had to remind the people that they had not been chosen because they were a great and mighty people but because they were the 'smallest of all nations' (Deuteronomy 7.7). Similarly, Amos had to warn the people of Israel that they were in danger of exaggerating the significance of their own salvation history:

> 'Are not you Israelites
> the same to me as the Cushites?'
> declares the Lord.
> 'Did I not bring Israel up from Egypt,
> the Philistines from Caphtor
> and the Arameans from Kir?'
>
> (Amos 9.7 NIV)

The history of Israel shows a tendency to change emphasis between the tribalism of Gideon and Ezra and the universalism of Ruth and Jonah. This tendency to replace the mission of God by the welfare of the nation led finally to the destruction of the temple and of the state. That destruction was repeated in the destruction of the body of Jesus upon the cross and the total elimination of Jerusalem. It was out of these tendencies towards idolatrous self-absorption and the destruction that followed that Christian faith emerged as a new vehicle for the universal restoration, the establishment of the kingdom of God on earth as it is in heaven. The reference to the body of Jesus in this context may surprise some but I am thinking of John 16.7:

> But very truly I tell you, it is for your good that I am going away. Unless I go away, the Counsellor will not come to you; but if I go, I will send him to you. (NIV)

and in the second letter to the Corinthians:

> Therefore from now on we recognize no one according to the flesh; even though we have known Christ according to the flesh, yet now we know Him in this way no longer.
> (2 Corinthians 5.16 NASB)

Christian faith institutionalized within churches and denominations is not immune from these tendencies. Again and again Christian history shows that Christians have consciously or unconsciously turned away from the mission of God for justice and peace towards the propagation of their own tribalistic religion or Christian faith has been identified with the interest of Christians and the welfare of the Church. So powerful is this tendency that it is possible to lose sight of the mission of God almost entirely and to replace it with the notion of ecclesiastical expansion. These experiences give a new and more disturbing meaning to the saying of the apostle that we preach not ourselves but Jesus Christ and him crucified.[26]

While I respect the intentions of those who divide people in Britain into the churched and the unchurched, and see it as their mission to transfer as many people as possible from the latter category to the former, I do not believe that this distinction is fundamental to the mission of God. If we take the biblical prophetic tradition seriously, we must say that a more fundamental distinction in the sight of God is between the rich and the poor, those at home and the aliens, those who seek for selfish power and those who set out to serve their neighbours, those who in the name of the national interest are ready to renew nuclear weapons and those who seek for peace and equality between the nations. Where do we look today to find the great reversal of which Jesus spoke? How can it be that the mission of God who wills that all people should be saved has been turned into a competitive ideology and an institution with the same survival instincts as any other institution?

Concluding questions and answers

Finally, I am aware that so profoundly has our understanding of Christian faith been contaminated by our culture of individualism, money and power, and by the replacement of the agent by the object, that my exposition of what

I regard as the mission of God today must give rise to many questions. I will anticipate some of these and no doubt there are many others that I have not noticed.

The mission of God and social service

What is the difference between the approach outlined here and social and political service? Are not the peace and justice issues I mention the responsibility of secular professions and of society as a whole? Should not the Church let them get on with it and concentrate on what we do uniquely – proclaim Jesus Christ?

First, I would say that anyone who struggles for justice, peace and the integrity of creation is an ally, and should be encouraged. What matters is not being different but getting on with the job. Nevertheless, the presence and activities of the Church are different in several important ways. Jesus asked his critics by whom did their own people cast out demons if his own exorcisms were the product of a partnership with Beelzebub. He went on to say that if, on the contrary, his works were done by the finger of God, then the kingdom of God had come among them (Luke 11.20). On the face of it, an exorcism is an exorcism no matter who does it, and a pain relieved is a pain relieved. But when the relief of suffering is done in the name of Christ, it becomes significant of something greater. In other words, Christian faith places the elements of individual and communal reform in a wider pattern of interpretation. This context is provided by Christian faith itself, which gives to the acting parties the vision of a whole historic destiny, in which God is working out the purpose and meaning of creation itself. Such an interpretation sustains meaning and hope in the most hopeless situation, and this gives to the Christian working for the coming of God's kingdom a strength and an endurance, a joy that others must find elsewhere, if at all. Thus the Christian may glimpse the transcendent beyond the other, and the ultimate future of transcendent otherness, while the secular person may not have such imaginative resources of interpretation to inspire and strengthen.

Secondly, the churches must exercise an influence upon secular society by occupying a significant place in civil society, and by the insistence on ethical and humane standards maintain a constant pressure on public life. This we may describe as the prophetic function of the Church.

Moreover, if the churches withdraw into purely religious activity (as the secular world would see it) and only preach Christ without lifting a finger to alleviate human suffering, our message will become mere words. We will lose the respect of the public even more thoroughly, and we will be in flagrant disobedience to Scripture. Nothing in my argument implies that the Church will not go on preaching Christ. In the context of striving for the kingdom of God, such preaching, which will expose the faith, hope and love which inspire us, will have much more credibility, and is more likely to draw people into the relevance of faith.

Finally, I do not claim that proclaiming and working for the kingdom is the only thing Christian life offers. There is still what Bonhoeffer described as 'the secret discipline', there is still worship, the study and interpretation of the Scriptures, the intellectual life of theology, the pastoral care of congregations, the carrying out of the rituals of the life cycle. However, I do maintain that in the context of mission as the kingdom of God, all these other meditations and activities take on a new urgency and relevance.

What about my personal and individual relation to Jesus Christ as my Saviour and Lord?

Although at first sight this might seem to be an example of the vertical, I have shown that in the days of his ministry, relationship with God through Jesus was the supreme example of prophetic horizontality. In these days of the Church, when Jesus is seated at the right hand of God in glory, he is to be found through human otherness, as we have seen.

However, I acknowledge that the prophetic tradition may be placed side by side with other traditions such as the mystical, the charismatic and the sacramental. I have emphasized the prophetic tradition because it is the one most relevant to the mission of God. If we are to mould the life of our churches upon the mission of God, it is to the prophetic tradition that we must look. That does not mean that I have no sympathy for and first hand knowledge of individual religious experience, especially as reconstituted in memory around the person of Jesus.

Christ-mysticism, however, is in danger today of becoming a kind of erotic spirituality in which it is easier to adore Jesus than to follow him. This erotic fascination, so neatly summed up in the comment 'Jesus is my girlfriend' has many of the features of a fetish. This is why I have little sympathy with the preacher at the most recent Good Friday morning service who said, 'I have nothing against social justice but the heart of the Christian faith is personal devotion to Jesus.' This is indeed the case, but what the preacher has forgotten is that I am to find Jesus through human otherness, and any religious experience of which Jesus is the content, but which is isolated from obligation to the human other, quickly degenerates into a kind of self-congratulatory spiritual self-enclosure. One can see this clearly in so many of the hymns about this kind of Christian experience, in which the believer's feelings of happiness, satisfaction and security have become the focus of faith. Such 'Happy Christians' need to hear again the words of the prophet James who says that without ethical commitment, faith is meaningless.

Does not prayer represent a vertical relation with God?

If prayer is naïvely addressed to God, it is necessarily addressed to the God-image within us, and psychoanalytic object-relations theory and attachment theory have helped us to realize the process whereby the God-image is created.[27] It is necessarily formed through absorption and projection of traces of God as perceived or imagined in other people, so even in direct prayer, we are in a bundle of life with others. Whether in sophisticated prayer it is possible consciously to pass through the other to the infinite, I cannot tell. This would mean approaching the God beyond God in earthly human experience, but I am sure that such communion with God, if it can be known, would be in love, and love of God is only formed through love to others.

The Church and the Eucharist

What then, of the Church? If, as the theologians from Asia, Africa and Latin America are always telling us, God becomes real in the pursuit of justice, we need have no fears for the Church once it pursues the mission of God along prophetic lines.

In the Eucharist, the person of Jesus Christ is reconstructed in memory and becomes a presence which is at least symbolic. Because of this way of memorializing Jesus, the presence of Jesus in his mission as the one who being sent also sends us transforms the Lord's Supper into an impetus for the mission of God. Being a communion, most usually taken together, and being a sacrament of reconciliation, it has powerful elements of prophetic faith. The broken bread brings us into a single body as we eat it, meaning that in the Body of Christ we become his body, the reconstructed social body. This is also why the sacrament is essentially inclusive, and should be open to all, so representing and creating that universal fellowship which is the objective of the mission of God.

What of 'the unchurched'?

Here I find significance in Isaiah 65.1: 'I revealed myself to those who did not ask for me; I was found by those who did not seek me. To a nation that did not call on my name, I said "Here am I, here am I".' I also remember the words of Paul when addressing the Greeks, God 'is not far from each one of us. "For in him we live and move and have our being" ' (Acts 17.27, 28) and in the idea that 'the word is near you, it is on your lips and in your heart' (Romans 10.8) and that Christ is 'the logos that enlightens every human being' (John 1.9).

Although the dangers faced by our species seem to be very threatening and the solutions hard to seek I do not believe that the Spirit of God, the Lord and giver of life, is finished with us yet.

11

What patterns of church and mission are found in the Acts of the Apostles?

Loveday Alexander

Mission-shaped Church? Fresh expressions of church? Yes, they're both there in the Acts of the Apostles – in fact, you could say Acts provides the original biblical template for both. But the book of Acts raises some hard questions too:

- The historical question: Did it actually happen? Is this mission-shaped picture of the Early Church real, or is it just a fantasy?
- The inter-faith question: Does it promote a supersessionist view of Judaism?
- The postcolonial question: is mission-shaped Church inherently colonialist?
- The ecclesiological question: Is mission-shaped Church inherently centrifugal, sectarian and anarchic?

In this chapter I want to look briefly at the 'mission-shaped' presentation of the Early Church in Acts before going on to look at these questions, focusing in more detail on one particular episode – the conversion of Cornelius and its consequences – which I believe can give us some biblical tools for thinking through what it means to live in a mixed economy Church.

Biblical foundations for mission-shaped Church

Luke's view of the Church is 'mission-shaped' right from the opening sequence of Acts, where the apostles receive their commission on the Mount of Olives. I like to read Luke's narrative as a series of explosions, working outwards from Jerusalem, as the 120 gathered in the upper room are first blown out onto the streets (2.1ff.), then 'scattered' from Jerusalem (8.1ff.), then launched into full-blown mission from Antioch (13.1ff.), finally reaching Rome in chapter 28. 'Growth' is constantly highlighted in the narrative (6.7; 12.24;

19.20): numerical growth (2.41; 4.4); geographical expansion (1.8; 8.25; 9.31; 11.19-20; chapters 13-20, 27-28); growth in ethnic diversity (8.27; 10.1ff.; 11.18, 20; 13.46-48; 14.11; 18.6; 28.4; 28.28). In fact, Luke's narrative focuses much more on mission and church-planting than on 'continuing' Church history; and Luke is only interested in the people in his story (apostles and others) when they are engaged in mission, or offering a theological apologia for mission, or suffering as a result of mission. If you're looking for a history of the Early Church, Luke's story is full of maddening gaps: but if you want an inspiring story of pioneer missionary work, Acts is the one to read.

Built into this familiar narrative structure are the two fundamentals in Luke's theology of mission. First, the missionary task in 1.8: defined not in the more churchy terms of 'baptizing and teaching' (as in Matthew 28.19), but as bearing witness to the risen Lord. The fundamental task of mission is to bear witness to Christ – to be, if you like, 'fresh expressions' in the world of God's living Word. And the witness is empowered by the gift of God's Holy Spirit, promised in 1.8 and acted out dramatically at Pentecost (2.1ff.). It is the gift of the Spirit that gives the tongue-tied apostles 'utterance' – the power of speech, the gift of communication – and sends them out into the streets of Jerusalem to be heard and (miraculously) understood by visitors from every corner of the known world (2.9-11). Without the Spirit, Luke implies, the mission would never have got started; the word would have stayed shut up in the upper room.

And note that this amazing gift is linked directly to the whole complex of events that Luke calls the 'ascension' of the Christ – that is, his passion, death, resurrection and ascension (Luke 9.51). It is the arrival of the ascended Lord into heaven (Acts 2.33) that acts as the trigger to release showers of blessing on the assembled group of disciples and turns them into the Church, a dynamic, prophetic organization whose whole *raison d'être* is the proclamation of the wonderful works of God – in terms that people can understand. The Spirit is poured out by the Risen Lord himself: that's why the ascension stands at the apex of Luke's two-volume construction, serving both as the climax to the Gospel and as the launch-pad for the mission of the Church in Acts. You can't have one without the other.

Similarly, it is very easy to read Acts as a 'fresh expressions' story: it's a story that is packed full of different ways of being church (even on a boat! 27.35). Virtually every episode offers us a 'fresh expression'. Luke shows very little interest in repeating or successful patterns of church growth, leaving us rather to assume that what he has mentioned once becomes a standard pattern. What interests him as a narrator is the new, the fresh – the wind of the Spirit blowing in unexpected directions.

Acts begins on a mountain-top, and moves to a prayer-meeting in an upstairs room (1.14). Pentecost (chapter 2) gives us an outburst of glossolalia that sounds like the pubs letting out, but turns into an impromptu sermon resulting in 3,000 baptisms (2.41) – though Luke never bothers to tell us where so many people were baptized, or how, or by whom. Chapter 3 starts with a visit to the temple to pray (perhaps the closest we get to conventional patterns of religious life), but Peter and John never get to say their prayers. A beggar receives new legs instead of spare change; the passers-by get another unscripted sermon in Solomon's portico (3.11).

But this attempt to use the traditional religious spaces to proclaim the gospel runs immediately into trouble: the new wine bursts the old bottles and incurs a hostile reaction: 'You can't say that 'ere!' (chapters 4, 5). Nevertheless, the unsayable goes on being said, the unstoppable word goes on being spoken – despite everything religious and civil authority can do to stop it – in the public spaces of the temple (5.12-14), in the streets (5.14-16), and in private homes (4.23). And that essentially is the narrative pattern that Acts is built on, a paradigm that repeats itself in Samaria, on the road to Gaza, in a soldier's front parlour in Caesarea, by the riverside in Philippi, on the Areopagus in Athens, in prison cells, in workshops, in the School of Tyrannus in Ephesus, in a hired lodging in Rome. Everywhere the word is proclaimed and church starts to happen – everywhere *except* (it seems) the conventional religious spaces of temple and synagogue, where the word is contested and finally cast out. And when it is cast out, the word – or rather the Spirit – creates its own religious spaces: not buildings, but communities, small groups practising charitable works (chapters 6, 9, 11), studying the Scriptures and teaching each other (chapters 17, 18), working out the ethical implications of their new-found faith (chapters 5, 19) – and sending out their own missionaries (chapters 13–14).

There is (it must be said) something appealingly anarchic about all this. Luke is remarkably uninterested in setting out a single, standardized pattern of church order or initiation: chapters 14 and 20 seem to imply that 'elders' were standard in the Pauline churches, but Luke never tells us in so many words. Similarly, it is notoriously difficult to derive a single pattern of initiation from Luke's narrative. The standard pattern of repentance > baptism > gift of the Spirit is implied by 2.35ff., but in fact the same elements recur frequently in different orders. Again, we should note the centrality of the Spirit in Luke's ecclesiology. What is most remarkable about the missionary practice of Acts is the cheerful insouciance with which Paul, within weeks (or so it would appear) of founding small cell groups of believers in Iconium, Lystra and Derbe, selects (local) elders for these tiny congregations, entrusts them to 'the God in whom they had believed' – and leaves them to it (chapter 14). As

Roland Allen has perspicaciously observed, at the heart of Paul's missionary practice is trust – trust in the people of God, but above all trust in the Spirit – and it is this core element of trust that he identifies as the missing ingredient in the (pre-war) practice of western missionaries in China and Africa:

> Do we not say 'newborn Christians' or 'infant churches,' as we call them, cannot possibly stand secure without our 'activities' to support and train them? Do we speak, or act, as if we did in fact rely, and teach them by our own action to rely, upon the Holy Spirit for their guidance and keeping? We often talk to them and to one another of reliance upon the Holy Spirit, but do our acts support our speech? In the main? In our daily practice in relation to them? I think not. From our preaching they might learn to rely upon the Holy Spirit for the establishment and expansion of the church; but from our other speech, from our obvious fear of the consequences of the removal of our education and organizations, they do not learn it; for we do rely upon *our* guidance.[1]

Hard questions

So far, so good. But this volume is about asking hard questions: and we need to look at some of the problems associated with telling Luke's story – and basing our own missionary practice on it – in today's world.

The historical question

Is mission-shaped Church a figment of Luke's imagination? That's a question I cannot avoid *as a historian* – and neither can anyone setting out to write a history of the Early Church. I personally would not share the radical scepticism expressed by some New Testament historians: I believe that Luke is doing an honest job according to his lights, and according to the material available to him. He is putting together the best story he can, based partly on personal reminiscences of the Pauline circle, and partly on more scattered local and community traditions.[2] And the Spirit-led, mission-shaped pattern of church that he describes is precisely *not* the pattern that was beginning to emerge at the beginning of the second century, which is where many scholars would now place the composition of Acts.

But even so, it's important that we recognize that Luke's story is not the only story that could have been told about Christian origins: for example, the story might have looked very different told from James' point of view.[3] Luke's story has a distinctively Pauline slant – and yet we know from Paul's letters that Paul himself might have told the story rather differently. Like all good historians, Luke gives us not raw data but a selective and purposeful retelling of the past, shaped by his own rhetorical purpose in the present (that's what history is). It's easier to see this with the Gospels, because we have four different retellings of the Jesus story, four distinctive camera angles if you like. With Acts, we have only one: which makes it harder (but more interesting) to pick out the distinctive angle of the story as Luke tells it.

Nevertheless, the historical question is not our prime concern here. However we estimate the accuracy of Luke's picture of the early decades of the Church, Acts provides us with a biblical paradigm for how the Church ought to be – even if it maybe wasn't quite like that.[4]

The inter-faith question (how we brought the good news from Jerusalem to Rome)

Is mission-shaped Church inherently supersessionist?
Acts charts the story of a splinter group, a sectarian movement within the broad church of Second Temple Judaism, 'This way that people call a sect' (24.14). The whole story – as James Dunn so graphically demonstrates in his chapter in this volume – can be read as the story of (and a theological justification for) a fresh expression, a new way of being God's people, and responding to God's Spirit, carefully placed within the whole long history of God's people going back to Abraham (cf. Acts 7). As we would expect from a tightly constructed apologetic narrative, it presents a carefully worked-out and selective re-reading of Israel's history, designed to show how everything in that history leads to the Pauline mission, and specifically to the bringing in of the gentiles.[5]

The problem is that if we're not careful, this story can be told in a way that is supersessionist and implicitly anti-semitic. I can't count how many times I've been shocked to hear sermons and read Bible study notes telling a story in which 'the Jews' are always the bad guys, and in which following the Spirit means leaving behind the traditional ways of 'Jewish religion'. That's a gross over-simplification of a complex argument, and it's essential in reading Acts that we slow ourselves down to listen to what is really going on and try to understand it from both sides. The speakers in Acts (and the speeches are central to the argument) use prophetic language that is pointed and often painful: but though Paul keeps announcing that he is 'turning to the gentiles' (cf.14.46; 18.6; 28.28), there is no corresponding turning away from Israel in Acts. The rejection of the message by successive synagogue audiences is part of Paul's theological justification for moving outwards to a gentile audience. It is also part of the thorny theological problem over the 'hardening' of Israel, reflected also in the gospels and in Romans 9–11. But every time Paul gets to a new place, he goes back to the Jewish community: the message of salvation and the offer of repentance are always on the table, for Jew and gentile alike (cf. 28.31).

The postcolonial question

Is mission-shaped church inherently colonialist? It is rather alarming to find Roland Allen, that great champion of 'indigenous churches', co-operating with Thomas Cochrane and Sidney Clark in setting up a missionary organization called the World Dominion Movement in 1917, 'initially based in three small rooms on the top floor of No.3, Tudor Street, in London's East End'. Cochrane had earlier compiled a 'Survey of the Missionary Occupation of China, with accompanying atlas'.[6] The titles are a salutary reminder of the colonialist spirit that is often associated with western missionary activity. In fact Allen himself was fully aware of this problem: at the 1926 Shanghai Missionary Conference, he shocked delegates by announcing, 'The Chinese have in fact lately been proclaiming that the spiritual force which they see in these activities is a capitalistic or an imperialistic spirit, or the spirit of a Western civilization striving to bring them into bondage to itself.' It was in response to this perception that Allen began to radicalize the missionary establishment by developing his 'indigenous principles' of 'self-support, self-propagation and self-government'.[7]

Mission has moved on since the 1920s, and Allen's principle of 'indigenous churches' is now widely accepted. But colonial habits die hard: the churches of western Europe and the USA still tend to assume some kind of primacy over the old 'mission' churches of Africa and Asia (even if it's a very Anglican primacy *inter pares*), some kind of recognition of their historic role as bearers of the gospel. In the new global Christendom, this casual assumption of 'Western-centric' primacy is becoming harder to sustain (as recent events in the Anglican Communion have made clear). In a trenchant critique of 'The demographic transformation of world Christianity and the twilight of "mainline" Protestant foreign missions', Thomas Hastings of Union Theological Seminary in Tokyo points out that the same colonial assumptions still prevail in many non-western churches. As far back as 1974, he notes, it was beginning to be acknowledged in some quarters that 'the West has been dismissed from its post as centre of religious cultural unity for the whole of Christianity'.[8]

But what do we put in its place? A simple one-member-one-vote democracy? A Darwinian 'survival of the fittest' (aka 'market forces')? A new, reversed colonialism, with the churches of the South reasserting domination over the churches of the North under the banner of 'traditional values'? These are urgent, practical questions crying out to be addressed with a profoundly theological critique – and not only within the Anglican Communion. Justo Gonzalez, writing as a Hispanic-American historian and theologian, reflects on the explosion of new ways of being church in Latin America in a post-liberation theology situation where (as another Hispanic-American theologian put it to me recently), 'Liberation theology voted for the poor; but the poor voted for the Holy Spirit.'[9] Rather than trying to locate a new centre for the postcolonial map of world church, Gonzalez speaks of the urgent need for 'a new catholicity' for a polycentric global Christianity. Hastings, building on the work of Andrew Walls, adds:

> In the heyday of the modern missionary movement, the churches of North America [and western Europe, we might add] saw themselves as 'senders' and the so-called 'younger' churches of Asia, Africa and Latin America as 'receivers'. Today, in the twilight of that movement, the Western churches have yet to awaken to the fact that, partly because of and partly in spite of the missionary movement, Christianity, which 'is itself increasingly marginal to Western intellectual discourse', is now 'a non-Western religion'. Given this new situation, [Andrew Walls also suggests], 'Perhaps there is now an obligation of Christians to "use means" better fitted for two-way traffic, fellowship, for receiving, than have yet been perfected'.[10]

We shall return to this point: because it seems to me that many of the issues being raised by Walls, Hastings, Gonzalez and others in relation to global Christianity are equally pertinent in microcosm to any consideration of 'fresh expressions' in a mixed economy Church.

The ecclesiological question

Is mission-shaped Church inherently centrifugal, sectarian and anarchic?
As we have seen, it is very easy to read Acts – indeed the whole of the New Testament – in line with a church/sect typology, reading the early Christian movement as a renewal movement within Second Temple Judaism. And (as we all know) this pattern is repeated time and time again in Church history. As each radical new 'sect' becomes established 'church' in its turn, charisma gives way to order: yesterday's fresh expressions become today's

tired, fossilized structures, and the Spirit has to get people moving all over again. It's a good story, encoded in the collective *Heilsgeschichte* (salvation history) of Protestantism. But it's also a dangerous story – and I'd like to suggest that it's time we asked ourselves some hard questions about this pattern of ecclesial historiography. It's dangerous, I believe, because it's built on a series of opposing concepts between what Pete Ward[11] calls 'liquid church' and 'solid church'; between order and charisma, between traditional structures and the freedom of the Spirit, between institutional hierarchy and prophetic vocation, between establishment and liberation – and binary oppositions always oversimplify.

The way it's normally told, this is an inherently centrifugal story, a story about moving out West, leaving behind the tired old centres and heading out for the wide open prairies (spot that 'pioneer' language!). That's great if you're on the wagon train – but what happens to the empty 'centre' you've left behind? This centrifugal pattern, of course, is exactly what we see in Acts. The narrative successively moves out from Jerusalem to Antioch, to Asia, and eventually to Rome; Jerusalem effectively disappears from view after chapter 15. This pattern reflects Luke's dominant interest in Paul (whose letters make it clear that he much preferred to operate as a pioneer missioner: cf. Romans 15.20–21). So Luke's narrative follows Paul as he becomes more and more freelance and breaks his links, first with Jerusalem, then with Barnabas and Antioch. That's Luke's narrative agenda: he's telling the story of how Paul got to Rome. But should it be part of our theological agenda? It also reflects the historical fact that Jerusalem did very soon (within Luke's lifetime) become an empty centre, devastated by war and abandoned by the Church. That's a fact of history: but does that make it also a fact of ecclesiology?

Gonzalez points out that any successful missionary movement runs twin risks: the risk of syncretism and the risk of sectarianism.[12] The problem of syncretism can be seen again and again in Church history, when the new (or fresh, or marginal) areas become so attuned to their local context that they risk losing touch with the core beliefs and values of the parent tradition. That has been a concern of church leaders down the centuries, and it is a legitimate concern today.

But, Gonzalez argues, there is an equal and opposite risk of sectarianism. Such a pattern of church growth is inherently fissiparous. As each group grows, it splits and creates splinter groups – a pattern seen time and again in Protestant history. And each of these sects has an inbuilt tendency 'to take its own sector of reality and experience for the whole'. We are in the realm of sectarianism when any group, 'no matter how orthodox, errs in that it considers its own sector of reality, its own limited perspective, to be the whole of reality, or the only allowable perspective'. On a world scale, the problem can be expressed in terms of the tension between local and global, between mission (in which each individual church is called and challenged to communicate with its own local context without losing its Christian identity) and ecumenism (in which each local church is called and challenged to maintain a two-way conversation within the whole Body of Christ). On a more domestic scale, that is precisely the challenge that faces the fresh expressions movement within a 'mixed economy' Church.

Learning to listen: the DNA of Luke's ecclesiology

Can the book of Acts provide us with any biblical resources to help us to resolve these questions? I believe so: and I believe the key is learning to listen. We need to listen more carefully to Luke's story, to be aware of the teleologies implicit in our own readings and alert to the possibilities of other readings from other places; and in doing so we shall find that learning to listen – and to trust the Spirit – is at the heart of Luke's vision of mission-shaped Church.

Let's look back for a moment to the 'mission-shaped' reading of Acts I gave at the beginning of this chapter. It will not have escaped your notice that this is a very 'Protestant' reading. Acts comes across as a story in which the traditional locations of sacred space, and the traditional mediators of the divine presence, are either marginalized or hostile, as the power of the Spirit moves out to the margins, and the disempowered, begging for alms at the temple gate, throw away their crutches and start walking and leaping and praising God. It's a story told time and again in Protestant history: the story of the Pilgrim Fathers, persecuted and driven out by the established Church; a story in which the guardians of traditional structures have to 'keep on building altars so that the fire from heaven can fall somewhere else'.[13]

But of course Luke has often been read (especially in German scholarship of the twentieth century) as a proponent of 'Early Catholicism', propagating a 'catholic' view of the Church, with Jerusalem, and the circle of the twelve, providing a strong focus for centralized authority as a defence against Gnosticism. On this reading, Acts seeks to underpin a vision of institutional stability in the face of the spiralling theological controversies of the second century, and in doing so sets the Church on a hierarchical trajectory that will eventually lead to the post-Constantinian vision of 'Christendom'. And that is a form of 'catholicity' that is often seen as the very antithesis of 'fresh expressions of church'.

What is interesting is that this 'catholic' reading of Acts is an equally legitimate reading that uncovers some overlooked features of Luke's narrative: it is plausible precisely in so far as it can be substantiated from the text. But then so can the fresh expressions reading! Both are selective: but both draw on aspects that are genuinely there in the text. And what I want to suggest is that both are there, not because Luke is careless or inconsistent in his ecclesiology (or because he hasn't read *Mission-shaped Church*). Rather, I would suggest that Luke's ecclesiology, his vision of what it means to be church, encompasses all the tensions inherent in the fresh expressions story – tensions between centre and periphery, between charisma and order, between 'liquid church' and 'solid church' – and refuses to allow us to be content with either end of the bi-polar division. It isn't a matter of compromise: what I find in Acts is something much more dynamic, something that looks much more like the 'double helix' pattern of the human genome. A kind of dance, you might say: or (to follow James Alison's vivid image) like being invited to a party by a host whose generosity includes all kinds of people we don't actually like or even agree with:

> It is not how I defend my own [viewpoint], but how I imagine, portray and engage with my adversary that is the only really important issue at hand ... The really hard work in Christian theology lies in the ecclesiological sphere: creating church with those whom we don't like ... And this means that a considerable point of the theological effort which I think is called for is the courtesy of constructing bridges for the benefit of others, being vulnerable on their turf, exercising magnanimity towards foes ... to [seek] ways to make room for us all to be wrong together, and yet all able to be rescued together, and all able to learn together.[14]

One of the best places to illustrate the 'double helix' of Lucan ecclesiology is the Cornelius narrative in Acts 10–11, a key passage in understanding Luke's vision of mission-shaped Church. The most effective way to follow the argument here is to read with the text of Acts chapters 10–11 open, following every twist and turn in the story alongside a fuller commentary on Acts (such as Gonzalez or Beverly Gaventa, or my own commentary in the People's Bible series[15]).

Peter and Cornelius / Cornelius and Peter (Acts 10)

The narrative focus here alternates all the way through between Peter's viewpoint and Cornelius's (and Cornelius gets first go: 10.1–8!). Luke won't let us get away with seeing mission as a colonial activity: Peter's task is 'to find out what God is doing, and get in on the act'. One of the best ways to feel the force of this is to do a dual-focus character study on this chapter, letting different groups (or people) explore what it's like being Cornelius in this story, and what it's like being Peter. I suspect that most of us find it easier to identify with Cornelius: we're gentiles, we can't see the problem, we just want Peter to get on with it. But Luke won't let us away with unthinking anti-semitism either: he walks us through Peter's dilemma step by step. Note the slow and deliberate crossing of thresholds in this story, the careful exploration, first of inviting the strangers into my world (10.23), then allowing myself to go with them into theirs (10.25). And let's not disguise the painfulness of Peter's dilemma by describing his problem as 'Jewish dietary regulations' – which makes it 'their' problem', not 'our' problem. To appreciate what's going on here, ask yourself: who told Peter that it was 'sacrilegious' (deeply, religiously wrong, taboo) for him to eat with gentiles (10.28)? Yes, of course Jews in Peter's day had differing attitudes to the *kashrut* regulations (just as Jews do today, just as Christians do on other issues like drinking or smoking). But the real source of Peter's dilemma is the Bible itself (cf. Leviticus 11). And when he gets there, faced with a bunch of people all expectantly awaiting a word from God, there is only one story that Peter can tell, the only story he's commissioned to tell – though he sounds as surprised as Cornelius to find that *this* story, the apostolic witness to Jesus, is for the gentiles as well as for 'the people' (10.34–43). So this story is as much about the conversion of Peter as the conversion of Cornelius.

Peter and Jerusalem / Jerusalem and Peter (Acts 11)

Luke's slow-motion narrative techniques also unravel any easy assumptions about the new and the old, centre and margins. Having discovered what God was doing, out there on the margins, Peter could have stayed there, doing his thing, enjoying being a pioneer. But he doesn't. Something makes him go back to report on his actions to the folks back home – and face a very negative reaction. Again, we need to be careful here to avoid the trap of anti-semitism (which is also the trap of cheap liberalism) – and Luke almost falls into it himself. We need to remember that the people who oppose Peter's mission in 11.22 ('those of the circumcision': compare Galatians 2.1) are *Christians*: this is a debate within the Church, a debate about the relationships (of authority, companionship, trust) between centre and margins, between fresh expressions and traditional structures. In this debate, the centre needs to learn the value of listening and silence (11.18) in order to hear what God is doing out on the margins. But Peter has something to learn too. By taking the risk of coming back to the centre, submitting his experience to the process of shared discernment, he too gains a deeper insight into the full significance of what happened in Caesarea (11.16).

Jerusalem and Antioch (Acts 11–13)

The relationship between these two churches plays out all the tensions between fresh expression and continuing church. The foundation of the Antioch church in 11.19-21 is a classic fresh expression, and the Jerusalem church reacts by sending down Barnabas to investigate (11.22-24). Depending on your point of view, this could be seen either as a reassurance or a threat – or perhaps both. But somehow, through Barnabas' gifts of discernment and encouragement, the 'church plant' becomes a church in its own right, actively maintaining links with the mother church (11.27-30; 12.24-25), and sending out its own missionaries (13.1-3).

Antioch and Jerusalem (Acts 15)

Saul and Barnabas depart on mission at 13.4, and return home to report back at 14.26-28. By the time they get back, the narrative dynamics are reversed: Antioch is now the primary focus of Luke's story line, and Jerusalem appears initially as a distant grumble on the horizon, the source (apparently: cf. 15.24) of a hard-line directive that looks set to undermine all that the Antioch church has achieved in building up an inclusive multicultural community (15.1). Again, it would have been easy for the fresh expression to go it alone, secure in its own conviction of the Spirit's leading. Instead, Paul and Barnabas take the risky step of coming back to the old centre for a process of mutual discernment, a process that requires disciplined attentiveness on both sides, spaces for silence and listening – and for testimony (telling stories) as the key to finding out what God is doing. And in that process, we find that the Spirit has not abandoned the old centre: the Spirit is part of the process of discernment (15.28), allowing the whole Church to move forward in a shared and costly commitment to catholicity.

In this long sequence, from the conversion of Cornelius through to the Apostolic Decree, Luke gives us the best chance to see how his theological vision of what it means to be church works out in practice – in the hard, painful process of learning to be faithful to God's Spirit, and to each other. We probably shouldn't be surprised to find that it's a vision that is deeply committed to catholicity, not in the sectarian sense but in Gonzalez's sense of 'that which is according to the whole, that in which all have a place', a catholicity that calls us to listen to each other:

> The written word of God, by its very structure and composition, calls us also to cath'holicity, to listen to what other interpreters from other perspectives find in the text and in the story. This requires a structure and a self-understanding that, like the canon of the New Testament, can bind the irreducible contributions of various perspectives in an indissoluble unity.[16]

To be on the margins, at the apparent edges (as Gonzalez remarks elsewhere) can be a privileged position:

> The place where we are, at this apparent edge, is where God is doing new things. And those who daily see the new things that God is doing in the world have the obligation toward God and toward the rest of the Christian world to go back to the old centers, which often have lost much of their vision, taking to them our renewed vision of what God is doing today.[17]

But when we do that, when we take that risk, we shouldn't be surprised – unless we've been seduced by our own sectarian rhetoric – to find that God's Spirit can be at work at the 'old centres' too, within the institutional structures, within the hierarchies, within the traditional ways of being church. We shouldn't be surprised to find this 'double helix' deeply embedded into the structure of Luke's story. After all, it is Luke who (knowing a thing or two about vintage wine, perhaps) adds to Mark's saying on new wine in old bottles the comment that 'No one wants new wine after tasting the old' (Luke 5.38). And it is Luke who, in the Song of Simeon (Luke 2.32) spells out the ecumenical vision of the Christ who comes as 'a light of revelation to the gentiles, and the glory of your people Israel'.

12

What does the gift of the Spirit mean for the shape of the Church?

Alison Morgan

Introduction

Few people today would dispute that we are living through one of the great transitional periods of history, a time of unprecedented challenge and change. As a context-dependent institution, this inevitably requires the Church to undertake a radical reappraisal of its mission and ministry – a reappraisal that should properly begin with a discussion of the Holy Spirit who both initiates and sustains our shared spiritual life as the Body of Christ. What can we learn from a study of the Holy Spirit that will help us to live our lives as Christian believers and witnesses in this changing cultural context? What insights may we gain about the gift of the Spirit from the story of creation and from the teaching of Jesus? What can we discover by looking at the relationship between Spirit and the Church in the New Testament, in different historical periods since then, and in our own experience? And above all, can we pull out from all these things some guiding principles to help us reshape our mission and ministry for a radically different future? I suggest that we can.

However, fresh insights usually depend on fresh methodologies. Theological reflection is essential, especially at times of change; but if we are not careful it can become divorced from real life. Alister McGrath has written about our need to engage in what he calls organic theology – theology which links directly to the life and mission of the Church. I would go further and say that I see a great need for embodied theology – theology that is rooted in our own experience. We live between the worlds of modernity and postmodernity, between a preference for the objective and a preference for the subjective. I am modern enough to prefer thinking and analysis as my main *modus operandi*, but postmodern enough too to know that we start from where we are at and tell our own stories – my faith is both conceptual and relational. If modern theology was sometimes an exercise in secular reductionism, postmodern theology is best seen as a conversation. I can only have a conversation as myself; and hope (with Henri Nouwen) that what I bring into that conversation is a function not just of who I am but also of where I am – as an individual within a context, a context that is shared.[1]

In the beginning: The Holy Spirit in creation

The work of the Spirit begins not in the Church but in the world. And so it was that, knowing nothing of Christ or of his Church, I nonetheless found the Spirit in the world around me – in a giant stag beetle encountered one day as a toddler in the garden; as I grew older, in the tiny football-rattle calls and bright red eyebrows of flocks of long-tailed tits, and the deep orange eyes of owls. For some, the sheer gratuitous variety of creation is evidence that there can be no creating and controlling God.[2] For me, the suspicion gradually grew that the opposite was the case. Could I explain the different reactions of garden birds as I held them in order to ring them – the astonishing variety of different shades and shapes of plant leaves on a single slope in the Canary Islands? The sight of the wind rippling over the silky golden heads of a field of ripe barley? Knowing nothing of Jesus' comparison between the wind and the Spirit, and unaware of Paul's words to the Romans that the invisible things of God can be understood through the things he has made, I first began to find the Spirit of God in the inexplicable mystery and variety of what I saw around me.

That was my beginning. What about God's beginning? Well, for God too the work of the Spirit starts, as Raniero Cantalamessa has noted, in the open air. Genesis 1 verses 1-2:

> In the beginning when God created the heavens and the earth,
> the earth was a formless void and darkness covered the face
> of the deep, while a wind from God swept over the face of the
> waters.[3]

The wind is *ruach*, the Spirit of God. This same word means wind, spirit, breath. And in the movement of this Spirit the world was created, day and night, sun and moon, land and water, plants and birds and fish and animals and insects, and finally man. What characterizes the world to which the Spirit of God gives birth as she sweeps over the waters at this moment of creation (the Hebrew word *ruach* is feminine)? It is diversity, and the whole of Genesis 1 bears witness to it. The world that is born is a model of extraordinary, and probably unnecessary, diversity; and this is what is striking about it. It's still there for us to see. And it is through this diverse world that we begin to know the Spirit of God – not in some abstruse or difficult way, but simply by opening our eyes. It indeed became commonplace from the earliest times, in a society where most could not read, for God to be apprehended in this way. Augustine pointed out that only the literate can read the book of Scripture, while everyone can read from the book of the universe. The medieval mystics taught that prayer should begin with the contemplation of the created world, for there we find the footprints of God, the thoughts of God, the music of God. In the thirteenth century Thomas Aquinas said that the diversity of creation is necessary in order to bear witness to the nature of God, 'so that what was wanting to one in the manifestation of the divine goodness might be supplied by another'. Bonaventure taught his monks that 'God is contemplated not only *through* material things as footprints, but also *in* them, inasmuch as he is in them in essence, power and presence'. In the sixteenth century Calvin talked about God communicating himself to us through his created works. In the eighteenth Jonathan Edwards described them as God's shadow, as his voice or language. In our own times Pierre Teilhard de Chardin wrote about all things being animated by a single spirit, and finding himself, as he wandered among them, approaching the point where the heart of the world is caught in the descending radiance of the heart of God. The Spirit of God leaves her traces in the world she made, and it is there that we first find her.[4]

The word *ruach* means wind, spirit, breath; the Spirit of God swept over the waters like a wind and left in her wake a created world of astonishing diversity. And in the very same movement, the Spirit of God breathed life into that world. So if the first thing we notice about the work of the Spirit is that she brings *diversity*, the second is that she brings *life*, the 'breath of life' as God puts it in Genesis 1.30 and again in 2.7. Life itself is a product of the Spirit. First the Spirit creates; then she breathes. As Job says, 'the spirit of God has made me, and the breath of the Almighty gives me life' (Job 33.4). The world to which the Spirit gives birth is not dead, not a painted canvas of carefully assembled still life; it's living, moving, breathing.

And as we read on we find it constantly stated in Scripture that the Spirit not only breathed life into God's creatures at the beginning of time, but continues day by day to sustain that life with her breath. The best-known passage is Psalm 104, a hymn to the continued dependence of the created world on the life-giving presence of the Spirit of God. Wolfhart Pannenberg summarizes:

> Every creature is in need of conservation of its existence in every moment; and such conservation is, according to theological

tradition, nothing else but a continuous creation. This means that the act of creation did not take place only in the beginning. It occurs at every moment.[5]

So the Spirit of God brings life, and renews life. This too is a constant theme of Scripture. The Spirit of God is daily at work to sustain and renew that which she has created. It is the Spirit of God who renews the ground and the grass, who sustains all creatures with her breath, who renews our strength and our days, our heart and spirit, and who one day will begin again with a new creation. The Spirit of God makes all things new, and it is on her that we depend in all that we are and do.[6]

What then do we take from this rapid overview of the role of the Spirit in the world? Two things: the world that is born as the Spirit sweeps over the waters is a diverse world, and it is a world that owes not just its initial life but its ongoing existence to the Spirit. The Spirit creates. The Spirit renews.

The teaching of Jesus

Now that's all very interesting. But is it relevant to a discussion of the Church, or is it merely of historical interest, relating to the days of the Old Covenant when the Spirit was not available to us directly and individually? In the New Testament we move from an emphasis on the role of the Spirit in creating and renewing the physical world to an emphasis on his work in the spiritual world (switching from the feminine Hebrew *ruach* to the neuter Greek *pneuma*). Does this mean that the New Testament talks about the Spirit in other ways, and that it would be better to think about the relationship between the Spirit and the Church in those ways?

John begins his Gospel with a deliberate echo of the opening words of Genesis 1, 'in the beginning': 'In the beginning was the Word ... All things came into being through him ... What has come into being in him was life.' The implication is clear. What is happening now in the person of Jesus is being said to be continuous, and not discontinuous, with what happened at the beginning of time. Spirit and Word are the two hands of God, working together; 'Spirit and Word belong together like breath and voice', Irenaeus said in the second century. Throughout the Old Testament we see an interplay between Spirit and Word, present above all in the active speaking of the prophets, and often personified in the Wisdom tradition. Both these strands come to fullness now in the person of Jesus, the living Word.[7]

And if we turn to the teaching of Jesus, we find that he too drew frequently on the created world, in metaphor, simile and parable. We might assume that he did so because that is what is there, just as we often draw on illustrations from computers and technical processes. But perhaps there's more to it than that. Perhaps Jesus drew on the created world when teaching about the spiritual world not just because it was convenient, but because there is an intrinsic affinity between them – because created things, as visible manifestations of the Spirit of God, themselves embody spiritual realities. Paul said that we understand invisible things through looking at visible ones, and he himself taught that way.[8]

Theologians have warmed to the theme. In the eighteenth century Jonathan Edwards suggested that the visible world was designedly made and constituted in analogy to the more spiritual, noble, and real world, and that the signs and types in the book of nature are representations of spiritual realities. In the 1930s the biblical scholar Charles Dodd suggested in his study of the parables that Jesus' use of the created world arises 'from a conviction that there is no mere analogy, but an inward affinity, between the natural order and the spiritual order'.[9]

So, when Jesus taught about the vine and the branches, the tree and its fruits, the mustard seed and the yeast, the wheat and tares, the farmer sowing his fields, the sparrow and the lilies, the fox and his hole, he regarded these things not so much as teaching aids as visible representations of spiritual principles. This, he says, is how things are.

What does this offer to us? Jesus had little to say about the Church, inevitably. But he had a great deal to say both about individuals and about the kingdom, and most of the examples I have just given relate to one or other of these topics. The Church is just what comes in between; it is the community of those who are 'called out' of the world and into the kingdom of God – that's what the word 'church' means. Pentecostal theologian Gordon Fee defines the Church as 'an eschatological community', a kingdom community, a travelling community called by Jesus and dependent, just like the created world, on the indwelling presence of the Spirit within it as it moves towards an eternal destination.[10] It's a community that is open to us to think and talk about as Jesus did, maybe in ways that differ from the ways we have grown used to thinking about it – for on the whole we have looked not to the created world but to the world of an industrialized human society for our illustrations; and perhaps that has influenced the way we do things.

The Holy Spirit in the New Testament Church

Let's move on, then, to focus on the Church itself – for the coming of Jesus inaugurates a new phase in the work of the Spirit. As Jesus is baptized, the heavens are torn open and the Spirit comes down. As Jesus is crucified, the dividing curtain of the temple is torn. Both events mark the crossing of a boundary, a boundary that hitherto had separated human beings from the direct presence of God. The Spirit is made available to the community of believers, the people of God who will constitute the Church. And as we begin to follow the fortunes of the Church through the New Testament, we find that the relationship between Spirit and Church echoes the relationship between Spirit and creation. The Spirit breathed life into all living creatures at the beginning of time, and so now he breathes life into the Church at the beginning of this new era in human history. John 20.22: Jesus breathed on the disciples and said 'Receive the Holy Spirit'. Acts 2.2, 4: 'suddenly from heaven there came a sound like the rush of a violent wind . . . All of them were filled with the Holy Spirit'. As Tom Wright has pointed out, the Spirit given afresh on the day of Pentecost is the *same* Spirit who brooded over the waters of chaos at the beginning. The Spirit who hovers now over Jesus in the form of a dove is the *same* Spirit who hovered with pregnant intent over the world at the moment of creation. She, or he, is the Spirit from whom all life comes, life both physical and spiritual.[11]

It follows that the Church, like the world, is to be characterized by the presence of the Spirit within it. The Church, in other words, is to be a charismatic community. Often we instinctively define it as so much less than that. But the Church can *only* be defined by the presence of the Spirit within its members. 'In the one Spirit we were all baptized into one body', Paul tells the Corinthians (1 Corinthians 12.13). We are 'a letter of Christ, written . . . with the Spirit of the living God'. Without the Holy Spirit, the Church is not church (2 Corinthians 3.3).[12]

As a charismatic community, we find that the Church is a diverse community. Diversity in unity is a major theme of the New Testament in relation to the work of the Spirit in the Church. The first thing that happens is that the gospel is announced in many languages to members of many people groups. Soon we see the coming together of people old and young, rich and poor, to share their lives and possessions as one. Paul's letters to the Ephesians, the Romans and the Corinthians speak of the members of the Church as members of a body, different in spiritual gifting but united in Christ. 'There are varieties of gifts, but the same Spirit' (1 Corinthians 12.4), who allots them individually as he chooses. It is noticeable that Paul offers no blueprints for church structure or organization other than this single principle of diversity in unity through the presence of the Spirit. Roland Allen and Vincent Donovan have famously remarked how different this is from our own ways of planting churches. And we might note how different too this kind of diversity is from the diversity celebrated in our current culture, where diversity means little more than difference. The diversity we find among ourselves as members of this charismatic community which we call Church is a diversity which, like the diversity of the created world, holds together in a unity which comes from the constant presence within it of the Spirit of God.[13]

If diversity in creation was our first theme from the work of the Spirit in the Old Testament, renewal of that same creation was our second. And this holds true in the Church too. The word 'renewal' has been somewhat caricatured in recent times, but the New Testament bears constant witness to the role of the Spirit in bringing renewal of life to the newly called people of God – new life, new birth, new creation, new hope, a new self, new tongues, new gifts, new teaching, a new people, a new commandment, good news; the list is endless. And if Paul offers no organizational blueprint for the Church, he offers no relational law either – his appeals to those struggling with issues of discipline are always appeals to turn to the Spirit, in whom they will find the resources they need. It is noticeable that in the letters to the seven churches revealed to John in the book of Revelation, each time the Spirit is speaking of the spiritual, not organizational, life of the church in question – and each time the message is different. I suspect that in our own churches the same will be true.[14]

The Holy Spirit and the shape of the Church in history

So the New Testament Church seems clearly shaped by the Spirit, diverse and yet unified, constantly renewed and resourced by his presence within it. It sounds simple; and yet history shows it is not. Diversity can easily slip back into chaos. The Spirit, like the wind, is hard to pin down and easy to misinterpret. We see the beginning of this process in Corinth, where diversity had obviously been grasped more readily than unity. The charisms were much in evidence in the Early Church, but by the third century it was felt that things were getting a little out of hand – particularly with regard to the prophetic Montanist movement, whose adherents believed they were experiencing the spiritual gifts of the end time. Meanwhile, creeds and liturgies were developed, and professional ministers grew in authority. Cyprian linked the charismatic gifts firmly with the office of bishop, and imperceptibly the wind of the Spirit became identified with the structures of the Church. The ascetic and monastic movements, and groups such as the Cathars, the Anabaptists and the Quakers sought with varying degrees of success to keep the Spirit at the centre of their communities; but by and large, as the years went by, the Spirit became not so much a living presence as a metaphor, a kind of shorthand justification, for the decisions of the Church.[15]

Charismatic ecclesiologists do not mince their words when they reflect on this process. José Comblin states that by the fourteenth century the Spirit was confined to sacraments, councils and the authority of the Pope, and had long been invoked only as a prop for everything the hierarchical Church had already decided. Jean-Jacques Suurmond remarks that if the Catholics imprisoned the Spirit in the Church, the Protestants imprisoned the Spirit in the word, and suggests that Luther's failure to see the structure of the community of Christ as a charismatic one meant that the exciting rediscovery of the priesthood of all believers turned out in practice to mean little more than prayer and Bible reading at home. The Orthodox Church fares little better, for there the Spirit is said to have become trapped in the sanctuary.[16]

It is undeniable that as time went on, the Church settled more and more into an ordered shape. It is customary to blame Constantine for the beginnings of this process, but the political struggles of the Middle Ages, the classical thought patterns of the Renaissance and the rationalist beliefs of the Enlightenment did nothing to disturb the pattern, and much has been written on the adaptation of the Church to the culture of modernity since then. Order was maintained – but the price of unity was to be, as so often before, the taming of apostles and the muzzling of prophets. The Pentecostal movement of the twentieth century represents a serious attempt to break free from an ecclesiastical straitjacket and reintroduce the Spirit to the life of the Church, but often division and denominationalism have been the result. The whole process was summarized by Dutch theologian Hendrikus Berkhof when he wrote that 'to a great extent, official church history is the story of the *defeats* of the Spirit'.[17]

And yet perhaps it's not as simple as that. It's fashionable to knock institutions, for we live in an anti-institutional age. To distinguish between institution and Spirit is not always helpful, for institutions are what happen when people come together; the word means little more than 'something that is'. What matters is our willingness to allow the presence of the Spirit to bring change to our institutions, to shape and renew them. If there is a key to the renewal of the Church, William Abraham remarks, it is to be found here; 'the foundation of the church's life is to be found by exploring to the full the riches of God made incarnate in Jesus Christ through the agency of the Holy Spirit here and now'. The traditions, canons and creeds of the Church merely provide the context for such an exploration.[18]

And history does indeed show this happening repeatedly, as the Church struggles in different periods to respond to the ever changing missionary context in the culture around it. Alone of all human institutions, the Church has the seeds of reformation and renewal built into its DNA, for alone of all institutions it is able to respond to the indwelling presence of the Spirit of God through Scripture and in prayer. It is the role of the Spirit to promote reform in the Church, to shape it and resource it, to help it be the incarnate Body of Christ in the world in which it is set. And as Michael Riddell rightly says, we stand now in one of those closed epochs which calls for vision and reformation. No one expected 40 years ago that the Spirit would once again be playing a dominant role in the Christian faith, or that it would be an even more profoundly significant event than the Reformation – but that is precisely what is being suggested now.[19]

The Holy Spirit and the shape of the Church today

What then of the Church today? How can we open ourselves to the patterns of diversity and renewal that have characterized the life-bearing work of the Spirit since the beginning of time?

Well, the modern world has not been a diverse world. Uniformity, not diversity, has characterized the period from the eighteenth to the twentieth centuries. The modern world is a predictable world, dominated by centralized hierarchies, long-term planning, and confidence in human ability to manage the present and the future. It is a world in which change is initiated at the centre. Its key values have been recognized as efficiency, calculability, predictability and control. And in many ways these are the things that have come to characterize the Church. We have inherited uniform buildings, centrally provided liturgies and hierarchically determined structures and processes. For some these things provide a reassuring link to the past; but for an increasing number both inside and outside the Church, they have become deeply unhelpful.[20]

And yet many of our attempts to bring ourselves up to date have been equally prescriptive, owing more to the secular culture than to the Spirit. Gothic buildings and Victorian pews have been replaced by converted warehouses and plastic chairs. Church growth literature offers new blueprints for missionary success. Copyrighted enquiry courses are available. Steven Croft has pointed to the way in which churches have unconsciously conformed to models of cinema, franchise, or unit of production, among others. So often we have tried harder, but not thought what we were doing.[21]

We went to a beautiful church on holiday in Norway – a brightly coloured modern stave church, all painted wood and welcome. They were having a family service and hoped to attract some new people. They had composed a special song for children. They held a quiz. They followed the service with a wonderful barbecue in the snow. But only one family came. Our next holiday was in this country. Another family service. There was a drama on Abraham led by a professor of theology from Oxford. A special children's liturgy, but still 'thy kingdom come' and 'trespasses', and a song with a Latin title called the Sanctus. The congregation was mostly retired; three children sat at the front and a baby cried at the back. We have to be more radical than this! 'We provide it and they join it' won't do any more, however carefully crafted our offering may be. It is, as Frost and Hirsch remark, no longer enough to take the car in for a service. It's time to revisit our whole transport policy.[22]

The world is moving on. We live now in a time that has been dubbed post-modernity, because in many ways it is a reaction to modernity. Postmodernity is characterized by decentralized networks, unpredictability, flexibility and uncertainty, and change is initiated at the periphery. It is a diverse, DIY and yet confused world; a world in which people are increasingly aware of the marginalization of the spiritual, emotional and aesthetic side of life, and increasingly experimenting with alternative spiritualities in order to answer the cry of their souls. It's an 'it-must-fit-me' world, a world in which truth claims are distrusted and authenticity is sought in experience. The last place most people now think of looking for answers to spiritual questions is the Church.[23]

Christian management guru Ken Blanchard observes that it is commonly asked, 'Which approach is better – improving what is, or creating what isn't?' The answer he gives is 'Yes!'. And that is our challenge. We have 2,000 years of tradition and experience on which to draw, and we live in a culture that is willing to experiment. Some gloomy things have been said. But perhaps we can take advantage of these postmodern waters to swim in new and more creative ways, to pay new attention to the resources we find in Scripture, and to open ourselves more fully to the presence of the Spirit among us – for word and Spirit have always been inseparable partners in the self-expression of God.[24]

To do that will mean to be willing not just to seek inspiration for the creation of a diverse Church, but also to allow the sustaining and renewing presence of the Spirit full reign in our lives; it will mean avowing our intent to be, in every way that we can, a genuinely charismatic community. The New Testament speaks of spiritual renewal in different ways, ways which have often been reduced to a restricted range of manifestations and expressed in increasingly predictable forms – charismatic renewal has become a bit of a subculture, if you like. Spiritual renewal, properly understood, should be a constant process, continuous as the flowing of fresh water, refreshing as a stream to the roots of a tree on parched land. It should be as fruitful as an orchard, as noticeable as salt in food and light in darkness, as inspiring as the building of living stones into a spiritual house which becomes a holy priesthood. Spiritual renewal is not an event that happens but a process that unfolds. And as a process, it has an outcome. God, said Cyprian in the third century, is building a people for his name. God is creating a kingdom. Rivers flow into the sea.[25]

What all this means is that one of the marks of spiritual renewal should always be an outward focus, a mission focus. A Church that is diverse and being daily renewed is a mission-shaped Church, a Church that is going somewhere, a Church that is genuinely an eschatological community, a kingdom community open not just to its current members but to those outside. 'As the Father sent me, so I send you' said Jesus as he breathed the Spirit upon the disciples (John 20.21). The Spirit of God is a missionary Spirit, active not only in the Church but also in the world.

Looking to the future

Now to the big question: What might all that mean in practice?

It has sometimes been the Church's experience that the Holy Spirit can bring chaos. Diversity of gifting, role and expression has at times in the Church's history almost overwhelmed her. So we tend – and we've done it spectacularly with the reinforcing ethos of modernism – to clip the Spirit's wings. The Church dislikes the consequences of immaturity, and maybe particularly so in England, where it's been remarked that we prefer slow evolutionary change, measured, discussed, weighted with checks and balances.[26] The Spirit of God, on the other hand, tears holes in heaven, and has a habit of descending with apparent total lack of discrimination on the most unlikely people. It's alarming stuff.

And yet if we return to Genesis, we find that the Spirit did not, as we fear, bring chaos into order, but rather order into chaos. It is precisely the misunderstanding that there is no alternative to order than disorder that has so often hampered our mission and ministry, and fuelled conservatism and institutionalism within the Church. Scripture shows the opposite trend at work. At the moment of the crucifixion, the sky darkens and the primordial chaos threatens once again; Jesus sends forth his spirit, and the universe regains its stability. In the microcosm of our own lives, chaos and confusion is similarly replaced by stillness and peace as we turn to Christ and welcome the Spirit to work within us. So it is that chaos is to be replaced, not by production-line uniformity, but by the pervading, organic, life-giving presence of the Holy Spirit. Only then is real growth possible.[27]

With that in mind, I'd like to propose four ways in which we might think about the gift of the Spirit and the shape of the Church.

A focus on Jesus

First, we will need to focus on Jesus, through whom the gift of the Spirit has come to us. Our primary preoccupation should not be the Church, which is after all a transitional body, an outpost of the kingdom for travellers on the way, but Jesus. Maybe because this is such an anti-institutional age, I find myself spending less and less time thinking about Church and more and more time thinking about Jesus. I find increasingly within myself this question – who is Jesus, and what does it mean to allow the Spirit to bring him to life in me? After all, it was through Jesus that the Spirit was given, and to Jesus that the Spirit bears witness.[28]

Others have felt the same. 'If ever there was a time to rediscover Jesus the Messiah, it is now', Frost and Hirsch suggest. 'It is possible that the story of Jesus may find a hearing once more, if it can be cleansed of its institutional accretions and retold in simplicity and honesty', Michael Riddell writes. 'Jesus emerged from the interviews with a good reputation', Nick Spencer reports from a series of discussions with people outside the Church.[29] Christianity is a person.

And yet, so often we focus our attention not on Jesus but on ourselves. 'We have reduced the gospel message so that it is inseparable from the institution of church', Neil Cole laments. If Jesus walked into a church on Sunday morning, what would change? Does he take part, or is he the star player left sitting with the subs on the bench? Is it Jesus we talk about, or is it church? Who is this Jesus? 'Who do you say that I am?', he asked the disciples. A church is shaped in large part by its answer to that question. It was to a church that Jesus said, 'I stand at the door and knock'. How ready are we to let him in?[30]

I think these are timely questions. Philosophers talk to us of the postmodern rejection of meta-narrative – of the idea that there is an overarching meaning to life. Postmodernism gives us a tremendous opportunity to re-examine who we are and what we are doing – but while we may agree with its rejection of the modern meta-narrative, we don't have to invent our own, for we have one. Social philosopher Ivan Illich once said that if you want to change society, you must tell an alternative story. We've got an alternative story. It's a story about Jesus.

Unity

Secondly, we need unity, a unity that comes from our identity as a community sustained by the Spirit in a world breathed by the Spirit. Unity, for us as for Father, Son and Spirit, will be expressed in a common vision and a shared purpose. If there is shared vision and purpose, then we can dispense with the centralization and control that is the natural human response when things are not going well. If we are united in our thinking and our praying, then there is room for experimentation, for diversification, for the empowerment of local leadership without which growth is impossible. These are commonplaces among experts on change and growth in secular organizations, but they apply no less to the Church. It has long been recognized that the Church must change if she is to stay the same. If we are united in our vision and purpose, we will be able to adopt a permission-giving approach which fosters the creativity we will need if we are to make that possible. I am always struck by the first scriptural reference to an individual being filled by the Spirit – it was the artisan Bezalel, charged with the crafting of the tabernacle in the book of Exodus.[31]

What might our purpose be? Well, one possibility is that suggested in the recent *Resourcing Mission* report of the Church of England – 'we suggest that [our] mission objective should be stated as to present to all people of England the good news of Jesus Christ as the hope of the world'. That is, after all, the task that Jesus left us.[32]

If this is right, it means that we must do theology together. It means sharing ideas, exchanging stories. It means being willing to take risks, to trust one another, to be humble. And it means being open to the new things the Spirit of God might do among us – for, as Jane Williams remarks, we have lost a great deal through fear of finding the Holy Spirit at work without our authorization.[33]

Diversity – or, letting a thousand flowers bloom

Thirdly, we need diversity. Robert Warren has said that in a period of transition we should let a thousand flowers bloom. One way of looking at the relationship between the Spirit and the Church is to say that we should cultivate diversity, not just because we live in an increasingly diverse culture, but because diversity is a fundamental characteristic of spiritual reality, an essential part of the self-expression of the Spirit of God in her life-giving act of creation. There are, I'm told, between one quarter and half a million species of flowering plants on earth.[34]

We live now in a world where a diversity that was once global has become local. I look out of my window, and beside the native lime and birch trees in my garden I see the Australian eucalyptus and Norwegian spruce next door. I live in a city where, instead of just English, 200 languages are now spoken. How can we presume that the Spirit who created and presides over such variety would have us express ourselves in any other way, once it presses all around us? How would he have us worship, where would he have us meet, how would he encourage us to reach out to others? Having gifted us spiritually, how would he have us use those gifts except as parts of a diverse, creative and developing community of believers?

I don't, of course, know the answer to those questions. But we have within us, as a charismatic community, the capacity to explore them. We can dream dreams, as the prophet Joel foretold that we would when the Spirit was poured out in days to come. Nothing can take place that has not first been imagined; so perhaps we should start by unleashing our imaginations. We live in an age where creativity is at a premium, and all too often we stifle it. We need to identify and release our prophets, recruit our Bezalels, set free our poets. It doesn't all have to be new stuff; we can look to our own traditions, bring out of our treasure not just what is new but also what is old. We live in a pick 'n' mix age, and we have an astonishingly diverse spiritual heritage to draw on. Let's borrow from one another and borrow from the past. We have much to learn and much to share.[35]

Depending on the Holy Spirit

Finally, to end where we began, we must depend on the Spirit, the Spirit who gave and sustains our common life. Diversity in itself is just postmodernism. We do need diversity of both form and approach, but it's the content that is the key, and the content is relationship with Jesus through daily dependence on the Holy Spirit. I came across a comment recently from a Korean pastor who had been visiting some mega-churches in the United States. 'What do you think?' they asked him at the end of his stay. He paused. 'Well, it's just amazing what you people can do without the Holy Spirit.' We mustn't let that be said of us.[36]

So, if we are going to count for anything in this postmodern world, the Spirit must remain the key to everything that we are and do. José Comblin predicts that the new era of Church will be under the sign of the Holy Spirit, and that charismatic experience will be valued more highly than at any time since the third century. If so, such experience will be understood not narrowly as the exercising of the gifts of the Spirit by individuals – although it will always be that too – but broadly as a renewed willingness to abandon our certainties and allow the wind to blow where it will. It has been said that what we need more than anything else is an adventure.[37] In particular, we need to allow our life and mission to be shaped by a God of life-breathing diversity who grows great big trees from tiny seeds, so that the birds of the air can come and make their nests in the branches.

There are a lot of birds out there.

13

Can fresh expressions of church make a difference?

Lynda Barley

Christian Britain

In recent years, social research findings have increasingly pointed the Church towards those beyond its walls. As we see our nation embracing greater diversity, this research is encouraging the Church to consider the hard question of the religious world view of those it seeks to serve. And, as we shall see, this exploration is beginning to reveal common insights to surprise us. Rather like the popular Sudoku puzzles there are patterns to ponder and connections to be made for the exploration to be relevant to the growing diversity of local contexts in which the Church witnesses to the gospel.

It is worth briefly reminding ourselves of the distance we have travelled as a nation in less than a decade. As I write this we are only seven years into the twenty-first century and yet our enthusiastic millennium celebrations seem a distant memory. How quickly all those hopes and expectations evaporated with recent global events! And we live today on an international stage where technology instantly plays out these events at a local and national level.

The world is changing at a faster and faster pace so that keeping in touch with it preoccupies the day-to-day living of the majority. Of arguably greater challenge to those who follow Christ's way is that we worship a God who holds the past, the present and the future. It presents the Christian Church with the hard question of how to follow this God who leads into the future 'making all things new'. How can the people of God continue to be the Church for England in the brave new world of the twenty-first century? Can fresh expressions of church make a difference?

Christian foundations

As this new millennium started, the government in England and Wales, for the first time, asked a question on personal religion in the national census. Religious affiliation was an emerging and sensitive issue as the nation increasingly reflected on its Christian roots. To the surprise of many policy makers, 7 in 10 households reported Christian affiliation, only 2 in 10 expressed no religious affiliation and less than 1 in 10 aligned themselves with other faiths.

A map of these results (see opposite) reveals significant differences across England, with the northern counties displaying noticeably higher levels of indigenous Christianity than their southern counterparts. Further academic research and numerous reputable national polls since that time have confirmed this currently stable picture of personal religious affiliation across Britain. It may be that many are holding to their Christian heritage as a default position, but there are other messages beneath the surface of Christian Britain.

Britain today is a country in transition in terms of its spiritual and religious inheritance. Its older generations were raised on regular attendance at Sunday school and church while its younger generations are largely in this sense 'unchurched'. Traditional church then is more likely to resonate with older, 'churched' people who have a church context to relate to. The growing numbers of unchurched need to be pointed towards their unknown God in a fresh way that relates to their everyday experience. As the apostle Paul related the gospel to the unknown Athenian gods of his day so the Church today must find fresh ways to build church for future generations.

In addition, faith and faith-related matters are becoming acceptable and worthy of discussion in public life again. Religious attitudes are developing further with each year of the twenty-first century. We see fresh signs of God's activity bubbling up all around us and urgent reflection is needed if the Church in England is going to avoid being left stranded. We will only continue to be the Church for England if we relate to emerging signs of God breathing his renewing life into this nation at this time.

Patterns of churchgoing today

In the lifetimes of most people today there has been a permanent shift in the religious attitudes and practice of our nation. Churchgoing, for example, has undergone a massive shift in social acceptability over the last 50 years or so. Recent studies to explore churchgoing in ordinary churches reveal some

Percentage of population stating religion as Christian

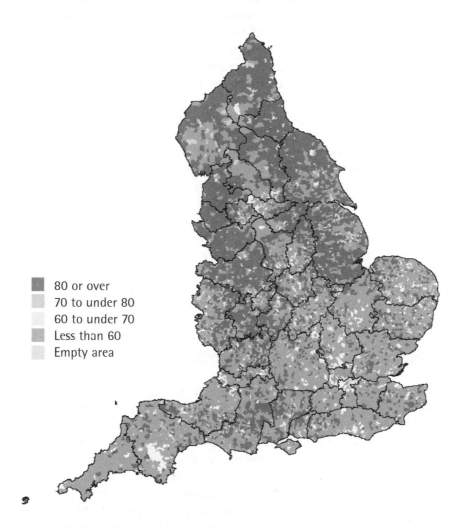

80 or over
70 to under 80
60 to under 70
Less than 60
Empty area

Data source: 2001 Key Statistics. Census Output is reproduced with the permission of the Controller of HMSO and the Queen's Printer for Scotland

interesting patterns too. Research, for example, by Wakefield Diocese into congregational church attendance in the late 1990s has recently been updated with interesting results.

Registers of everyone attending church worship in the Almondsbury deanery were maintained for eight weeks in October and November 1997, 2000 and

2006. One problem subsequently discovered was that those attending fresh expressions of church were not considered to be eligible for this exercise! Ways need to be developed to include emerging fresh expressions into an expanded vision of church. They may be fledgling churches but they are partners within the Body of Christ from whom, in the spirit of mutual support, we have a lot to learn. When financial agendas, for example, exclude fresh expressions of church, connections between us are undermined and we are the poorer.

Despite the consequent omission of two fresh expressions of church, the church attendance picture across the 17 churches of the Almondsbury deanery was only slightly less positive than national trends. Over almost a decade three churches showed strong growth while seven churches suffered serious decline. Regular attendance at midweek services almost doubled and became a significant element in church life, while on Sundays the number of regular weekly attenders dropped a little. The total number of people attending church worship across the deanery also dropped a little but the most significant change was in the number of people who attended Sunday worship once or twice a month. Their numbers decreased by a third over the nine years. Their attendance had become still less frequent so that the proportion of one-off attenders over the eight weeks increased from 52 per cent of Sunday church attenders in 1997 to 60 per cent in 2006.[1] The impact of this cannot be underestimated, for on an ordinary Sunday morning the usual congregation consequently declined by 1 in 6 (17 per cent).

The findings in this quite typical deanery and the experience of cathedrals in recent years illustrate how people will attend worship at times convenient to their lifestyles while at the same time fighting shy of regular commitment. Professor Grace Davie has helpfully reminded us that we live in an age where duty has been replaced by consumer choice.[2] People will no longer necessarily attend church worship from any sense of obligation. It must be relevant to their lives and easily accessible. Christians must meet their neighbours where they are and not just in the physical sense. The products we offer need to be contextualized for their modern-day market without compromising their Christian essence. The decline in Christian baptisms, for example, confirms that people will no longer necessarily come to the church without prompting.

Perhaps then it is a surprise to discover that our churches are being increasingly used on a growing variety of other occasions by the vast majority of our nation. Over the first seven years of the new millennium, survey results have consistently shown that 85 per cent of adults in Britain have been in a church or chapel in the previous year and for an increasing number of reasons. In particular, these results emphasize the importance of being open and available for our busy neighbours. Two in ten people report they have visited a place of worship in the last year because 'they were walking past and felt the need to go in'.[3] Churches that find ways to be open and accessible are frequently rewarded with new contacts to pray for and a new vision for their place in the local neighbourhood. Churches also provide a quiet place, sacred space for reflection and peaceful surroundings away from the busy world. The same national research discovered that two in ten adults visited a place of worship in the last year because it was 'a quiet space' while seven in ten saw churches and chapels as 'a quiet space or sanctuary'.

Alongside this appeal for open and accessible church we should consider something that on the face of it could hardly be called a fresh expression of church – our cathedrals. Since the turn of the millennium, our English cathedrals have made particular efforts to reflect on their roles in modern-day Britain. They have taken a step back to consider their mission and ministry from the outside, from the perspective of those with whom they come into contact day by day, week by week. They have been able to follow what God is doing and to begin to respond as they are able. In some respects they were already there open almost all hours for a 24/7 society seeking convenient and accessible opportunities for worship that provides personal satisfaction without undue commitment. Cathedrals offer opportunities to observe professionally led worship anonymously and with minimal participation. The modern-day reticence towards commitment of any sort and its preoccupation with individual experience can be positively developed into a fuller faith through cathedral worship.

As cathedrals have reflected on their situations, they have been surprised to observe the attendance of adults and of children at midweek services of worship to be steadily increasing. Sunday observance in our cathedrals remains static but services during the week are attracting more adults and more children and young people. Over the first six years of this millennium, attendance at ordinary cathedral services grew 18 per cent to approximately 25,000 adults, children and young people – that is, on average, 600 people in each cathedral participating in cathedral worship each week. The role of cathedrals as a modern-day educational resource has also gradually grown but more marked still is the growth of congregations at special services and particularly those at Christmas. Over the same six-year period, attendance at cathedral services for Christmas Eve, Christmas Day alone rose by 38 per cent to approximately 130,000, or an average of 3,100 adults, children and young people in each cathedral. There are, in fact, many stories of bulging Christmas congregations in both our parishes and cathedrals. As cathedrals and churches respond with additional alternative services, so new congregations are being discovered. Something special is going on at Christmas!

Open to churchgoing?

A study in Kendal, Cumbria by the University of Lancaster compared the spiritual experiences of congregation members to those of people involved beyond the church in body, mind and spirit holistic experiences.[4] The study showed people trying out spiritual things for themselves, drifting away from the churches. Other research has confirmed this drift and found that nationally, a quarter of people outside our churches have drifted away from churchgoing due to lack of time or other pressures.[5] More recent national studies have found that overall around 50 per cent of adults in Britain today have drifted away from regular churchgoing. Usually they have attended church or Sunday school as a child or teenager but for various reasons their churchgoing has lapsed. In addition, 30 per cent have never attended church or Sunday school with any regularity, so generating the following picture of regular churchgoing in Britain today.[6]

Experience of churchgoing composite result, Great Britain

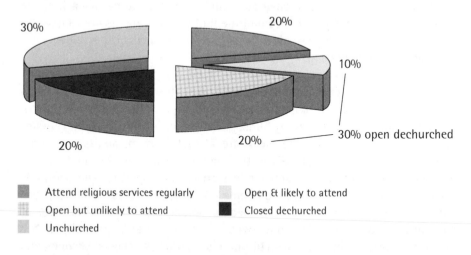

Attend religious services regularly

Open but unlikely to attend

Unchurched

Open & likely to attend

Closed dechurched

Sources: British Social Attitudes 2004, European Social Survey 2002, Gone but not Forgotten 1996/7, Tearfund 2005/6, ORB 2005, Populas 2006

It is immediately striking how the growing proportion of unchurched currently matches the proportion who are dechurched but open to churchgoing, each having very different relationships, both positive and negative, towards church. As we look closer at the large numbers who have drifted away from church-going, the dechurched, we find that a significant number (10 per cent of the adult population) are not only open to return but consider the possibility likely. Younger people are less likely to have attended church or Sunday school regularly than older generations. In fact, 60 per cent of 60-year-olds, 40 per cent of 40-year-olds and 20 per cent of 20-year-olds have childhood experiences of church and churchgoing while many others are not necessarily closed to the possibility.[7]

In modern-day Britain different generations have very different experiences of church. Strikingly, older people are not only more likely than other generations to be regular churchgoers, but they are also more likely to be dechurched. A quarter of people over retirement age attend church at least once a month while four in ten of this age group are dechurched.[8] In contrast, approaching half of young adults under 25 years of age are unchurched, they have no experience of regular churchgoing (or Sunday school attendance) and only one in ten attends church regularly at least once a month. When we consider adults in their forties we find a more pluralistic picture: 15 per cent attend church at least once a month while more than three in ten are dechurched and three in ten unchurched.

Overall, ignoring church background, a third of adults have been found to be closed to churchgoing, while a third, although open to churchgoing, consider the possibility unlikely at least in the next two years. Of significant encouragement and challenge to the Church are the additional one in eight (12 per cent) who thought it likely that they would attend church in the next two years. In this context, fresh expressions must make a difference. For the significant number for whom traditional, inherited church is not relevant flexible, adaptable fresh expressions of church are well placed to be responsive to their spiritual needs.

The response to these survey findings generated the headline in one national newspaper 'We've given up on churchgoing but not on Christianity'.[9] So, we need to ask the question, When exactly do people go to church? It appears that modern-day Britons only go to church on specific occasions and for specific purposes. Their Christian lives do not necessitate regular attendance at church worship. In fact, the more distant people are from regular churchgoing the less likely they are to be open to church attendance as we currently know it. Three in ten of those who still attend church on occasions through the year consider themselves likely to return to regular church attendance compared to half that number of dechurched and a meagre 4 per cent of the unchurched.[10] At Christmas, in particular, we see many occasional churchgoers who relate to the Christian traditions of their childhood. In fact, over half of people who only attend church once a year attend church at Christmas and four in ten attend weddings, baptisms or funerals. If we are to be the Church for modern-day England, new ways of being church must be found alongside traditional, inherited church. A significant and growing minority have no experience of church and little Christian heritage to return to. They seek spiritual nourishment relevant to their modern lifestyles – work or school based perhaps and frequently through visual or electronic communication.

Fresh expressions making a difference?

As more and more have caught the vision behind incorporating fresh expressions into a mixed economy of church (or perhaps 'mixed ecology' of church as proposed by Angela Tilby in chapter 7), a national enquiry has revealed the amazing speed of its development in the life of our church. In 2005 half of Church of England parishes indicated to their dioceses that since the turn of the millennium they had been involved in some sort of fresh expression of church or that they intended to do so in the following two years.[11] Definitions have subsequently become more formalized but this perhaps surprising result reflects a quiet acceptance of new and socially relevant ways of being church, of reaching out in locally contextual mission.

Parishes in 2006 engaged with fresh expressions of church

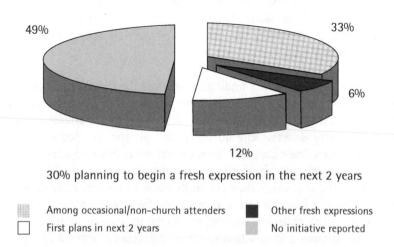

49% 33%

6%

12%

30% planning to begin a fresh expression in the next 2 years

▦	Among occasional/non-church attenders	■	Other fresh expressions
☐	First plans in next 2 years	▨	No initiative reported

Parishes were asked whether, since 2000, their churches had begun any new regular activities, which they would regard as a fresh expression of church. The definition offered was that a fresh expression of church is 'a new and/or different way of being church in and for a changing culture'. Examples that people gave included youth congregations, new initiatives in schools, community- or network-based churches, cells, things that can genuinely be (or that became) church for those who take part. One third (33 per cent) reported involvement in such initiatives among people who, at most, only attend church occasionally. Nearly the same proportion (30 per cent) were planning a fresh expression in the following two years, and for one in eight (12 per cent), this would be their first involvement in a fresh expression of church. Although smaller churches were less likely to be involved in fresh expressions, the enquiry found that in a quarter of dioceses over half the parishes have been involved in fresh expressions of church in the previous five years. Churches reported more than 216,100 people equally spread among both adults, and children and young people to be involved in these fresh expressions. This is a significant number of people even more so when we recall that the average number of church attenders in church each week across all Church of England parishes has been at the same level of 1.2 million for several years. Adding fresh expressions of church could increase this by an additional one in six people. Of course, many fresh expressions of church will be jointly sponsored with several churches perhaps of different denominations coming together but the impact on the church over just five years is clearly significant. That this could be longer lasting than hasty contrived experiments was observed by Archbishop Rowan to General Synod in February 2007:

> Essentially the Fresh Expressions programme is not simply about a kind of scattered set of experiments . . . it's about that gradual, but I think inexorable shift, in the whole culture of our church that has been going on in the last few years, and which will undoubtedly continue to grow and develop.

Also in 2005, the independent research organization Christian Research conducted its own interdenominational survey of church attendance. On Sunday 8 May 2005 it counted 3.2 million people, 6.3 per cent of the population of England in church. It estimated that at least 125,000 were involved in fresh expressions or 'the explosion of ethnic churches' particularly in London.[12] The report observed that without these adults, children and young people the steady loss in church attendance on Sundays it evidenced in its surveys since 1987 would have continued at the same rate.

The estimate above of 216,100 attending fresh expressions of church in which

Church of England churches are involved can be reconciled with the 2005 Sunday interdenominational count if we recall that by no means all fresh expressions of church meet on Sundays and by no means all fresh expressions are included in parish-based church attendance counts. In our 24/7 society churches and fresh expressions of church are all spreading their worship activities over the seven day week. Sunday is no longer the only day when the local church gathers. Indeed, many churches are successfully embracing a multi-congregation model with different worship styles on different occasions throughout the week, sometimes in varying venues.

A more cautious interpretation then is that fresh expressions of church are making a significant contribution towards arresting the continuing decline in church attendance and, in particular, the decline in traditional Sunday church attendance across all denominations. More positively, the Church of England experience suggests that fresh expressions of church are not always seen (and counted) as full expressions of church. Their impact could be more considerable and has the potential to significantly change the fortunes of church attendance in the twenty-first century – in short, to make a material difference.

Refreshing church

In modern-day Britain individual experience and well-being is paramount. Even those who are open to returning to church come seeking immediate spiritual relevance from their Christian roots and their inherited rites of passage – baptisms, marriages and funerals. Our growing Christmas congregations may reflect this searching. Elsewhere, for example, in Europe the German EKD church faces a divided country similar to our own although split on historic rather than generational grounds. Two in ten attend religious services at least once a month in West Germany while in East Germany the figure is just 8 per cent.[13] When surveyed, six in ten of adults in West Germany say they believe in God while in East Germany the figure is under half this. Many in West Germany can relate to past religious experience but many in East Germany question the need for religious faith in any form. This is in noticeable contrast to Britain where, although religious experience is fading there is a growing appreciation of the spiritual dimension to human life and a desire to take personal responsibility for it. In 2004 *The Times* newspaper sponsored research among what it termed the i-generation. These were adults of 18 to 30 years of age, so-named to reflect their individualistic, self-centred, me, me, me approach and their reliance on electronic information technology. After several days reporting the results, *The Times* commented that this generation was 'willing to believe but its spiritual needs are not being met in church'.[14]

Faith in Britain may have been secularized in recent years but secularization has not taken over. As I write, there are front page newspaper stories relating to the tragic disappearance of a couple's small daughter entitled 'Madeline's mum prays for a miracle'.[15] It is not uncommon to see prominent reports by the press of prayerful support by clergy and congregations of individuals and communities suffering loss or tragedy. The Soham murders and the Boscastle floods are notable instances. Often the outside world looks to local church leaders to speak on behalf of their community at such times of tragedy. Research is showing that local churches are increasingly valued for the core values they bring to their neighbourhoods. They are also valued particularly for their worship and sacred space together with the opportunities they provide for marking before God individual rites of passage through life – baptisms, marriages and funerals. All the signs are that churches, in turn, are discovering a growing confidence to develop this role, going beyond the comfort of their church walls.

The future

Our churches know things have to be done differently for the twenty-first century. Although that in itself does not create fresh expressions, it has taken the growing diversity of spiritual experiences and faith positions in our nation to show us the reality of God doing new and sometimes diverse things. Faith is bubbling out under the surface of modern-day Britain, particularly at times of apparent bewilderment and tragedy. Spiritual exploration is becoming acceptable both within church life and outside it.

A spiritually diverse, pluralistic nation needs a diverse Church where groups of Christians, local churches and mother churches each respond to God's leading where they are whether it be in work or other meeting places, local neighbourhoods or elsewhere. In attracting new spiritual and religious searchers fresh expressions of church must invigorate the Church not stand apart from it or, worse, draw people away from it. One danger is that if, for example, they are seen as requiring less commitment, they could become alternatives to church rather than refreshing expressions of church. Maintaining parish links will be important if they are to continue to be part of the mission of a Church that is there for the nation and broader than the strength of its Sunday worshipping congregation.

Across our nation signs are emerging of a twenty-first century that will cause a reshaping of our Christian inheritance in ways that will need to be culturally responsive yet rooted in gospel values. Christians in different localities will need to respond in fresh ways if they are to be relevant expressions of God's love where they are. Holding this growing diversity will, I believe, encourage the Church, like the nation it serves, to revisit and refresh its Christian roots. The contribution of fresh expressions of church towards this revitalization will then make a God-given difference towards re-equipping the Church for modern-day England.

14

How does a mixed economy Church connect with contemporary spirituality?

Martin Warner

Like many of my generation, I'm struck by the huge gap between family life today and what I recollect from my own childhood and adolescence. I rely for my information on university contemporaries, their children who are my godchildren, the pupils of our Cathedral School, our best asset at St Paul's, and finally – an invaluable source of information – the 'Living with Teenagers' column in the Family section of *The Saturday Guardian*. It has to be admitted that this column is relentlessly middle class, although that doesn't invalidate it (more on that point later).

The writer of 'Living with Teenagers' is, understandably, anonymous. She is the mother of Ed, Becca and Jack, who live, as their names might suggest, in Islington. There are episodes that are excruciatingly unpleasant (Ed's language to his parents), startlingly explicit (Becca's tampons), and hideously painful (Jack's lies).

But between the tears, frustration, disappointments and sheer exhaustion of parenting these children (done mainly by mum), there are moments of extreme tenderness that take us to the heart of a metaphor often used in the Scriptures to describe divine–human relationships: parental love.

Mum looks at Becca and thinks 'how beautiful the 15-year-old female face is: clear, aloof, untroubled.' In a conflict with Ed, his mum discovers 'something about the toddler solemnity of his face (that) so makes me want to believe him'. And it's the memory of youth, vulnerable childhood, that constantly wells up in a mother's view of her youngest, Jack, 'when he was eight or nine years old – small and bendy enough for me to grab him and kiss the top of his head, take in the biscuity smell of his hair'.

'Living with Teenagers' has now been running for just over a year, and never once in all that time has there been any reference to religion – or at least none that has given it consideration as something that people in Islington would take seriously. There have been, distressingly enough, plenty of expletives associated with God but no real talk of God. And, interestingly, no explicit use of the 's' word that is so common in the city, where many people from Islington work. The 's' word is now quite common in Human Resources departments of city firms, and it stands for spirituality.

In 'Living with Teenagers' we come as close to spirituality as I think we are likely to get when the Islington family goes on holiday to Cornwall. Total disaster is averted (in the minds of the children) when Jack discovers the television, which 'some weirdo' had hidden in a cupboard and there's a 'once-in-a-lifetime moment: sibling solidarity'. This is the teenagers' shared perspective on the catastrophe that is Cornwall, the land of nothing to do.

But a deeper truth, a truth about being human, is also revealed in this place, as mum herself perceives, when 'the pale-faced, black-hooded trio, like a clutch of rejects from *Lord of the Rings*' is finally persuaded to have a cup of tea and a slice of sponge cake. And 'as they chew, some of the sad, urban tightness in their faces starts to loosen'. 'I reckon this holiday will do them a world of good', is mum's verdict.

And that's precisely where I want to hold our attention as we turn to what we are calling a mixed economy Church.

The term 'economy' does, of course, have its origin in the word for a household. It's a term that Paul uses very clearly in 1 Corinthians 9.17 to describe his vocation in the household of the Church, a vocation in which he is specifically commissioned by God. And this vocation relates not simply to the material ordering of the life of the Church, referred to in another early Christian document as 'the administration of human mysteries'.[1] But it relates also to God's plan for our salvation, described in Ephesians 3.9 as 'the plan of the mystery hidden for ages in God who created all things'.

Starting from the 'human'

We are living in a culture that has little or no understanding of God, neither of the concept nor the experience of God. So our starting point as Christians seeking to invite our contemporaries to explore the enterprise of prayer and spirituality is no longer the divine, but the human, that which, as Christians, we believe is made in the image of God.

This is not about seeking to replace God with humanity: secular culture has already done that. This is about recovering humanity as needing the divine in order to be fully itself. Recovery confronts us with the need for a particular kind of economy. Indeed, that is the very word that the second-century Christian writer, Irenaeus, uses for outlining the way in which God is revealed to humanity in Jesus Christ, 'through many economies' is actually what he says, in order that 'the human race may not be remote from God, and so cease to exist'.[2]

Humanity from a Christian standpoint

Our starting point for prayer and spirituality in a mixed economy Church must be a clear, scriptural and doctrinal Christian anthropology. Far from being a programme for individualism, this lays out for us the scope of the nature of the Church and the reason for our use of body language to describe it. And in this regard I have always valued the clarity of vision that undergirds the texts of the Second Vatican Council.

The opening paragraphs of the document about the Church begin with the statement, 'Christ is the light of humanity'.[3] The focus here is on the human race in its entirety. The statement being made is about who each of us is as a member of that race and, within this vision, the destiny of those whose hearts are directed towards justice – the just men and women of every age – are what is defined as the completion of the Church's mission, when, ' "from Abel, the just one, to the last of the elect" will be gathered together with the Father in the universal Church'.[4]

What was important about *Lumen Gentium* was that it did not claim exclusive identification with the Roman Catholic Church. It states that 'the Catholic faithful, others who believe in Christ, and finally all mankind [are] called by God's grace into salvation'. Relationship with each other in Christ is, in the vision of this document, indivisible from relationship with the entire human race whom Christ also redeems.

This recognition of the intimate bond between those who are united with Christ by faith through baptism, and the wider constituency of the human race, is similarly articulated by Vatican II's Pastoral Constitution on the Church in the Modern World. Its introduction begins: 'The joy and hope, the grief and anguish of the men and women of our time, especially those who are poor or afflicted in any way, are the joy and hope, the grief and anguish of the followers of Christ as well.'

This document, also known by the Latin of its opening introductory words, *Gaudium et Spes* (Joy and Hope) goes on to articulate the importance of culture as integral to the dignity of the human person, to the essential nature of being human, revealed in intellect, conscience, the capacity for truth and the desire for freedom.

So, it states, when we as human beings fulfil our vocation to use the gifts of creativity in areas such as the arts, we 'greatly contribute towards bringing the human race to a higher understanding of truth, goodness and beauty, to points of view having universal value; thus humankind will be more clearly enlightened by the wondrous Wisdom which was with God from eternity, working beside him like a master craftsman, rejoicing in his inhabited world, and delighting in the sons of men'.[5]

In this regard, we are hearing nothing that has not already been said before. At the end of the second century, Clement of Alexandria surveyed the infusion of wisdom in the Greek philosophical culture of his day and was able to assert that 'God is the source of all good; either directly, as in the Old and New Testaments, or indirectly, as in the case of philosophy . . . "a school teacher" to bring Hellenism to Christ'.[6]

And it is with that sense of confidence in God as the source of all that is good, explicitly in the Christian Scriptures, in a hidden fashion in other manifestations of wisdom, innate and intrinsic to human identity, that I wish to return to our Islington family, on holiday in the apparent catastrophe, for the teenager members, that is called Cornwall.

What do we have to say to them about prayer and spirituality, living as they, and we do, in a mixed economy? We find ourselves in a mixed economy of Church life that, in its liturgical points of reference, ranges from *The Book of Common Prayer*, via cyberspace to the *Alpha* course. They, seeking to be fully human and fully alive but without the ability to make reference to God, find themselves in a mixed economy of belief in what is real and what is not, who they are and what their lives are for. In both instances, the points at which we explore the truth, whether about God or about who we are as the creatures God has made, cannot be predicted or determined. It could be surfing in Cornwall that enables some to find God through a fresh expression of church on surfing beaches there. For our secular *Guardian* family the experience of interdependence might raise a challenge to self-interested consumerism and open up an enquiry about relationship as what constitutes human existence. They might be prompted to ask themselves about the scope of that relationship in time and, through death, beyond time.

Holding on to the understanding of Church in its relation to humanity that I have tried to outline, together with some sense of a Christian anthropology (described by Irenaeus as part of the economy of divine self-revelation in Jesus Christ), I want to explore how we might match the experiences of our Islington family with the economy of prayer and spirituality in Christian practice and tradition today.

Fresh experiences of life

In this matching, I believe fresh expressions of the life of the Church are not about any new and distinct organization, but about new and distinct experiences in the life of those who have never before encountered Christian faith. Based on our Christian anthropology, we would expect that this fresh expression, or fresh experience, is possible because fundamental aspects of human life, such as family relationships, holiday, and the experience of beauty, are the media of divine revelation. And the challenge for the Church today is how to make encounter with points of congruity between human life and divine revelation accessible in ways that invite further exploration.

Perhaps a good place to begin is where we left our Islington family: on holiday. The notion of a time of rest is itself rooted in the Judaeo-Christian tradition of Sabbath. Our word 'holiday' also has connections with a calendar of liturgical celebration in which time is made holy by re-creation. Similarly, the term 'vacation' connects us with the idea of freedom, free from labour, but also free for a purpose; this is about being 'free to . . .' or 'free for . . .' and so the phrase, *vacate Deo*, free for God, is at the heart of that time that we, perhaps less helpfully, describe as retreat.

Looking at her teenage children as they lapse into the recreational experience of tea and cake in Cornwall, our Islington mum notes that the 'sad, urban tightness in their faces starts to loosen' and concludes, 'I reckon this holiday will do them a world of good.' That's a verdict that is true of people of all ages who work, especially those who work in London. It is also true of our society for other reasons, because life is fast, noisy, filled with sound but little communication, overcrowded with people but devoid of relationship, relentlessly graphic and visual, but lacking coherent vision and perspective.

In the mixed economy of the Church I see a need for us to safeguard Sabbath experience and to limit activism. The gift of rest is essential to our capacity for appreciation of the divine life, as much as it holds within it the means of release from patterns of behaviour that can damage and harm not only ourselves but also other people, especially those we love most.

For nine years I worked at the Shrine of Our Lady of Walsingham in Norfolk. Like Cornwall, there were aspects of life there that teenagers would recognize as catastrophic and at times I would have sympathized with them. The nearest supermarket was 35 miles away – need I say more! But I also recognized that those who came on pilgrimage represented a very mixed economy. In many instances they were regulars, but never without some who had little or no Christian faith and who came in search of release from 'sad, urban tightness'.

This was equally so for tourists who happened across Walsingham as a place of historic interest and medieval charm. Holidaying in north Norfolk, and understandably drawn by a fantastic coast and unspoilt countryside, they discovered a freedom in the natural environment that released them to respond to something within themselves that this rest, this Sabbath, held within itself.

I am not saying that all tourists became pilgrims, or were necessarily converted. But I do believe that in Walsingham they encountered something numinous, something of the spirit that is integral to human identity, something that refreshed them. It was for them a fresh expression of something that, if they pursued it, would lead them to an experience of God through the existing witness of the Church's life. And I believe that this is also part of the ministry of many of our church buildings and cathedrals. In such places space – freedom from being targeted by some kind of consumerist marketing is also assured by a high degree of anonymity, which should be a matter of choice, unimposed and therefore quite different from exclusion. This is invaluable to a person for whom faith and the life of the spirit is exploratory and tentative.

In many instances these places provide a certain kind of freedom, they are vacation places, in which the spirit is released, is 'free to . . .' or 'free for . . .' an exercise of imagination and inquiry that the time and space constraints of contemporary life inhibit and often extinguish. Although there is no substitute for visiting an actual place, the existence of web sites that provide this kind of space are of increasing importance to those who seek to sustain contact with their interior life in the context of a busy working schedule. So, for example, I know of clergy and laity who use the www.sacredspace.ie web site for their daily prayer time: I know of one person who downloads its guided meditation material on to his i-pod and uses it throughout the morning in an inner-city parish. But I also know that this electronic economy, or medium for seeking the revelation of divine life is fed and deepened by its material, temporal, liturgical equivalent.

Liturgy and new dimensions to life

I also want to suggest that our Islington family on holiday is modelling something of the reciprocity between givenness (Cornwall) and free will (opting in to tea and cake) that is characteristic of liturgical worship. The variety of liturgical texts that we now have can aid – or inhibit – this (on the whole I think that there are too many words).

As we see most obviously in the rite of marriage, liturgical texts are given to us, placed on our lips, to open up dimensions of life that we may not know how to articulate for ourselves, since the sacred is an aspect that is unfamiliar to us. We have to have confidence in the words that are ours to give, in their content, time-honoured quality, and capacity to communicate truth. Here, again, we find that what already exists in the life of the Church, its liturgy, becomes a fresh expression of something natural-but-transformed when experienced by those who have no faith or knowledge of God. Ministry of word and place has to be very carefully attuned to the needs of those who experience themselves thus transformed. This ministry needs to be confident about inviting exploration of places and words of faith that express congruity between life devoid of knowledge of God and Christian witness.

Part of my work at St Paul's centres on our engagement with contemporary art. The impetus to do this is a bit obvious, with the cathedral and Tate Modern staring at each other across the river. Conversations with artists, especially those who do not profess any Christian faith, have been among the most fascinating I've experienced. They understand precisely this point about congruity, even though it's not Christian witness they are seeking to connect people with. But they are engaged in touching the spirit within the human person, entering a different dimension of life, transcending or re-imagining the mundane. They can see how similar our enterprises are.

Remembering

Returning again to our Islington family, no small part of the dynamic of their life as seen through parental eyes was the force of memory. Mum's recollection in Ed of a 'toddler solemnity' or of Jack being 'small and bendy enough for me to grab him and kiss the top of his head' was a vital part of the relationship that had moved beyond that stage of life but was still informed by it.

Ancient cathedrals and parish churches have walls that are thick with memories, often carved in stone tablets and ornate monuments. They are a constant source of interest to tourists, and very obviously not only when the names on them are famous. In St Paul's I see people poring over ledger stones of long-dead clergy, musicians, minor artists and unsung benefactors, and I wonder at the attraction.

The attraction is not factual. These are not PhD students or people tracing their family tree, but they are people who, in no other place, are invited to exercise memory for its own sake and, in so doing, to encounter that store of thought, experience and reality that is themselves in relation to a range of other times and people to whom they will forever be connected. This is where we locate the heart and movement that issues in intercessory prayer – remembering. Remembering is what we do. It also what we ask God to do. It is at the heart of our intention in the Eucharist, and the foundation of our hope of resurrection – that God will re-member, collect together every scattered part of ourselves, in to an integrity and beauty that is redeemed and perfect. It is in the precious freedom to remember that the motive to light a candle and say a prayer is located.

There is an important distinction to be made here. On the one hand, there is something vague that contains a high degree of nostalgia and, on the other hand, we discern a sense of connectedness in time that holds together past, present and future. And this 'holding together' is the continuum that forms the Christian tradition of engagement with the eternal Word who encapsulates in himself the alpha and the omega – the beginning and the end of time. There is a marked strain of this thought in Celtic Christianity, particularly the Irish tradition, and it is perhaps because of this intuitive sense of loss and searching in that tradition that it speaks so immediately to many people today.

The Irish poet Denis Devlin wrote that 'it is inside our life the angel happens', a perception expanded by another Irish writer, John O'Donahue: 'Your angel is as ancient as eternity itself and has a memory that is older than the earth. Your angel was there when the eternal artist began to dream you ... Your angel is aware of the secret life that sleeps in your soul.'[7]

Healing lives

This leads to another match between the experience of life in today's secular culture and the fresh expression of it as transformed by recognition of congruity with the ministry of the Church. The match lies in the need for, and experience of healing. One of the important aspects of maternal love for Ed, Becca and Jack is the recollection of their capacity for innocence in childhood that is, as they grow up, more heavily obscured but not lost. And it is in the glimpse of what was and is still there that the hope for a different, better way of being emerges.

No small part of the attraction of the *Alpha* course and its marketing is the narrating of lives that have been recovered from chaos by attention to dislocation and loss of control. Whatever the particular economy of your church community, the invitation into an environment of safety in which it is possible to explore the areas of our life that are damaged, is both essential for the community's well-being and profoundly attractive to today's society.

When terrible disasters occur, anywhere in the world, one of the features of the scenes that follow, as a hideous truth sinks in upon a whole community, is the isolation of people who are grieving. Standing in their twos and threes, they are not only numb with pain, they also long for a shared context in which to give expression to their feelings. In St Paul's, this has brought together people from across the faith traditions in profoundly important acts of worship that have expressed something that testifies to what I have been describing as a Christian anthropology. Grief at the loss of loved ones in the Tsunami, the Iraq conflict, or the London bombings was the driving force for this search for healing, variously described, but often as 'closure'.

Placed in the wider framework of ordinary life, the need for healing in the sphere of one's soul, and therefore beyond the sphere of psychotherapy, valuable though that may be, is expressed in a growing appreciation of the use of a spiritual director. In the Diocese of London, the London Centre for Spirituality trains women and men, lay, ordained, and religious, in the art and skill of spiritual direction. They now have an extensive directory of people who have completed a three-year course in spiritual direction and are available for this ministry.

But this is a tradition in which not everyone is necessarily comfortable. We also recognize that house groups are an essential element in church growth. It is in these small, intimate, safe gatherings that a similar form of spiritual openness can be explored and fostered, in the context of prayer and Christian nurture.

This tradition of spiritual direction is an attractive ministry because it is not tied to any institutional structure: the art of conversation between two people on a journey together is essentially scriptural, and innately human. It is an exact point of congruity between the template of church economy and the needs of today's society. There is a point when Islington mum notes with satisfaction an extremely rare outbreak of sibling solidarity on their holiday. She is touching on something more profound than simply the cohesion of her own family: she is recognizing the importance of common ground in which to be and to be known, unashamedly, as yourself.

The availability of someone to whom one can go, in whom one can confide, who understands a shared humanity, and who is in a category that is not determined by sexual attraction or manipulation, is sadly rare. The categories of brother, sister, friend belong to the texture of the Christian language. They also hold an economy for the world that has expended its energies on patterns of relationship (boyfriend, girlfriend, lover, partner, ex) that too easily exclude this economy and the benefits is offers.

Truth in beauty

This also touches on another aspect of the economy of the Church in its understanding of beauty. Back to our Islington mum: she refers to her three children as a black-hooded trio. It's a fashion statement, of course, but as is always the case with fashion, it's also more. What is this saying? It may be that's it's a symptom of adolescence that my hood is providing space to be myself at a time when things are happening to me that I don't understand and am finding difficult to cope with.

But there are other discourses along these lines that are more damaging and longer lasting. Every confessor and spiritual director will know that a considerable part of their task is helping the penitent or directee to overcome tendencies towards self-doubt or worse, self-hatred. In part this is fuelled by a fashion-conscious world that is ruthless in its impact.

When Islington mum comments on her daughter's beauty, she touches on something that is both personal, but also universal: 'the 15-year-old female face'. The description she then gives, 'clear, aloof, untroubled' is a common – though generally critical – description of many Renaissance portraits of the Blessed Virgin Mary.[8] It is, unwittingly, a statement about moral beauty that informs who we are as persons by the kind of lives that we live. And, in this regard, the vision is as much spiritual as it is moral and ethical.

It is when we can see beauty outside the synthetic creations of fashion and cosmetics that we appreciate what the freedom of the gospel truly is.

I mentioned that my own sources of information about the economy of family life are relentlessly middle class. It is here that something of the spirituality of a mixed economy Church must challenge the prevailing culture of a success-driven, celebrity-acclaimed, media-led social economy.

When the Second Vatican Council's statement *Gaudium et Spes* was written, it had the consequence of turning the attention of the Roman Catholic Church to those areas where grief and hope were most severely challenged. Alongside the work of great Christians in our own communion, Janani Luwum and Desmond Tutu, for example, we see set the example of the martyr Oscar Romero, Mother Teresa of Calcutta and John Paul II.

In our own time these are the better-known examples of people who have reminded us that the poor are our teachers: that wherever human dignity is compromised by the culture of death, Christians should cry out in protest.

In our society, the economy of the household of the Church has to be one in which this understanding of beauty in the life of every human being informs its spirituality. It contributes to our determination that human dignity must never be violated, by sexual, material, or economic abuse, since beauty is, in the case of every human being, both physical and moral. It is physical because flesh and blood is the economy of divine revelation – as Irenaeus taught us – and moral because it is determined by our behaviour.

The question of beauty points to one last, and in many ways most potent, possibility of congruence between the mixed economy of the Church's life and its discovery as a fresh expression by those in our contemporary society who have never experienced themselves in that dimension.

We recently had the privilege of showing in St Paul's a work entitled 'Moon Mirror' by the German artist Rebecca Horn. At the opening of this exhibition of an intriguing sculpture of light and glass, a reporter challenged us with the observation that buildings like St Paul's are largely redundant, since it is art galleries, like Tate Modern, that are the cathedrals of today.

It was an interesting point, but not persuasive. We at St Paul's are fascinated by the possibilities that the Millennium Bridge opens up between our two buildings. But what we also find interesting is the fact that galleries are filled with images all looking for a narrative; we have a narrative, and are confident and content to allow images to illuminate and enrich it. And it is here that we identify a congruity between the economies of Church and world in what I have been attempting to identify as a fresh expression of life transfigured for people of no explicit faith.

People are today drawn in huge crowds by the attractive and accessible pull of our public art galleries, where narrative, imagination and image intersect. Here, in the visual gymnasia of the imagination we find the human person revealed, in artist and viewer, as one who bears the image of God in creativity and the capacity to work with the Holy Spirit, even when it is present in ways that are profoundly anonymous to the artist.

Graham Howes, in his recent book, *The Art of the Sacred*, relates observations by Matisse on the 'tempestuous' experience of painting the Stations of the Cross. Matisse writes: 'You have to know them so well by heart that you could draw them blindfold.' Matisse was not a conventional Christian, but he did buy into the economy of Christian faith in God, finding in the figure of the human person 'the so-to-say religious feeling that I have towards life' and acknowledging the significance of divine inspiration by saying, 'When I work ... I feel somehow aided by someone who makes me do things that are beyond me.'[9]

This quotation opens up for us an example of how artistic inspiration crosses in and out of the boundaries of institutional religion and is evidence of the intuitive spirituality that I have been suggesting is the foundation of a Christian anthropology. As a reflection of the divine beauty, art, in its many forms – painting, sculpture, architecture, music, sport, gardening, film, fiction, poetry, drama, dance, etc. – is the expression of mystery that is within us, that is God given and spirit filled, and it is the guarantor of our humanity, as Kazuo Ishiguro brilliantly suggests in his novel, *Never Let me Go*.[10]

This is, I hope, a good place to draw my reflections to a close and invite you to continue yours. In the context of our exploration of prayer and spirituality in a mixed economy Church, it is from our understanding of a Christian anthropology that the significance of beauty emerges. It points us to mystery and suggests that material yet inapprehensible dimension of life for which we also use the word 'sacrament'.

Here, in the mixed economy of the sacred and the material, boundaries between Church and society, faith and identity, Christian and human, realization and potential seem to be more porous that we might have imagined. In our secular culture Christians have good reason for quiet confidence that the attraction of beauty will express itself afresh as an ensign of what it means to by fully human. Its attraction is captured famously and definitively as a fresh expression in the human economy of wisdom by one of the greatest agents of Christianity. In the fourth century St Augustine of Hippo reflected it was 'late that I have loved you, O Beauty so ancient and so new'.[11]

15

Mapping ecclesiology for a mixed economy

Steven Croft

> There is a simplicity on the near side of complexity which is worthless. There is a simplicity on the far side of complexity which is priceless.
>
> *Oliver Wendell Holmes*

If you have engaged seriously with the chapters in this book you will know, as I do, that rethinking what it means to be the Church is at present a complex but essential task. We have not yet reached the point of simplicity beyond complexity.

Our churches are seeking to emerge from Christendom as dynamic, missionary communities shaped by the love of God made known in Jesus Christ with a passionate commitment to see God's kingdom come in our society and in God's world.

This process has meant first (in both time and priority) a significant engagement with the mission of God. This engagement has been resourced practically through new beginnings in evangelism, mission and new ways of being church. It has been resourced theologically, primarily through engagement with Scripture and with the global Christian community.

Engaging with mission has led, inevitably to fresh reflection on what it means to be church in a changing context: to different attempts to re-imagine church. The different authors in this book each bring different perspectives and questions to what is a multi-faceted question.

My aim in this final chapter is to draw some of these threads together and offer an outline map of the field of current reflection about the Church.

Finally, I want to offer in conclusion a compass as an essential help to navigation where the map may not yet have sufficient detail.

My perspective is that we are at present reasonably good at thinking about mission as a church (and very much better than we were ten or fifteen years ago). However, collectively we remain poor at thinking about the Church. There is some knowledge and understanding of the biblical traditions on ecclesiology (though this is often incomplete). But there is general ignorance of the wider Christian and specifically Anglican and Methodist traditions on what it means to be the Church.

It is vital that we reverse this situation. How can we seek to re-imagine what it means to be the Church and create new Christian communities if we lack the language and ability to talk and reflect about what it means to be the Church in dialogue with Scripture and our tradition? I don't mean, of course, that every minister and church member should be able to talk in technical theological language about ecclesiology. The end point should be that people are able to talk with depth and simplicity about what it means to be church in language that inspires and gives life to new and existing communities. But like any other skill or language this one needs to be intentionally learned.

Ecclesiology: mapping the discipline

My starting point is that thinking and reflection on the life of the Church is not a small area of theology but a significant and large field. What I am attempting to map and describe here is not therefore a small area like a garden or an English village but something much more complex (about the size of the Lake District).

Conversations and debates on ecclesiology can often be frustrating in part because clergy in particular often talk at cross purposes. It is rather as though a group of people sit down to talk about music and one has in mind the classical music tradition, a second thinks the conversation is about the latest singles chart and the third is talking about learning the trombone. When someone says in a church meeting: 'I have severe reservations about what is proposed on the grounds of ecclesiology', I have found this can mean many different things. One person may be talking about what is at the heart of what it is to be church. Another may be really saying something about church governance or the ordained ministry or the place of the sacraments. Another may even be trying to intimidate the rest of the people in the room by deploying the 'e' word because they think they understand what it means and no one else will.

Christians have been reflecting on the life and nature of the Church for 2,000 years. It should be no surprise that a particular and large theological discipline can be broken down into different areas. The study of the New Testament involves a number of key but distinct disciplines: New Testament Greek, the evolution of the text, history and archaeology, theology and, of course, the normal divisions between the Gospels, the epistles of Paul and the other writings. Someone who is beginning to study the New Testament for the first time needs a map of these basic disciplines in order to find their way around and begin to explore the text for themselves. The same can be said, of course, for any area of human knowledge and study: economics, biology or cookery. After a while, these subdivisions of the subject become second nature but they are a necessary first stage in mastering a discipline.

Thinking about the Church and its life is no different – so here I set out the beginnings of a beginners' map, which divides the territory into five areas and five kinds of reflection:

Distilled ecclesiology: drawing out the essence of the Church

To distil something is to attempt to get right to the heart of what it is or is about. In a time of stability, when everyone thinks they know what the Church is, this kind of activity has low priority. But in a time of mission in a changing culture, it becomes an essential task. If we are seeking to change existing communities or help to build fresh expressions of church, we must be able to distinguish the heart of the enterprise (such as love or the sacraments) from the culturally specific (such as pews, organ music or a particular style of dress).

Several of the chapters in this book aim in this way to get right to the heart of what it means to be the Church – the people of God – particularly Martyn Atkins, James Dunn and John Hull.[1] Their three perspectives are not, I think, mutually incompatible. We can set others next to them as ways of attempting to distil in an idea or a few sentences what it means to be the Christian community.

My own favourite verse in the New Testament for this is Mark's earliest description of the call of the first disciples – the new community, which Jesus calls into being at the beginning of his ministry. It is clear from a number of passages in Mark's Gospel that we are meant to see ourselves, as it were, in the life of the disciples. It is worth, therefore, paying careful attention to one of the earliest New Testament descriptions of the life of the community formed by Jesus:

> [Jesus] went up the mountain and called to him those whom he
> wanted, and they came to him. And he appointed twelve, whom
> he also named apostles, to be with him and to be sent out.
>
> (Mark 3.13–14 NRSV)

Mark intends us to understand from these two verses that the Church is
initiated by Jesus as we respond to an encounter with the risen Lord and to his
call (the Greek term *ekklesia* means, literally, those who are called out). The
calling of twelve signifies both a continuity with and a re-founding of
the people of God as the new Israel. Most profoundly of all, Mark catches in
the story of the call of the twelve the entire rhythm of Christian discipleship:
to be with Jesus (in community) and to be sent out. Worship, fellowship and
mission are the essence of the life of the Church. The DNA – the life – of every
Christian community is contained in this simple rhythm. Our connection in
Christ is also our connection to his body through time and in eternity.

Acts 2.42 is often used in local church situations as a statement of distilled
ecclesiology:

> They devoted themselves to the apostles' teaching and
> fellowship, to the breaking of bread and the prayers.

This Lukan summary is helpful in a different way from Mark's two verses. It
provides what has become a classical fourfold statement of the elements or
activities that sustain Christian community and help it grow to maturity (in
ways echoed by Lindsay Urwin in his own chapter in this volume). However, the
two statements taken together illustrate well the difficulty of relying too
much on any single Bible verse or statement or definition to capture the
whole of what it means to be and live as God's Church. The verses from Mark
have nothing about the means by which the Church is sustained and is 'with
Jesus'. The verse from Acts says nothing about Jesus at all and, unless the
whole of the following paragraph is included, has no explicit missiology.

A third sentence, often cited as capturing the essence of the Church, is the
line which articulates the four marks of the church in the Nicene Creed:

> We believe in one, holy, catholic and apostolic church.

Notwithstanding Martyn Atkins's very helpful commentary on these four
elements (above pp. 25–6), this line remains a brilliant example of distilled
ecclesiology and, indeed of the simplicity that lies beyond complexity. *Mission-
shaped Church*, in my view, makes excellent use of these four marks in

189

connecting them to a directional metaphor: seeing the life of the Church in four spatial relationships. This directional language is particularly helpful in enabling pioneers to think through the different ways in which a community might grow to maturity:

- All expressions of church are drawn into a journey with an UP dimension – the journey towards God in worship, which must equally be about seeking God and becoming like God in holiness . . .

- The Church is led into a journey containing an IN dimension. It is a dimension of relationships, in order to express in practice the oneness of the Trinity and of the Body of Christ . . .

- The nature of the Church includes being sent onto the journey OUT. The sending in mission embraces the breadth of the five marks of mission. This journey on and out is fulfilment of our apostolic call . . .

- To be church we are called to walk on a journey which has an OF dimension. No one exists of themselves or by themselves . . . Both the Church militant and the Church triumphant are expressions of interdependence in the OF dimension as the Church seeks signs of being catholic.[2]

Finally, one of the most widely quoted and liberating contemporary examples of distilled ecclesiology is Rowan Williams's sentence from the preface to *Mission-shaped Church*:

> If 'church' is what happens when people encounter the Risen Jesus and commit themselves to sustaining and deepening that encounter in their encounter with each other, there is plenty of theological room for diversity of rhythm and style, so long as we have ways of identifying the same living Christ at the heart of every expression of Christian life in common.[3]

Like the earlier examples, the point of a statement like this is not that it claims to be complete but that it enables us to see more clearly what lies at the heart, the essence of being the Church of Christ. That perception in turn helps us to place other elements in a new perspective.

Descriptive ecclesiology: enriching our vision of the Church

If you are encouraging someone to visit or rediscover the wonder of a particular place, then you need to describe it in such a way that captures its particular essence. Other people's words can be immensely helpful. I love the city of Durham where I lived for 11 years but it's hard to beat Bill Bryson's words in terms of capturing its essence:

> I got off at Durham ... and fell in love with it instantly in a serious way. Why, it's wonderful – a perfect little city . . . If you have never been to Durham, go there at once. Take my car.[4]

However, once people have seen right to the heart of what's there, then more information is needed. The Durham tourist information web site would be no use at all if it simply consisted in short and inspiring phrases.

So, a more extended and descriptive ecclesiology is needed which ranges more widely over the different aspects and facets of the Church, which looks at the biblical material in more depth;[5] or which works systematically through the doctrine of the Church down the ages;[6] or which takes a particular doctrine or emphasis and works its implications through in the life of the Christian community.[7]

This kind of descriptive ecclesiology might be very focused and examine the jewel that is Christ's Church from one particular aspect. It may be at a high academic level. But it is also needed at a popular and accessible level, inspiring many ministers and members of the Church with the vision and scope and purpose of God's one, holy and apostolic people.[8]

In one sense, most of the chapters in this book are engaged in some kind of descriptive ecclesiology but, particularly, those by John Hull, Loveday Alexander, Alison Morgan and Martyn Atkins look at particular aspects of the life of the Church and describe them for us. This kind of endeavour is vital in all kinds of contexts today. Circuits and deaneries all across the country are engaged in producing mission action plans or engaging with the challenge of reduced resources in terms of full-time or stipendiary ministry. All too often such documents are produced and implemented with significant consequences for local church life and mission yet they contain no reference whatsoever to what the Church is or is called to be. We might as well be talking about maintaining factories or schools. Without a real attempt to think theologically about the nature of the Church any plan for the future is destined to evolve into a dead and deadly managerialism. In a time of change, we need to understand what it means to be the people of God in depth and in detail. This is primarily a theological task.

My own efforts to work at a descriptive ecclesiology attempts to do so under four headings. Each might be thought of as a separate range of mountains in the Lake District. Even when the headings have been filled out they need expanding and developing so that the details of the landscape are filled in:

1. The called community: the Church in relationship with God;

2. Members of one body: the Church in relation to herself;

3. A light to the nations: the Church in relation to God's world;

4. Pilgrims in progress: the Church in relation to time.[9]

This kind of descriptive ecclesiology will need also to engage with the biblical images of the Church. According to one study there are over 90 in the New Testament. On examination, they can all be seen to have something to say about Jesus Christ, something to say about fellowship and relationship with one another and something to say about mission to God's world. Like any summary of the essence of the Church, the different New Testament images need to be used together rather than in isolation. No single picture is complete in and of itself.[10]

The last heading in my own study – the Church in relation to time – highlights an aspect of describing the Church that is particularly important in balancing the rest. As Nicholas Healy has pointed out,[11] it becomes rather easy but actually quite dangerous to describe the Church in perfect terms as an ideal community (or even simply to paint a vision of what it should be in idealistic terms). This has been the overwhelming trend of recent Catholic and Protestant ecclesiology. The danger is that this idealized picture loses all points of connection with the reality of church as we experience it and therefore ceases to affect the way we are in practice. The risk is that we become either completely disillusioned with the community we are part of in relation to this ideal[12] or we may be so full of this idealized picture that as a Church we become arrogant in relationship to God's world. We need to hold together therefore the picture and vision of God's call to the Church with the actual experience of living in community, of engaging in mission and keep both in the perspective of the present time: we live in the period between the ministry, death and resurrection of Jesus and the end of time and Christ's return. In that period, the Church, like every other part of creation, is subject to every kind of failure and weakness, suffering and pain.

Healey calls ecclesiology back to this eschatological perspective and to working within what he describes as the 'theodramatic horizon' and away from a reliance on idealized perspectives. Such a horizon:

> provides the church with a framework within which it can

develop self-critical responses to the various challenges and opportunities of the present ecclesiological context.[13]

More colloquially, the Church can become so heavenly minded in terms of its own identity that it is no earthly use. Healey's framework, and Angela Tilby's similar emphasis on the need for reflecting on the Church as it is not as we would like it to be, form a bridge between this kind of thinking about church and the fifth section of the map explored below.

Discerning and defining ecclesiology: determining what is church and what is not

In periods of rapid change and pluralization, it has been necessary for a particular Christian community to set out clear definitions of what may or may not be legitimately described as a church and to discern accurately when a particular community meets them and can be recognized as such. Here inspiring phrases are not enough on their own and extensive descriptions give too much information.

Loveday Alexander describes the process of dialogue, trial and reflection by which the gospel was proclaimed to the gentiles as narrated by Luke in Acts 10–15. As part of that journey there are key moments of discernment when the apostles discern that what is taking place is a valid Christian community and can be recognized and authorized as such. One such moment occurs in Acts 11:

> Among them were some men of Cyprus and Cyrene who, on coming to Antioch, spoke to the Hellenists also, proclaiming the Lord Jesus. The hand of the Lord was with them, and a great number became believers and turned to the Lord. News of this came to the ears of the church in Jerusalem, and they sent Barnabas to Antioch. When he came and saw the grace of God, he rejoiced, and he exhorted them all to remain faithful to the Lord with steadfast devotion; for he was a good man, full of the Holy Spirit and of faith. And a great many people were brought to the Lord. Then Barnabas went to Tarsus to look for Saul, and when he had found him, he brought him to Antioch. So it was that for an entire year they met with the church and taught a great many people, and it was at Antioch that the disciples were first called Christians.
>
> (11.20-26)[14]

Note that Barnabas does not come to Antioch and apply a definition. He comes with open eyes and ears and sees the grace of God. What is happening in Antioch may not look a lot like what he knows church to be in Jerusalem. But Barnabas is able through that rare quality of goodness (he is the only church leader so described in Acts) to discern that this is indeed a work of God and a genuine Christian community. Discernment is a matter of the heart and of character as well as an intellectual exercise. By the end of the passage, Luke is able to describe the group in Antioch as he describes the group in Jerusalem: as church.

So any attempt at definition must be applied only as a tool in a discernment process as the Holy Spirit continues to create and do new things as both Dunn and Morgan argue in this volume. Nevertheless, a definition can be convenient shorthand for that process of discernment and such definitions have been vital at key moments of transition in Christian history.

Article XIX of the Thirty-Nine Articles remains the most relevant example for Anglican purposes:

> The visible Church of Christ is a congregation of faithful men, in which the pure word of God is preached and the Sacraments be duly ministered according to Christ's ordinance in all those things that of necessity are requisite to the same.

In the eighteenth century the Church of England applied its corporate discernment to whether the Methodist Societies were in fact to be recognized as church and (with hindsight) conspicuously lacked the wisdom and grace of Barnabas.

We are living in a similar time of transition and change where the challenge before us will be to recognize and discern new communities. Within the Church of England, the provision of the new Bishop's Mission Order in the Dioceses Mission and Pastoral Measure creates the possibility of legally recognizing new ecclesial communities alongside parishes. What theological criteria will be applied to determine how and when something might be called church? The Code of Practice to the Measure offers guidance, building on the four relationships and five values articulated by *Mission-shaped Church*[15] but this guidance will need to be applied by those who are well formed in their ecclesiology and with the capacity and goodness to discern what God is doing.

At a very local level also, one of the very helpful shifts which take forward the development of fresh expressions of church is the ability given to discern that something that began as an activity of the Church or an aspect of community service has become for those who are part of it, church and is to be seen and developed as such. Recognizing and discerning this multiplicity of smaller communities as church seems absolutely within the spirit of the New Testament, which is actually rather generous in its use of the term *ekklesia*.[16] It also involves a letting go of the old and persistent paradigm that the *real* Church is the assembly that meets on Sunday mornings for the parish Eucharist in a stone building with wooden pews, an organ and a robed cleric (male).

Derived ecclesiology: ministry, order and practice in church life

The remaining two areas on the sketch map focus on the more practical aspects of church life. First, how should the Christian Church order its life for its own well-being and flourishing and for the sake of its engagement in God's mission?

How should ministry and responsibility be ordered? Should there be recognized orders of ministry? How should they be selected, trained, deployed and supported? How should the Church administer its sacramental and preaching life? How should the Church administer a common purse? Should the community own property? How should it exercise discipline on those who depart from the teaching of the Church? How should a community order its own priorities and its demands on the life of its members?

This itself is a large area of reflection and study embracing church governance, ordained ministry, worship and sacramental life and mission. It focuses both on large questions of principle and vital matters of detail such as how many people should count the collection and how often there should be a central prayer meeting.

From the very beginning of its life, the Christian community has needed to wrestle with these questions. They are ecclesiological questions in that the answers to them are derived in different ways from the broader nature of the calling to be God's Church and God's mission. We are not just any human society. We have a particular call and particular values. In Acts 1 the early decision to replace Judas was so that the apostles would again number 12. This is not just to make an even number but is a theological statement about the relationship between Israel and the new community. The tensions in Acts 6 about the exercise of ministry are, at one level, about the structures and complexity of the community outgrowing its ideal of mutual care as presented in the earlier summary passages. Within the New Testament, the Corinthian correspondence and the Pastoral Epistles, in particular, address these concrete and practical questions by continually referring them back to the first principles of Christian community.

As we have seen, in a period of comparative stability for the Church where things are more or less seen to be 'working', these areas of ecclesiology are not particularly significant. Churches reach settled answers and develop due processes to all the normal, regular questions. The connections between (for example) the procedure for selecting Anglican or Methodist ministers and the New Testament principles about ministry become lost in the mists of time. However, in periods of rapid change and of seeking to establish new Christian communities, these questions again become vitally important.

One of the particularly demanding but also fulfilling tasks of pioneer ministry is helping a new church grapple with the detailed questions of how, for example, to reflect on its common finances and policy of giving money away. In that new situation it is little use to appeal to established custom and tradition: 'We have always done it this way in the circuit or diocese of Barchester.' It will become important to find and develop arguments from first principles – which is exactly the challenge Paul faces in 1 and 2 Corinthians. Alternatively, an existing Anglican church may accept the need to use the Lord's Prayer in public worship because it says so in the *Common Worship* rubric (or because the bishop says we must). A new community will need to go back to first principles and discover how and why that practice came about and why it remains a good and helpful common discipline. The resulting dialogue is a three-way one: between the new community, the primary values of the Christian community articulated in the Scriptures and the received tradition of the denomination or stream in which the new community is founded which may be challenged or reaffirmed as part of the process of dialogue. It is this dialogue which gives what some have helpfully called the Ancient-Future dynamic to conversations around practice in the emerging Church and fresh expressions of church: a desire to reach behind the present tradition to the values which give it life and meaning for today.[17]

As Angela Tilby points out, there are well-developed ecumenical documents, which have articulated common received wisdom on many of these matters and these will be an extremely helpful resource.[18] Lindsay Urwin's chapter is a powerful appeal for establishing good and appropriate sacramental practice on the basis of first principles and values, which I suspect will have significant impact within the fresh expressions movement. Graham Tomlin, Tim Dakin, John Drane and David Wilkinson all reflect in slightly different ways on the derived practice of the Church and, in so doing, appeal to particular values as a foundation for the practice they are advocating. If we are to develop mature communities effectively, both pioneers and permission givers will need to become adept at this style of reaching wise pastoral conclusions in dialogue with Scripture and the tradition.[19]

Developmental ecclesiology: contrasting the actual with the ideal

The final area of the map is closely related to the fourth but is rapidly becoming a whole new discipline of study. It is variously known as practical ecclesiology or congregational studies and is concerned with the in depth examination of the life of local churches often accompanied by the drawing of conclusions for their life and witness. As an emerging discipline, practical ecclesiology makes systematic use of the human sciences, particularly social anthropology, as tools to listen more deeply to local communities and discover what is actually happening and tests this against the rhetoric and espoused values of these communities.[20] As described above, this approach builds on the need identified by Nicholas Healy to deal with and reflect on the Church not as an abstract ideal but as a concrete reality.

This new discipline presents new possibilities and potential for the demanding enterprise of growing the life of new communities and may in the future better safeguard church leaders of all kinds against believing too readily their own rhetoric and somewhat rose tinted view of the communities they serve and lead.[21] Although the discipline itself is new the practice of contrasting the reality with the ideal goes back, of course, to 1 Corinthians which turns on exactly this dynamic.

In practical theology similar disciplines of study are emerging, which bring together the disciplines of the human sciences with the skills of theological reflection but which reflect on the evolving situation in society and apply the insights gained to Christian mission and the life of the churches.

Many of the essays in this book make a contribution to this kind of developmental ecclesiology but especially the chapters by John Drane, Lynda Barley and Martin Warner, all of which turn around a dialogue between what is observed in the Church and the broader culture and different aspects of the Christian tradition.

In a rapidly changing context, these disciplines come to the fore in terms of what is needed in the ordained whether they are primarily engaged with developing fresh expressions of church or refreshing and renewing existing communities.

The compass

Any kind of map is immensely useful as we enter the unexplored territory of the future. As we go forward, we will need the different discourses of

- distilled
- descriptive
- discerning/defining
- devolved and
- developmental

ecclesiology as we explore what it means to be the Church in a changing world.

However, I suspect that for many years to come there will still be a sense that we are, together, pioneering in terrain that is still unexplored. In this sense, it is true to say that it is the whole Church that is emerging from Christendom and modernity, not simply one section of it.

In this unexplored territory, a compass will be of even greater use than a very sketchy map of the terrain. From the Day of Pentecost, the Church itself has had a compass by which to measure its direction and on which to centre its life. The compass is and remains the person of Jesus Christ – the same yesterday, today and forever. The Church is his Body, his bride, his pilgrim people travelling home to his eternal hope and rest. In times of perplexity, anxiety and occasional despair, the one safe refuge and direction for the Christian Church is to follow and pattern our lives on Christ as our compass and to trust in his guidance towards a fruitful and hopeful future.

Until that moment comes, like the very first disciples, according to Mark, we are called to be with Jesus and to be sent out.

Notes

Introduction

1. Much of this practical wisdom is being distilled into Share: the online guide to fresh expressions: www.sharetheguide.org
2. Steven Croft (ed.), *The Future of the Parish System*, Church House Publishing, 2006.

Chapter 1   Fresh expressions in a mixed economy Church

1. *Breaking New Ground*, Church House Publishing 1994; *Mission-shaped Church*, Church House Publishing, 2004.
2. In this respect the working party are remarkable close to developing good practice in commercial and international leadership as exemplified in the book *Presence: Exploring profound change in people, organisations and society*, Peter Senge, C. Otto Scharmer, Joseph Jaworski and Betty Sue Flowers, Nicholas Brearley Publishing, 2005.
3. The report has not only been translated into German but has been widely commended and is forming the basis of strategy within the Evangelische Kirke Deutchland (despite the heading in the accompanying material: *Was kann aus England Gutes kommen?*): *Mission bringt Gemeinde in Form*, translated by Michael Herbst, Aussaat, 2006. The General Synod of the Church in Australia has also produced a parallel report and strategy: *Building the Mission Shaped Church in Australia*, General Synod Office of the Anglican Church in Australia, 2006. Fresh Expressions is currently dealing with serious lines of enquiry for help and information with the Church in Canada, Holland, France and New Zealand.
4. *Mission-shaped Church*, p. 34.
5. We have used this list of categories as a way of subdividing the Fresh Expressions directory on our own web site (with permission to tick as many as apply) but added two more: fresh expressions for children and fresh expressions for under fives and their families.
6. This process is well chronicled in respect of schemes for pastoral re-organization to enable mission by Nick Spencer in *Parochial Vision*, Paternoster, 2004, chapter 6.
7. *Mission-shaped Church*, p. vii.

8. Martyn has also recently published a book on the subject: *Resourcing Renewal: Shaping churches for the emerging future*, Inspire, 2007.
9. *Changing Church for a Changing World: Fresh ways of being church in a Methodist context*, The Methodist Church, 2007.
10. This is the Archbishop of Canterbury's phrase first used in the General Synod debates in February, 2004.
11. Full details of the Measure and the Code can be found through the Fresh Expressions web site and on the Church of England web site, General Synod Session, February 2007 group of sessions.
12. Again full details are on the Fresh Expressions web site and on the web site for the Church of England's ministry division of the Archbishops' Council.
13. St Paul's Theological Centre, Holy Trinity Brompton and the Westminster Theological Centre at St Mary's Bryanston Square.
14. See, for example, recent policy statements produced by the Dioceses of Canterbury and Liverpool or the policy developed by the Wolverhampton and Shrewsbury District.
15. The definition, printed above, was developed over a series of meetings by the Fresh Expressions core team in collaboration with representatives from the Church of England Mission and Public Affairs Division, the Methodist Church Evangelism and Church Planting Department, Church Army, Anglican Church Planting Initiatives, the Church Pastoral Aid Society and the Church Mission Society. Those consulted therefore included three members of the MSC working group (Graham Horsley, George Lings and Chris Neal) to ensure continuity with the group's work.
16. The best description of what it means to be incarnational I have found is in Michael Frost, *Exiles: Living missionally in a post-Christian culture*, Hendrickson, 2006, pp. 54ff.
17. One of the best ways to begin to understand fresh expressions of church is to watch one or both of the DVDs: *expressions: the dvd 1. Stories of church for a changing culture* (Church House Publishing, 2005) and *expressions: the dvd 2. changing church in every place* (Church House Publishing, 2006). Both are produced and directed by Norman Ivison. The examples given in this section draw one from each DVD.
18. See also Lucy Moore, *Messy Church*, Bible Reading Fellowship, 2005.
19. *Mission-shaped Church*, p. 34.
20. David Bosch, *Transforming Mission: Paradigm shifts in theology of mission*, Orbis, 1991.
21. The two most read texts are *Missionary Methods: St Paul's or ours?* (1912) and *The Spontaneous Expansion of the Church: And the causes which hinder it* (1927).
22. The relationship between these two terms and streams is an interesting subject in itself and is addressed in part by John Drane at the beginning of his chapter.

23. Vincent Donovan, *Christianity Rediscovered*, Fides/Claretian, 1978 and SCM Press, 1982, 2001. The impact of Allen on Donovan's thinking is described in chapter 3.
24. See for example, *The Household of God*, SCM Press, 1953, reprinted 1998; *The Gospel to the Greeks*, SPCK, 1986 and the recent *Lesslie Newbigin, Missionary Theologian: A reader*, ed. Paul Weston, SPCK, 2006.
25. John V. Taylor, *The Go-Between God*, SCM Press, 2002, reprinted 2004; The *Christlike God*, SCM Press, 1992, reprinted 2004. I am indebted to Canon Tim Dakin, current General Secretary of CMS, for pointing out that the core of the ideas in *Mission-shaped Church* are contained in chapter 7 of *The Go-Between God*: 'The Evangelical Spirit and the Structures of Mission'. I am told it was also Taylor who coined the phrase 'Mission is finding out what God is doing and joining in' but I have not been able to discover the reference.

Chapter 2   What is the essence of the Church?

1. Some parts of this essay are reproduced in Martyn Atkins, *Resourcing Renewal: Shaping churches for the emerging future*, Inspire, 2007.
2. P. T. Forsyth, 'Revelation, Old and New', a sermon delivered under the auspices of the Guilds of St Cuthbert's Parish Church, Edinburgh, 1911.
3. David J. Bosch, *Transforming Mission: Paradigm shifts in theology of mission*, Orbis, 1991, p. 390.
4. Paul R. Stevens, *The Abolition of the Laity: Vocation, work and ministry in a biblical perspective*, Paternoster Press, 1999, p. 6.
5. Cited by Rui Josgrilberg, 'The Holy Spirit and the Spirit of Globalization', a paper read at the Eleventh Oxford Institute of Methodist Theological Studies, Oxford, August 2002.
6. Cited by Robert Warren, *Building Missionary Congregations*, Church House Publishing, 1995, p. 31.
7. Lesslie Newbigin, *The Household of God: Lectures on the nature of the Church*, SCM Press, 1953, p. 143.
8. See Bosch, *Transforming Mission*, pp. 389ff.
9. Lesslie Newbigin's missional ecclesiology is found in many places in his own work, particularly *The Gospel in a Pluralist Society*, SPCK, 1989. Useful summaries can be found in many places, but particularly by writers of the North American 'The Gospel and our Culture' Network, e.g., see George Hunsberger's, *Bearing the Witness of the Spirit*, Eerdmans, 1998.
10. A constant theme in Moltmann's work, supremely in *Theology of Hope*, SCM Press, new ed., 2002; but significantly also in *The Crucified God*, SCM Press, new edition, 2001, *The Church in the Power of the Spirit*, SCM Press, revised ed., 1992. More recently, see *The Spirit of Life*, SCM Press, 1992 and *The Coming of God*, SCM Press, 1996. Tim Chester's recently published *Mission and the*

Coming of God: Eschatology, the Trinity and mission in the theology of Jürgen Moltmann, Paternoster, 2006 is an excellent overview.

11. See Dan Beeby, *Canon and Mission*, Trinity Press International, 1999, for a good overview.

12. See *After our Likeness: Church as the image of the Trinity*, Eerdmans, 1998, and *God's Life in Trinity*, Augsburg Fortress, 2006.

13. This is a theme found in the work of Dietrich Bonhoeffer in several places. For a more contemporary account of some of the issues, see Nicholas Healy, *Church, World and the Christian Life: Practical-prophetic ecclesiology*, Cambridge University Press, 2000.

14. See, for example, Leonardo Boff's apologetic for a reinvention of church in *Ecclesiogenesis*, Collins, 1986.

15. See Paul Minear, *Images of the Church in the New Testament*, James Clarke, 2007 (originally published in 1961).

16. *Decoding the Church*, Baker Books, 2002, pp. 22ff.

17. *Mission-shaped Church*, Church House Publishing, 2004, p. 99.

Chapter 3   What is the role of sacramental ministry in fresh expressions of church?

1. Evelyn Underhill, *Worship*, Nisbett, 1936, p. 68.

2. Augustine, *In Jo. ev.* 80, 3 PL 35, 1840.

3. Newman, *Parochial and Plain Sermons*, Vol. VI, Sermon 17.

4. Ephraem, Sermon 3, 2.4–5.

5. *The Book of Common Prayer*, Introduction to the Ordinal.

6. The question of novelty is complex in the developing life of the Church. But an example of novelty as opposed to renewal might be the use of other elements in the Eucharist, say cookies and coke when bread and wine are available as a means of 'relating' to the particular culture. Another might be the use of a lay person to preside at the table in a lay led youth congregation, because of a misguided idea that to introduce a priest would be an 'intrusion'.

7. Danny Baker in *Christian Herald*, March 2005.

Chapter 4   What is at the heart of a global perspective on the Church?

1. See Frances Young and David Ford, *Meaning and Truth in 2 Corinthians*, SPCK, 1989, for an exploration of the economy-of-overflow in the love of God.

2. Though I presume a Trinitarian basis for mission spirituality, and its outworking in what has come to be known as communion ecclesiology, I shall not outline this perspective and its variety of interpreters. See Dennis Doyle: *Communion Ecclesiology: Visions and versions*, Orbis, 2000, chapter 10. A communion ecclesiology includes in its approach an understanding of church marks, dimensions and aspects as found in the history of the Church's development.

What I'm proposing is a communion-in-mission-ecclesiology rooted in God's mission in the world and expressed in various shapes of the Church.

3. This alternative adjective to 'missionary' is now being widely used. See Christopher Wright, *The Mission of God: Unlocking the Bible's grand narrative*, InterVarsity Press, 2006, p. 24.

4. Relying on Philip Sheldrake and others I suggest that spirituality is a (missional) combination of a scriptural-theological vision, a prayerful relationship with God and a practical way of life. On evangelical spirituality and mission see Ian Randall: *What a Friend we have in Jesus*, Darton, Longman & Todd, 2005, especially chapter 9.

5. Stephen B. Bevans and Roger P. Schroeder, *Constants in Context*, Orbis, 2004, p. 13.

6. *Constants in Context*, chapter 1.

7. See Mark Chapman, *Anglicanism: A very short introduction*, Oxford University Press, 2006; T. Yates, 'Anglicans and Mission' in S. Sykes, J. Booty and J. Knight (eds), *The Study of Anglicanism*, SPCK, 1998, pp. 483–97.

8. Andrew Porter, *Religion Versus Empire*, Manchester University Press, 1996, p. 50.

9. See Waldron Scott's monograph: *Karl Barth's Theology of Mission*, InterVarsity Press, 1978, pp. 22f. Barth was criticizing the lack of a goal beyond the Church in the three Reformation marks of Church: the true preaching of the word, the right celebration of the sacraments and the exercise of church discipline.

10. David Runcorn, *Spirituality Workbook*, SPCK, 2006, p. 18 *my emphasis*.

11. After a while, the mission societies generated their own 'church problem'! See Peter Beyerhaus and Henry Lefever: *The Responsible Church and the Foreign Mission*, World Dominion Press, 1964.

12. Andrew Walls, *The Cross-Cultural Process in Human History*, Orbis, 2002, p. 78.

13. Roland Allen, *Missionary Principles – and Practice*, Lutterworth, 1913/2006, p. 51.

14. This kind of approach to mission and truth contrasts with that of Islam. See Taylor's comments on the theology of power later in *The Go-Between God*, SCM Press, 1972, pp.188f.

15. *The Go-Between God*, p. 115.

16. Samuel Escobar's comment on the changing nature of the global Church is pertinent, representing a tri-continental 'insurgent' Southern perspective: 'Precisely at the point in which the influence of Christianity declines in the West the new global order has brought the so-called Third World into the heart of North America and Europe' (*The New Global Mission*, InterVarsity Press, 2003, p. 18).

17. Max Warren, *The Calling of God*, Lutterworth, 1945, p. 63.

18. *The Go-Between God*, p. 151, *my emphasis*.

19. David Cunningham, 'The Trinity', in Kevin Vanhoozer (ed.), *The Cambridge Companion to Postmodern Theology*, Cambridge University Press, 2003, p. 16.

20. See Adrio Konig, *The Eclipse of Christ in Eschatology*, Eerdmans, 1989, chapter 2.
21. See N. T. Wright: *New Heavens, New Earth*, Grove Biblical Series, No.11, 1999, for a biblical basis.
22. See Andrew Wheeler's extraordinary testimony in his book *Bombs, Ruins and Honey: Journeys of the Spirit with Sudanese Christians*, St Paul's, 2006.
23. Peter Heslam, *Globalization: Unravelling the new capitalism*, Grove Books, 2002, p. 13.
24. Andrew Walls, 'Evangelical and Ecumenical: The Rise and Fall of the Early Church Model', in J. R. Krabill et al. (eds), *Evangelical, Ecumenical and Anabaptist Missiologists in Conversation*, Orbis, 2006, pp. 36f.

Chapter 5 Is there evidence for fresh expressions of church in the New Testament?

1. As in N. T. Wright, *Jesus and the Victory of* God, SPCK, 1996.
2. Eduard Schweizer in G. Kittel (ed.), *Theological Dictionary of the New Testament*, Eerdmans, 1968, Vol. 6, p. 396.

Chapter 6 Can we develop churches that can transform the culture?

1. http://www.youtube.com/watch?v=30SuZayHS2k
2. Richard H. Niebuhr, *Christ and Culture*, Harper Collins, 1975.
3. John Howard Yoder, *Authentic Transformation: A new vision of Christ and culture*, Abingdon, 1996.
4. Stanley Hauerwas, *A Community of Character: Toward a constructive Christian social ethic*, University of Notre Dame Press, 1981, p. 74.
5. John Gray, *Heresies Against Progress and Other Illusions*, Granta, 2004, p. 44.
6. Hauerwas, *Community of Character*, p. 49.
7. *Community of Character*, p. 3.
8. Stanley Hauerwas, *Vision and Virtue: Essays in Christian ethical reflection*, University of Notre Dame Press, 1981, p. 7.
9. *Vision and Virtue*, p. 13.
10. Dallas Willard, *Renovation of the Heart: Putting on the character of Christ*, NavPress, 2002, p. 21.
11. See Graham Tomlin, *Spiritual Fitness: Christian character in a consumer culture*, Continuum, 2006, for a development of this metaphor.
12. Dallas Willard, *The Spirit of the Disciplines: Understanding how God changes lives*, Hodder & Stoughton 1988, p. 87.
13. Leaders of Fresh Expressions might need to take especial note of this: it is easy to adopt a culture of superiority over more traditional forms of church that is critical and condescending, and which in turn breeds a spirit of criticism and condescension. Such attitudes normally come home to roost one day!

Chapter 7   What questions does Catholic ecclesiology pose for contemporary mission and fresh expressions of church?

1.   Clement of Rome, *Epistle to the Corinthians*, XL111.4.
2.   Irenaeus, *Against All Heresies*, III.1
3.   *Mission-shaped Church*, Church House Publishing, 2004, p. 100. Also *Draft Code of Practice to the Dioceses*, Pastoral and Mission Measure 4.3.4, p. 34.
4.   ARCIC Agreed Statement on Eucharistic Doctrine (Windsor, 1971) and subsequent elucidations.
5.   *Baptism, Eucharist and Ministry*, WCC Faith and Order paper no 111, the 'Lima Text', 1982.
6.   E. R. Dodds, *Pagan and Christian in an Age of Anxiety*, Cambridge University Press, 1965.
7.   My grateful thanks go to the Revd Jamie Hawkey, The Revd David Neaum, the Revd Vicky Johnson and the Revd Dr Michael Beasley from Westcott House, and also to James Hill from Ridley Hall and the Revd Vanessa Herrick, all of whom have offered helpful comments and suggestions.

Chapter 8   What does maturity in the emerging Church look like?

1.   For some Americans who are experimenting with new forms of church within a generally fundamentalist-evangelical context, 'emergent' seems to be preferred as a way of distancing themselves from the use of the term 'emerging Christianity' (not 'church') by more radical scholars such as Marcus Borg, to describe 'a "neotraditional" form of Christianity ... a "seeing again" of the most central elements of the Christian tradition.' Cf. Borg's, *Jesus: Uncovering the life, teachings, and relevance of a religious revolutionary*, HarperSanFrancisco, 2006, pp. 298–9. Others who are operating in a more global – and theologically diverse – context often wish to distance themselves from 'emergent' because it has become a commercial brand in the USA, and use of the term 'emerging' is a way of establishing a distinctive identity.
2.   For a more extensive discussion of this taxonomy, see John Drane, 'Editorial', in *International Journal for the Study of the Christian Church* 6/1 (2006), pp. 3–11. On the emerging Church more generally, Eddie Gibbs and Ryan K. Bolger, *Emerging Churches*, Baker Academic, 2005, offer a good overview, though with a tendency to impose a homogeneity on the emerging Church that goes beyond the evidence. The somewhat intemperate critique by D. A. Carson, *Becoming Conversant with the Emerging Church*, Zondervan, 2005, fails to recognize any diversity within the movement and as a consequence includes some who would not be part of the emerging Church by any definition adopted here (e.g. British Baptist Steve Chalke), while limiting the discussion to only one very narrow strand, predominantly that represented by the writings of Brian McLaren. Given the grass-roots nature of the movement, it is a fundamental mistake to try and understand it only by reference to those who publish books on the theme, as if

they were necessarily representative of the bigger picture, which is why the research of Gibbs and Bolger is a more reliable guide, as it is based on ethnographic study of specific local manifestations of emerging church.

3. Alan Jamieson, *A Churchless Faith*, SPCK, 2002; Alan Jamieson, Jenny McIntosh and Adrienne Thompson, *Church Leavers*, SPCK, 2006; Steve Taylor, 'A New Way of Being Church', University of Otago, PhD thesis 2005.

4. Dave Tomlinson, *The Post-Evangelical*, Triangle, 1995. It must be significant that this was republished in an expanded form as part of Zondervan's *emergent ys* series, aimed at the emerging Church market: Dave Tomlinson, *The Post-Evangelical*, revised North American edition, Zondervan, 2003. For a more personal account of much the same story, see Gordon Lynch, *Losing My Religion?*, Darton, Longman & Todd, 2003.

5. The reference only to Western nations is intentional: the rise of the emerging Church as defined here is largely a Western phenomenon – depending on one's perspective, either a product of or a response to the pervasive influence of post-modernity. It could plausibly be argued that indigenous churches such as those that are mushrooming in Africa ought also to be included in the 'emerging' spectrum, for they are indeed non-traditional in relation to the inherited patterns. But to include them here would be a diversion from the main purpose of this volume.

6. In some respects, this description could also apply to what is generally called 'altworship' ('alternative worship'), though that is not automatically the same thing as emerging church. There is a need for further discussion to tease out the similarities and differences between these two movements within the mainline Church, but this is not the place for it.

7. Typified in the sort of developmental patterns implied by Erik H. Erikson's 'eight ages of man', cf. his *Childhood and Society* 2nd ed., Norton, 1950.

8. Cf. Ray S. Anderson, *The Shape of Practical Theology*, InterVarsity Press, 2001, pp. 102–12, where he asks 'which century is normative for our theology?', and goes on to argue that in any authentically biblical theology there must always be an 'eschatological preference' looking to the future. Cf. also Anderson's essay, 'The Praxis of the Spirit as Liberation for Ministry', in *The Soul of Ministry*, Westminster John Knox Press, 1997.

9. See Richard Florida, *The Rise of the Creative Class*, Basic Books, 2002; *Cities and the Creative Class*, Routledge, 2004.

10. Paul H. Ray and Sherry Ruth Anderson, *The Cultural Creatives*, Three Rivers Press, 2000, p. 44.

11. The precise terminology may be less important than the reality that it represents: that growing numbers of people are moving beyond the McDonaldized systems we have inherited, and are seeking new ways to reinvent institutions of all sorts, from the bottom up. For more on this, see my forthcoming book *After McDonaldization*, Darton, Longman & Todd, 2008.

12. For a theologically well-grounded account of this mindset in relation to the emerging Church and the Bible, see Ray S. Anderson, *An Emergent Theology for Emerging Churches*, InterVarsity Press, 2006.

13. *The Truman Show*, directed by Peter Weir, written by Andrew Niccol, starring Jim Carrey as Truman Burbank, Laura Linney as Meryl, Ed Harris as Christof, Noah Emmerich as Marlon. Released by Paramount Pictures, 1998. For more reflection on this film, see John Drane, *Cultural Change and Biblical Faith*, Paternoster, 2000, pp. 154–73.

14. Cf. Donald E. Meek, *The Quest for Celtic Christianity*, Handsel Press. 2000; Ian Bradley, *Celtic Christianity: Making myths and chasing dreams*, Edinburgh University Press, 1999.

15. And which continues to be advocated by Stanley Hauerwas, a scholar who (surprisingly) is highly regarded in certain sections of the emerging church. For a classic statement of this position, see Stanley Hauerwas and William H. Willimon, *Resident Aliens*, Abingdon, 1989.

16. David J. Bosch, *Transforming Mission*, Orbis, 1991, pp. 389–93.

17. A good example of this would be *The Tribe* of Los Angeles, an emerging church that is recognized as a regular parish within the National Association of Congregational Christian Churches of the USA. Its regular meetings take place in the Subud Center in downtown Los Angeles (Subud is a worldwide spiritual movement with roots in Indonesia), and *The Tribe* has also become a significant spiritual component of the Burning Man Festival, an annual event that takes places in the Nevada Desert, combining Bacchanalian elements with spiritual search. See www.tribeofla.com and, on *The Tribe* and Burning Man, James G. Gilmore, 'Divine Appointments: patterns of engagement between burning man and emerging churches', Fuller Seminary Dissertation, 2006 – available at: http://emergingchurch.info/research/jimgilmore/gilmore_divine_appointments.pdf

18. http://www.sanctus1.co.uk/whoweare.php

19. Richard H. Niebuhr, *Christ and Culture*, HarperSanFrancisco, 2001, originally published 1951. For a critical analysis of this approach, see Craig A. Carter, *Rethinking Christ and Culture: A post-Christendom perspective*, Brazos Press, 2006.

20. Cf. George Ritzer, *McDonaldization: The reader*, 2nd ed., Pine Forge Press, 2006.

21. Cf. John Drane, *The McDonaldization of the Church*, Darton, Longman & Todd, 2000.

22. The classic study of our growing individuality and its consequences is Robert D. Putnam, *Bowling Alone*, Simon & Schuster, 2000. See also Ethan Watters, *Urban Tribes*, Bloomsbury, 2003.

23. For introductory treatments of emergence theory, see John H. Holland, *Emergence: From chaos to order*, Oxford University Press, 2000; Steven

Johnson, *Emergence: The connected lives of ants, brains, cities, and software*, Penguin, 2001; Richard Pascale, Mark Millemann and Linda Gioja, *Surfing the Edge of Chaos*, Random House, 2001.

24. Daniel H. Pink, *A Whole New Mind*, Riverhead Books, 2006, p. 1.
25. William J. Bausch, *Storytelling, Imagination and Faith*, Twenty-Third Publications, 1984, p. 28.
26. For more on this, see John Drane, 'From Creeds to Burgers: religious control, spiritual search, and the future of the world', in James R Beckford and John Walliss, *Theorising Religion*, Ashgate, 2006, pp. 120–31. Also in abridged form in George Ritzer, *McDonaldization: The reader*, 2nd ed., Pine Forge Press, 2006, pp. 197–202.
27. It has become fashionable in some circles to hold up the Anabaptist tradition as a form of Christianity that is somehow untainted by Christendom. There are certainly connections between some aspects of the emerging Church and Anabaptist principles, and there is no doubt that this tradition is offering fresh insights into the nature of Christian community that are being welcomed in many circles. But to imagine that this therefore represents a pristine model of church that comes without any of the baggage of the past requires some rewriting of history. Anabaptists – and the Free Churches more generally – rejected the coercive aspects of Christendom, but still operated on the underlying Constantinian notion of a culture that would be directed and owned by Christians.
28. In this respect, emerging Church has some interesting similarities with base Christian communities.
29. *The Tribe* of Los Angeles, mentioned earlier, is one of only a handful of emerging churches that I have come across that are led by women (and in that particular case, a woman who does not fit the other stereotype of emerging church people always being in their twenties or thirties).
30. Cf. Robert E. Webber, *Ancient-Future Faith*, Baker Academic, 1999; *Ancient-Future Evangelism*, Baker Academic, 2003; *Ancient-Future Time*, Baker Academic, 2004.
31. Gert Rüppell, *Ecumenical Letter on Evangelism*, World Council of Churches, December 1995, p. 6.

Chapter 9 What are the lessons from evangelism and apologetics for new communities?

1. A. Kirk, *What is Mission?*, Darton, Longman & Todd, London, 2002, p. 61.
2. V. Roberts, 'Getting the Message Out', in *Guarding the Gospel*, ed. C. Green, Zondervan, 2006, pp. 143–50.
3. B. Stone, *Evangelism After Christendom*, Brazos, 2007; J. A. Kirk, *Mission under scrutiny: Confronting contemporary challenges*, Fortress, 2006; G. G. Hunter, *Radical Outreach: The recovery of apostolic ministry and evangelism*,

Abingdon, 2003; S. Croft, R. Frost, M. Ireland, A. Richards, Y. Richmond and N. Spencer, *Evangelism in a Spiritual Age*, Church House Publishing, 2006.

4. D. Wilkinson, 'The Art of Apologetics in the Twenty-first Century', *Anvil*, 2002, 19, pp. 5–17; J. G. Stackhouse, *Humble Apologetics: Defending the Faith today*, Oxford University Press, 2002.

5. A. McGrath, *Bridge-Building: Effective Christian apologetics*, InterVarsity Press, 2002, p. 9.

6. W. R. Shenk, 'Contemporary Europe in Missiological Perspective', *Missiology: An International Review*, 2007, XXXV, p. 135.

7. R. Frost, 'The Future of Evangelism', *Epworth Review*, 2007, 34, p. 54.

8. A. Outler, *Evangelism in the Wesleyan Spirit*, Tidings, 1971, p. 19.

9. K. C. Dean, *Practicing Passion: Youth and the quest for a passionate Church*, Eerdmans, 2006.

10. J. W. Drane, *Do Christians Know how to be Spiritual?: The rise of new spirituality and the mission of the Church*, Darton, Longman & Todd, 2005.

11. M. Booker and M. Ireland, *Evangelism – which way now?*, Church House Publishing, 2005.

12. For example, T. Cawkwell, *The Filmgoer's Guide to God*, Darton, Longman & Todd, 2004; P. Plyming, *Harry Potter and the Meaning of Life: Engaging with spirituality in Christian mission*, Grove Books, 2001; W. D. Romanowski, *Eyes Wide Open: Looking for God in popular culture*, Brazos Press, 2001; D. Wilkinson, *The Power of the Force: The spirituality of the Star Wars films*, Lion, 2000.

13. R. Beckford, *Jesus Dub – Theology, Music and Social Change*, Routledge, 2006; G. Lynch, *Understanding Theology and Popular Culture*, Blackwell, 2005; C. Oswalt, *Secular Steeples: Popular culture and the religious imagination*, Trinity Press International, 2003; C. Detweiler, and B. Taylor, *A Matrix of Meanings: Finding God in popular culture*, Baker Academic, 2003; R. K. Johnstone, *Reel Spirituality: Theology and film in dialogue*, Baker Academic, 2001.

14. R. F. Lovelace, *Dynamics of Spiritual Life*, InterVarsity Press, 1979, p. 126.

15. G. Cray, 'Focusing church life on a theology of mission', in *The Future of the Parish System* ed. S. Croft, Church House Publishing, 2006, p. 62.

16. D. Alexander, 'Is Intelligent Design Biblical?', 2006. http://www.cis.org.uk/ resources/articles/article_archive/EN_IDarticle.pdf

17. A. Lovas, 'Mission Shaped Liturgy', *International Review of Mission*, 2006, 95, pp. 352–8.

18. M. J. Quicke, 'Prophetic Preaching for a Missional Church', in *Text and Task: Scripture and mission*, ed. M. Parsons, Paternoster, 2005, pp. 218–33.

19. J. Moltmann, 'The Resurrection of Christ: Hope for the World', in *Resurrection Reconsidered*, ed. G. D'Costa, Oneworld, 1996, p. 73.

20. L. Newbigin, *The Gospel in a Pluralist Society*, Eerdmans, 1989, p. 227.

21. *Mission-shaped Church*, Church House Publishing, 2004, p. 20.

22. R. Allen, *The Spontaneous Expansion of the Church: And the causes which hinder it*, Lutterworth Press, 2006.
23. J. Hull, *Mission-shaped Church: A theological response*, SCM Press, 2006.
24. M. Arias, 'Global and Local: A Critical View of Mission Models', in *Global Good News: Mission in a new context*, ed. H. A. Synder, Abingdon, 2001, p. 64.
25. J. Edwards, *Some Thoughts Concerning the Present Revival in New England and the Way It Ought to Be Acknowledged and Promoted*, Diggory Press, 2006.
26. G. Lings, 'Fresh Expressions growing to maturity', in *The Future of the Parish System* ed. S. Croft, p. 145.
27. J. Verkuyl, *Contemporary Missiology*, Eerdmans, 1978, p. 184.

Chapter 10 Mission–shaped and kingdom focused?

1. John M. Hull, *Mission Shaped Church: A theological response*, SCM Press, 2006.
2. Ken, Gnanakan, *Kingdom Concerns: A biblical theology of mission today*, InterVarsity Press, 1993, p. 208. Gnanakan rightly emphasises that 'A righteous vertical relationship is demonstrated in righteous horizontal relationships' (p. 92), but he continues 'Reconciliation must begin with the vertical dimension, with people made right with God' (p. 147), thus indicating his failure to grasp the radical nature of horizontal transcendence. Gnanakan's source for this distinction is Visser't Hooft, 'The Mandate of the Ecumenical Movement', Stockholm, 1925 reprinted in Normal Goodall (ed.), *The Uppsala Report 1968*, pp. 313–23.
3. Willem Visser't Hooft, *The Uppsala Report*, was seeking for the right balance between the two dimensions when he said 'The whole secret of the Christian faith is that it is man-centred [*sic*] because it is God-centred. We cannot speak of Christ as the man for others without speaking of him as the man who came from God and who lived for God' (p. 318), but Jesus Christ was a man, a human person and in that person we see God. Thus the whole secret of Christian faith is that it is God-centred because it is person-centred.
4. The Message.
5. G. W. H. Lampe *A Patristic Greek Lexicon*, Clarendon, 1961 refers to Athanasius using the word *homoios* to assert the likeness of the humanity of Christ to that of general humanity (p. 954) and also points out that the use of the word was attacked on the grounds that the 'distinction between Father and Son is thereby abolished' and that as late as the first century one word was being used to explain the other.
6. Note that the word *homoousion* is not listed in Liddell and Scott – Stuart Jones and Robert McKenzie (eds), *A Greek-English Lexicon*, Clarendon, 1968.
7. Liddell and Scott indicate that *Homoios* meant having the same rank or station and refers to Plotinus in the third century AD using the word to describe angles which were equal. It is also used in mathematics to describe the square of a

number as being the product of two equal factors. Stuart Jones and Robert McKenzie (eds), *A Greek-English Lexicon*, p. 1224.

8. Karl Barth has an extensive discussion of the meaning of the two great commandments in his *Church Dogmatics*, volume 1, part 2, T&t T Clark, 1956, pp. 381–454. Although a quick reading might suggest that my interpretation is more radical than that of Barth, a careful study of these pages shows that Barth rejects the idea that the vertical is completely collapsed into the horizontal mainly because 'We cannot believe in our neighbour' and thus it would be misleading 'to confuse or confound the two demands' (p. 413). Moreover, Barth's eschatological interpretation means that love of the neighbour takes place in this world whereas love of God is eternal. However, love of the neighbour is 'the inevitable outward side of that which inwardly is love to God' (p. 412) and 'we cannot love God without this loving, as it were, manifesting itself' (p. 413). In this comment 'this love' refers to love of the neighbour. This is quite consistent with my own comment 'the vertical has no independent existence as far as human beings are concerned' i.e., as far as our lives in this world are to be lived.

9. José P. Miranda, *Marx and the Bible: A critique of the philosophy of oppression*, SCM Press, 1977, pp. 36–44.

10. Walter Brueggemann, *Theology of the Old Testament*, Fortress, 1997, p. 25: 'From its beginning, Israel's covenant was a political theory of justice.' Brueggemann is quoting with approval the work of George Mendenhall.

11. In the 1928 revision of the Prayer Book the words were still omitted but in *The Alternative Service Book* (1980) there is an alternative which places the words 'who brought you out of the land of Egypt, out of the house of bondage' in brackets, a feature which is also found in *Common Worship*, p. 250. The effect of this is to minimise the role of the liberating God and to emphasize God as the general law-giver.

12. Brueggemann, *Theology of the Old Testament*, p. 30

13. Brueggemann, *Theology of the Old Testament*, p. 613.

14. Emmanuel Levinas, *Of God Who Comes to Mind*, Stanford University Press, 1998, p. xiv.

15. Levinas, *Of God Who Comes to Mind*, p. xv.

16. Levinas, *Of God Who Comes to Mind*, p. 13.

17. *Of God Who Comes to Mind*, p. 72.

18. John MacMurray, *The Search for Reality in Religion*, Friends Home Service Committee, 1965, p. 72.

19. C. B. Macpherson, *The Political Theory of Possessive Individualism*, Oxford University Press, 1964.

20. Levinas, *Of God Who Comes to Mind*, p. 73.

21. *Of God Who Comes to Mind*, p. 77.

22. *Of God Who Comes to Mind*, p. 105.

23. Ernst Bloch, *The Principle of Hope*, Blackwell, 1986, Vol. I, pp. 290–300.
24. Emmanuel Levinas, *Totality and Infinity: An essay on exteriority*, Duquesne, 1969, pp. 68f.
25. Levinas, *Totality*, pp. 254–5, 270–3. On the other hand, Levinas also speaks of 'The imperitive of gratuitous love which comes to me from the face of another', *God Who Comes to Mind*, preface.
26. In my studies of the theology of Isaac Watts (1674–1748) I have shown how the British congregations of the early eighteenth century turned away from the mission of God for justice and peace and concentrated upon the adoration of their own religious belief structure. See John M. Hull, 'From Experiential Educator to Nationalist Theologian; the Hymns of Isaac Watts', *Panorama: International Journal of Comparative Religious Education and Values*, Vol. 14, No. 1, Summer 2002, pp. 91–106; 'Isaac Watts and the Origins of British Imperial Theology', *International Congregational Journal*, Vol. 4, No. 2, February 2005, pp. 59–79.
27. Ana-Maria Rizzuto, *The Birth of the Living God: A psychoanalytic study*, University of Chicago Press, 1979; John McDargh, *Psychoanalytic Object Relations Theory and the Study of Religion: On faith and the imaging of God*, University Press of America, 1983.

Chapter 11   What patterns of church and mission are found in the Acts of the Apostles?

1. Roland Allen, *Selected Writings*, ed. David Paton, World Dominion Press, 1960, p. 98; cf. p. xvi: 'For thirty years he pleaded that the Church (overseas) be placed on its own feet, that is, for an indigenous Christianity. This, he held, could not be imposed from the outside, for an indigenous Church is not simply a Church that is master in its own house, but a Church that had the gift of the Holy Spirit and knew what this gift meant for its own life.'
2. For more details on this, see C. K. Barrett's well-moderated conclusion in the Introduction to Vol. 2 of his *International Critical Commentary on the Acts of the Apostles*, T&T Clark, 1998 or Ben Witherington III, *Acts: A socio-rhetorical commentary*, Eerdmans, 1998.
3. Cf., for example, Richard Bauckham, 'James and the Jerusalem Church', in Richard Bauckham (ed.), *The Book of Acts in its First Century Setting 4: Palestinian setting*, Paternoster/Eerdmans, 1995, pp. 415–80.
4. A point made persuasively by Luke T. Johnson, *Scripture and Discernment: Decision making in the Early Church*, Abingdon, 1996, chapter 4.
5. I have argued this point at greater length in the introduction to my *Acts: The People's Bible Commentary*, Bible Reading Fellowship, 2006, and more fully in my *Acts: Black's New Testament Commentaries*, Continuum, forthcoming. My own view is that Acts is an apologetic narrative addressed to Jews, a last-ditch attempt to win over the heart and soul of Diaspora Judaism in the spiritual

power vacuum created by the disastrous failure of the revolt against Rome in 66–70. It's effectively Luke's answer to the question put (with remarkable equanimity) to Paul, by the leaders of the Jewish community in Rome, in 28.22: 'Tell us about this sect.'

6. Hubert Allen, *Roland Allen: Pioneer, priest, and prophet*, Forward Movement, 1995, pp. 95, 92.

7. Allen, *Selected Writings*, p. 90; Hubert Allen, *Roland Allen*, p. 94.

8. Thomas Hastings, 'Unity and Diversity in the "One Body of Christ": Rethinking the Church's Missional and Ecumenical Vocation', in *KIATS Theological Journal* (*Journal of the Korea Institute for Advanced Theological Studies*) 1/1, 2005, pp. 23–38 (esp. p. 35 n. 27).

9. Justo L. Gonzalez, *The Changing Shape of Church History*, Chalice Press, 2002, chapter 1.

10. Hastings, 'Unity and Diversity', p. 37, citing Andrew Walls, *The Missionary Movement in Christian History*, Orbis, 1996, pp. xix, 260.

11. Pete Ward, *Liquid Church*, Paternoster, 2002.

12. Gonzalez, *Changing Shape*, pp. 69–70.

13. I associate this memorable phrase with Charles Williams, *The Descent of the Dove*, Fontana Library, 1963, but cannot now trace the reference.

14. James Alison, *Undergoing God: Dispatches from the scene of a break-in*, Darton, Longman & Todd, 2006, pp.169–73.

15. Justo L. Gonzalez, *Acts: The Gospel of the Spirit*, Orbis, 2001; Beverley Gaventa, *Acts*, Abingdon, 2003; Loveday Alexander, *Acts: The People's Bible*, 2006. Good studies also in Anthony B. Robinson and Robert W. Wall, *Called to be Church: The Book of Acts for a new day*, Eerdmans, 2006, chapters 9, 10; Johnson, *Scripture and Discernment*, chapter 5.

16. Gonzalez, *Changing Shape*, pp. 71, 77.

17. Gonzalez, *Acts: The Gospel of the Spirit*, pp. 179–80.

Chapter 12   What does the gift of the Spirit mean for the shape of the Church?

1. Alister McGrath, *The Future of Christianity*, Blackwell, 2002, chapter 6. See also the protest of John Drane that academic theology has conformed to a secular model and failed to refer to the concrete situation of the Church, thus contributing to its decline – *The McDonaldization of the Church*, Darton, Longman & Todd, 2000, chapter 1. For theology as a conversation see Mark Cartledge, *Encountering the Spirit: The Charismatic tradition*, Darton, Longman & Todd, 2006, p. 121. Nouwen quotes Carl Rogers: 'I have found that the very feeling which has seemed to me most private, most personal and hence most incomprehensible by others, has turned out to be an expression for which there is a resonance in many other people. It has led me to believe that what is most personal and unique in each one of us is probably the very element which

would, if it were shared or expressed, speak most deeply to others', *The Wounded Healer*, Darton, Longman & Todd, 1994, p. 74.

2. E.g. Richard Mabey, *BBC Wildlife*, March 2007: 'the intricacy of the living world means, I suspect, that Intelligent Design is mathematically impossible as well as biologically improbable' – and yet in the same article he describes listening to 'a sacred oratorio of sound', experiencing 'a moment of communion', being 'part of a larger being'.

3. NRSV. Other translations use the verb 'hover' rather than 'swept', and 'Spirit of God' or 'divine wind' rather than 'wind'. See R. Cantalamessa, *Come, Creator Spirit: Meditations on the Veni Creator*, Liturgical Press, 2003, p. 8.

4. Augustine, *Exposition on the Psalms* 45.7 (quoted Cantalamessa, *Come, Creator Spirit*, p. 95). Footprints – Meister Eckhart (quoted Matthew Fox, *Western Spirituality*, Bear & Co, 1981, p. 220). Thoughts – Maximus the Confessor (quoted Ray Simpson, *Church of the Isles*, Kevin Mayhew, 2003, p. 204). Music – Honorius of Autun (quoted Matthew Fox, *Original Blessing: A primer in creation spirituality*, Bear & Co, 1983, p. 70). Thomas Aquinas, *Summa Theologiae* (quoted in Ian Bradley, *God is Green*, Darton, Longman & Todd, 1990, p. 32); Bonaventure, *Journey of the Mind into God*, chapter 2, internet edition www.catholic-forum.com/saints/stb16012.htm; John Calvin, *Institutes I.v.1* (quoted Alister McGrath, *Bridge-Building: Effective Christian apologetics*, InterVarsity Press, 1992, p. 33); Jonathan Edwards, *Images or Shadows of Divine Things*, Yale University Press, 1948, pp. 44, 61. Pierre Teilhard de Chardin, *Hymn of the Universe*, Collins, 1965, pp. 35–6. For more quotations and examples see Alison Morgan, *Praying with Creation*, ReSource booklet no. 4, ReSource, 2006.

5. Wolfhart Pannenberg, *Towards a Theology of Nature*, Westminster/John Knox Press, 1993, p. 34.

6. See Psalm 104.27-30, 90.5-6; Isaiah 40.31; Lamentations 5.2; Ezekiel 36.26; Isaiah 65.17. For a discussion of the Spirit's role in creating and renewing the world see Christopher J. H. Wright, *Knowing the Holy Spirit through the Old Testament*, Monarch, 2006, chapter 1; and Alison Morgan, *Renewal in Scripture*, ReSource booklet no. 3, ReSource, 2006.

7. Irenaeus is quoted in Jean-Jacques Suurmond, *Word and Spirit at Play: Towards a charismatic theology*, SCM Press, 1994, Part II, chapter 1, p. 41. Suurmond discusses the relationship between Spirit, Word and the Wisdom tradition in Part II, chapters 1–2.

8. Romans 1.20. Commentators often point to 1 Corinthians 15.35-49 as an example.

9. Jonathan Edwards, *Images or Shadows of Divine Things*, Yale University Press, 1948, pp. 65, 109; Charles Harold Dodd, *The Parables of the Kingdom*, Nisbet, 1935, pp. 21–2.

10. Gordon Fee, *Paul, the Spirit and the People of God*, Hendrikson Publishers, 1996, chapter 5.

11. For the tearing of the heavens in Mark 1.10 and 15.38 see N. T. Wright, *Mark for Everyone*, SPCK, 2001, pp. 5 and 216. Wright spoke about the work of the Spirit in a lecture 'Inciting Insight – the Holy Spirit in the church', Fulcrum conference, Islington, 29 April 2005. See also his *Simply Christian*, SPCK, 2006, p. 103.

12. William Abraham, *The Logic of Renewal*, Eerdmans, 2003, p. 158: 'the church is from beginning to end a charismatic community, a community brought into existence, equipped, guided, and sustained by the Holy Spirit.' Often we see the church more as an institution, a building, a gathering of people with shared values, a hierarchy of officers. For a helpful discussion of the nature of the Church from different perspectives see José Comblin, *The Holy Spirit and Liberation*, chapter 3; Neil Cole, *Organic Church: Growing faith where life happens*, Jossey-Bass, 2005, chapter 3; Brian Hathaway, *Beyond Renewal: The kingdom of God*, Word (UK), 1990, chapter 5. For Paul see 1 Corinthians 12.13; 2 Corinthians 3.3.

13. Unity and diversity is also a key theme of Jesus' prayer to his Father on behalf of his disciples and their successors in John 17. For the Early Church see Acts chapters 2, 4, 5. For Paul see Romans 12, 1 Corinthians 12, Ephesians 4 (the quote is from 1 Corinthians 12). See also Roland Allen, *Missionary Methods: St Paul's or ours?*, Eerdmans, 1962 (first published 1912); Vincent Donovan, *Christianity Rediscovered: An epistle from the Masai*, SCM Press, 1982. An excellent discussion of what this might mean in the contemporary Church is to be found in Michael Frost and Alan Hirsch, *The Shaping of Things to Come: Innovation and mission for the twenty-first-century church*, Hendrikson, 2003.

14. For renewal in the New Testament see Romans 7.6; 1 Peter 1.3; 2 Corinthians 5.17; Ephesians 4.24; Mark 16.17; 1 Corinthians 12.7ff.; Acts 17.19; Colossians 3.11; John 13.34; Luke 4.18. For Paul see Romans 7.6; Peter 1.3, 2 Corinthians 5.17; Ephesians 4.24; Mark 16.17; 1 Corinthians 12.7ff.; Acts 17.19; Colossians 3.11; John 13.34; Luke 4.18; and Alison Morgan, *Renewal, What is it and What is it for?*, Grove Books, 2006. For Paul's approach to the Church see Roland Allen, *Missionary Methods*, section IV, 'St Paul's method of dealing with organized churches'. The locus classicus would be Romans 7–8. The nearest Paul comes to offering an organizational structure for the Church is Ephesians 4, in which he talks about different leadership giftings. For the letters to the churches see Revelation chapters 1–3.

15. Aquinas had said that everything which could be received from the Holy Spirit had already been given and was now to be found in the Church – see Comblin, *The Holy Spirit and Liberation*, chapter 1. A good charismatic history of the Church is given by Mark Cartledge, *Encountering the Spirit: The charismatic tradition*, Darton, Longman & Todd, 2006; see also David Allen, *The Unfailing Stream – A charismatic church history in outline*, Sovereign World,

1994. For Montanism see T. D. Barnes, *Tertullian, a historical and literary study*, Clarendon Press, 1971, chapter 5, and Henry Chadwick, *The Early Church*, Pelican, 1967, chapter 2.

16. Suurmond, *Word and Spirit at Play*, III, 1 'Church history,' especially pp. 63–9; Comblin, *The Holy Spirit and Liberation*, especially pp. 184–6 and chapter 3, 'The Holy Spirit in the Church'.

17. For the accommodation of the Church to modernity see the excellent collection of essays in *Faith and Modernity*, ed. P. Sampson et al., Regnum Books, 1994. Berkhof is quoted by D. J. Hall: *The End of Christendom and the Future of Christianity*, Trinity Press International, 1995, p. 18.

18. William Abraham, *The Logic of Renewal*, p. 21.

19. For the relationship between Church and culture in history see Alison Morgan, *The Wild Gospel*, Monarch, 2005, chapter 4. For Michael Riddell see his *Threshold of the Future – Reforming the church in the post-Christian West*, SPCK, 1998, p. 93. For comparison between the current situation and the Reformation see José Comblin, *The Holy Spirit and Liberation*, p. 60.

20. For modernism and the Church see Eddie Gibbs and Ian Coffey, *Church Next – Quantum changes in Christian ministry*, InterVarsity Press, 2001, p. 30; and George Ritzer, *The McDonaldization of Society*, Pine Forge Press, 1993, discussed by John Drane, *The McDonaldization of the Church: Spirituality, creativity and the future of the Church*, chapter 3.

21. See the critique of modern church buildings by Jonny Baker in Eddie Gibbs and Ryan Bolger, *Emerging Churches: Creating Christian community in post-modern cultures*, SPCK, 2006, p. 175. For models of church see Steven Croft, *Transforming Communities: Re-imagining church for the twenty-first century*, Darton, Longman & Todd, 2002, chapter 4. Many of the initiatives mentioned here have brought great growth to the church. But what works in some places does not work in others. It is not the initiatives themselves, but their adoption as blueprints that is unhelpful; one size no longer fits all.

22. Michael Frost and Alan Hirsch, *The Shaping of Things to Come: Innovation for the twenty-first-century Church*, Hendrikson, 2003, p. 35. The book offers an eloquent advocacy for a church which is not 'attractional' but 'missional' in its approach – i.e. one which engages with people by going to them rather than expecting them to come to it.

23. See the research by Yvonne Richmond in Coventry, in Nick Spencer, *Beyond the Fringe – Researching a spiritual age*, LICC, Cliff College Publishing, 2005. Michael Moynagh dubs postmodernity 'an experience economy' – *Changing World, Changing Church*, Monarch, 2001, p. 8.

24. Ken Blanchard and Terry Waghorn: *Mission Possible: Becoming a world-class organization while there's still time*, McGraw-Hill, 1997, p. xxi. Cf. the comment by Steven Croft, *Transforming Communities*, p. 160: 'This generation of Christian ministers is called to transitional leadership: to maintain the present structures

of church life but to develop within and alongside them new and creative ways of being church.' Less optimistic statements have been made by Michael Riddell, 'The greatest barrier to the gospel in contemporary Western culture is the church. The forms of the church, its life and pronouncements; these act to prevent people from hearing the liberating story of Jesus', in his *Threshold of the Future*, p. 57; Howard Snyder, 'the church will increasingly have to choose between a charismatic and an institutional or bureaucratic model for its life and structure', in his *Radical Renewal: The problem of wineskins today*, Touch Publications, 1996, p. 194. Many of the Church's problems have lain in its failure to fully acknowledge both word and Spirit. Word without Spirit leads to a rationalistic faith. Spirit without word leads to a potentially heretical faith – as with the Cathars, the Quakers and others.

25. See Comblin's remark that 'experience of the Holy Spirit cannot . . . be reduced to the charismatic manifestations so highly prized by the Corinthians', *The Holy Spirit and Liberation*, p. 41. Bible references in this paragraph: John 7.38; Jeremiah 17.7-8; Galatians 5.22; Matthew 5.13-14; 1 Peter 2.4.

26. See the comment in *Mission-shaped Church*, Church House Publishing, 2004, p. 132.

27. The point is powerfully made by Raniero Cantalamessa, *Come, Creator Spirit*, chapter 2, 'The Holy Spirit changes chaos into cosmos'.

28. Our English word 'church' in fact comes from the Greek *kuriakos*, meaning 'belonging to the Lord' – see Owen Chadwick, *A History of Christianity*, Phoenix, 1995, chapter 1.

29. Frost and Hirsch, *The Shaping of Things to Come*, p. 113; Michael Riddell, *Threshold of the Future*, p. 115; Nick Spencer, *Beyond the Fringe*, p. 19.

30. Neil Cole, *Organic Church*, chapter 4. See also Sally Gaze, *Mission-Shaped and Rural*, Church House Publishing, 2006, pp. 172–3; and the tale of two churches told by Martin Down, *Speak to these Bones*, Monarch, 1993.

31. For decentralization see Ken Blanchard, *Mission Impossible*; Stephen Covey, *The Eighth Habit – From effectiveness to greatness*, Simon & Schuster, 2004. Cole cites Hock, founder of Visa, saying an organisation can dispense with command/control if it holds common purpose and principles – people will behave creatively in accordance with them (Neil Cole, *Organic Church: Growing faith where life happens*, Jossey-Bass, 2005, p. 124). See the comment by Gibbs and Coffey, 'If denominational structures are in place primarily as instruments of control, then the identity problem is probably insurmountable. But if these vertical structures can be dismantled to provide financial and personnel resources by which local churches can be effectively serviced, their diversity celebrated and a variety of models assessed, then structures can play an important role', *Church Next*, p. 71. The practical implications of such an approach are explored by Bob Jackson, *The Road to Growth*, Church House Publishing, 2005. For Bezalel see Exodus 35.30–35.

32. *Resourcing Mission for a twenty-first-century Church*, Church House Publishing, 2006, p. 21. See Matthew 28.19-20 and John 20.21-22.
33. Fulcrum conference, Islington, 29 April 2005.
34. *Building Missionary Congregations*, Church House Publishing, 1996 (a concept perversely taken from the *Little Red Book* of Mao Tse-Tung: 'Letting a hundred flowers blossom and a hundred schools of thought contend is the policy for promoting the progress of the arts and the sciences and a flourishing socialist culture in our land', *Quotations from Chairman Mao Tse-Tung*, Foreign Languages Press, Peking, 1968 pp. 302–3). Bob Jackson has remarked that perhaps our greatest mistake under modernism was to treat all churches as if they were oak trees, able to grow to any size and live forever – *Hope for the Church*, Church House Publishing, 2004, p. 132. For the number of plant species see www.plant-talk.org/stories/28bramw.html
35. For Joel's prophecy see Joel 2.28-29 and Acts 2.16-18. For treasures new and old see Matthew 13.52.
36. Quoted by Neil Cole, *Organic Church*, p. 50.
37. José Comblin, *The Holy Spirit and Liberation*, p. 41: 'We are witnessing a resurgence of experience of the Holy Spirit. If this is the case, it is a phenomenon unique in the history of the church since the third century. It is a complete inversion of the course the church in the West has followed since then.' See also p. 19. The call for adventure is given by Sue Hope, *Mission-shaped Spirituality*, Church House Publishing, 2006, p. 108.

Chapter 13   Can fresh expressions of church make a difference?

1. The Diocese of Wakefield Statistics Project 2006.
2. Grace Davie writing, for example, in *The Future of the Parish System*, ed. S. Croft, Church House Publishing, 2006.
3. National survey by Opinion Research Business on behalf of the Archbishops' Council (2005)
4. Paul Heelas and Linda Woodhead, *The Spiritual Revolution*, Blackwell, 2005.
5. National survey by ORB (2001) for the Archbishops' Council.
6. National survey by ORB (2005 and 2007) for the Archbishops' Council.
7. National survey by ORB (2005) for the Archbishops' Council.
8. Churchgoing in the UK, Tearfund 2007.
9. *Daily Mail* newspaper, 4 May 2007.
10. *Churchgoing in the UK*, Tearfund, 2007.
11. Research towards fresh expressions of church, Research and Statistics Department, Archbishops' Council, February 2007; www.cofe.anglican.org/information/statistics
12. Peter Brierley, *Pulling out of the Nosedive*, Christian Research, 2006.
13. *British Social Attitudes* Seventeenth Report, National Centre for Social Research 2000.

14. iGeneration Survey by Populas for *The Times* newspaper, September 2004.
15. The *Express* newspaper, 24 May 2007.

Chapter 14   How does a mixed economy Church connect with contemporary spirituality?

1. *Epistle to Diognetus*, 17.1.
2. Irenaeus, *Against Heresies*, iv.xx.6.
3. *Lumen Gentium* is the title of the document, and is translated as 'light of humanity', rather than 'light of the nations', the more literal meaning, by Fr Colman O'Neill OP, in the English language version authorized by the Roman Catholic Church in 1975. See Austin Flannery OP (ed.), *Vatican Council II: The Conciliar and Post Conciliar Documents*, Dominican Publications, 1977.
4. *Lumen Gentium* 2.
5. *Gaudium et Spes* 57.
6. Clement of Alexandria, *Stromateis* i. v; cf. Galatians 3.24.
7. John O'Donohue, *Eternal Echoes*, Bantam Books, 2000, p. 194.
8. See Marina Warner, *Alone of All Her Sex*, Picador, 1990, especially Part 3 'Bride'.
9. Graham Howes, *The Art of the Sacred*, I. B. Tauris, 2007, p. 102.
10. Kazuo Ishiguro, *Never Let Me Go*, Faber, 2005. 'Your art would reveal what you were like. What you were like inside ... We took away your art because we thought it would reveal your souls. Or to put it more finely, we did it to *prove you had souls at all*', p 238.
11. Augustine of Hippo, *Confessions*, Book 10, paragraph 38.

Chapter 15   Mapping ecclesiology for a mixed economy

1. Martyn Atkins argues that the essence of the Church lies in its derived nature: the people of God draw their identity and nature from the life of God, Father, Son and Holy Spirit. As such the Church is primarily the community shaped by the mission of God in and to creation: this is our essential nature. James Dunn seeks to go back to fundamentals by looking at the essence and character of earliest Christianity as seen in the New Testament and argues that the dynamics of mission and beginning in fresh ways is at the heart of what it means to be God's people. John Hull presents a powerful case for the mission of God which shapes the Church being as much if not more about our 'horizontal' relationships with the rest of creation than our 'vertical' relationship with God in prayer and worship.
2. *Mission-shaped Church*, p. 99 (abbreviated).
3. Rowan Williams has expanded this sentence in 'Theological resources for re-examining church' in S. Croft (ed.), *The Future of the Parish System*, pp. 49–60.
4. Bill Bryson, *Notes from a Small Island*, Doubleday, 1995.
5. See for example, Kevin Giles, *What on Earth is the Church? A biblical and*

theological enquiry, SPCK, 1995; Paul S. Minnear, *Images of the Church in the New Testament*, Westminster John Knox Press, 1960, 2004.

6. Hans Küng, *The Church*, Burns & Oates, 1968; Jürgen Moltmann, *The Church in the Power of the Spirit*, SCM Press, 1977.

7. John D. Zizioulas, *Being as Communion, Studies in Personhood and the Church*, St Vladimir's Seminary Press, 1985.

8. One of the best popular books remains David Watson, *I Believe in the Church*, Hodder & Stoughton, 1978. There is a great need for similar visionary books for today's context.

9. Steven Croft, *Transforming Communities*, Darton, Longman & Todd, 2002, chapters 7–10.

10. This point is made particularly well by David Hope, former Archbishop of York in 'Changing Church, Unchanging world', a sermon preached at the University of Cambridge in 2001 and published in *Signs of Hope*, Continuum, 2001, pp.139–50.

11. Nicholas Healy, *Church, World and the Christian Life: Practical-prophetic ecclesiology*, Cambridge University Press, 2000.

12. There is plenty of evidence out there that this actually happens. See Leslie Francis and Philip Richter, *Gone but not Forgotten*, Darton, Longman & Todd, 1998; Alan Jamieson, *A Churchless Faith*, SPCK, 2002.

13. Nicholas Healy, *Church, World and Christian Life*, p. 154.

14. Acts 11.20–26. Note Luke's careful use of the term 'the church' (with the definite article) first in Jerusalem and then at the end of the passage in Antioch.

15. *Mission-shaped Church*, pp. 81ff. The five values are that a missionary church is focused on God the Trinity, is incarnational, is transformational, makes disciples and is relational. For a longer exposition see Graham Cray, 'Focusing church life on a theology of mission' in *The Future of the Parish System*, pp. 61–75. For these criteria and others to be applied to new communities see the Code of Practice to the Measure, February, 2007 Draft, p. 30. Angela Tilby presents the case that these values and those of the Lambeth Quadrilateral may not be sufficient – and I would agree in that they are not aiming to present a complete and descriptive ecclesiology. However, the missiological question is: Are these elements sufficient to discern that a particular community is church in the Anglican tradition? And there I would say they provide exactly the framework needed for a flexible discernment process of recognizing what God is doing and joining in.

16. See a concordance or dictionary on the use of the term 'church' and also James D. G. Dunn, *The Theology of Paul the Apostle*, T&T Clark, 1998, p. 542: 'Paul could speak both of the whole congregation in a place as "church" and also of individual house groups within that congregation as "church" (1 Cor. 1.1; 16.19). The one was not seen as detracting from the status of the other.'

17. See for example, *Ancient-Future Evangelism* (and the evolving series) by Robert E. Webber, Baker Books, 2003 (www.ancientfutureworship.com) and Ian J. Mobsby, *Emerging and Fresh Expressions of Church: How are they authentically church and Anglican?*, Moot Community Publishing, 2007.
18. See in particular, *Baptism, Eucharist and Ministry*, WCC, Geneva, 1982.
19. It is partly for this reason that the discipline of ecclesiologically informed theological reflection needs to lie at the very heart of all formation for ministry. See Roger Walton, 'Theological Reflection', in Steven Croft and Roger Walton, *Learning for Ministry*, Church House Publishing, 2005, pp.149–63.
20. For recent British examples see *Congregational Studies in the UK: Christianity in a Post-Christian Context*, ed. Matthew Guest, Karin Tusting and Linda Woodhead, Ashgate, 2004; *Studying Local Churches: A handbook*, ed. Helen Cameron, Philip Richter, Douglas Davies and Frances Ward, SCM Press, 2005 and Martyn Percy, *Engaging with Contemporary Culture: Christianity, theology and the concrete Church*, Ashgate, 2005.
21. For a distilled and practical text book for leaders of traditional churches and fresh expressions which makes good use of this methodology see Eolene Boyd-Macmillan and Sara Savage, *The Human Face of the Church*, Canterbury Press, 2007.

Index